THE ALAMO

Date Due	
JAN 2 1 2003	

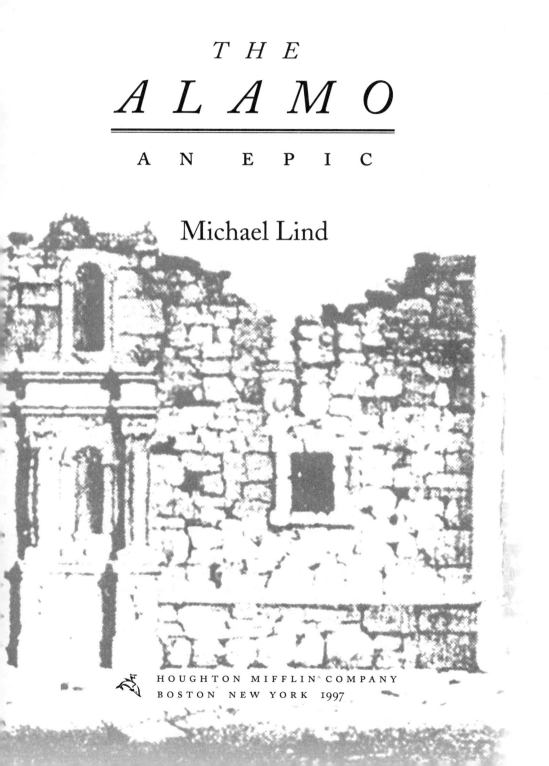

THE
ALAMO
A N E P I C

Michael Lind

HOUGHTON MIFFLIN COMPANY
BOSTON NEW YORK 1997

Copyright © 1997 by Michael Lind

All rights reserved

For information about permission to reproduce selections from
this book, write to Permissions, Houghton Mifflin Company,
215 Park Avenue South, New York, New York 10003.

For information about this and other Houghton Mifflin trade and reference
books and multimedia products, visit The Bookstore at Houghton Mifflin on the
World Wide Web at http://www.hmco.com/trade/.

Library of Congress Cataloging-in-Publication Data

Lind, Michael.
The Alamo : an epic / Michael Lind.
p. cm.
ISBN 0-395-82758-2
1. Alamo (San Antonio, Tex.) — Siege, 1836 — Poetry.
2. Texas — History — Revolution, 1835–1836 — Poetry.   I. Title.
PS3562.I482A79   1997
811'.54 — dc20   96-43416   CIP

Book design by Anne Chalmers
Typeface: Adobe Caslon

Printed in the United States of America

QUM 10 9 8 7 6 5 4 3 2 1

Illustration of the Alamo church: Executive Document 32, U.S. Senate, 31st Con-
gress, 1st session. Photograph of Dickert rifle, courtesy of The Alamo. *The Odyssey* by
Homer, translated by Robert Fitzgerald, copyright © 1961, 1963 by Robert Fitzgerald
and renewed 1989 by Benedict R. C. Fitzgerald. Reprinted by permission of Vintage
Books, a division of Random House, Inc.

This poem is dedicated

to the men and women

of the Armed Forces

of the

United States of America

and their families

ACKNOWLEDGMENTS

I would like to express my gratitude to Steven Fraser, my editor at Houghton Mifflin. His enthusiastic support of this unconventional project has been as important as the skill he has brought to the task of publishing *The Alamo*. I am grateful as well to Wendy Strothman, executive vice president of Houghton Mifflin. The assistance of Kristine Dahl, my agent at International Creative Management, has been indispensable.

I would also like to thank Dana Gioia for his generous encouragement and insightful criticism. I am indebted to Frederick Turner for his example and his friendship over many years. Robert McDowell has provided astute and helpful criticism. Thomas M. Disch and Bruce Bawer have been enthusiastic readers and helpful critics.

The Alamo was begun on the campus of Yale University in the spring of 1984, and the last lines of Book Twelve were written at the Chelsea Hotel in Manhattan in the spring of 1996. At every stage of this enterprise, Decherd Turner has provided assistance and encouragement. Thomas S. Langston has read and provided helpful comments on every draft. At different points during the last twelve years I have also benefited from the enthusiasm and suggestions of Lance Bertelsen, Stanley Werbow, Bobbie Sanders, Earl Shorris, Kevin

McMurtry, Richard Linklater, and Edward T. Chase.

I owe special thanks to Nicol Rae for encouraging me to undertake this project during a visit to the Alamo in the winter of 1983. Finally, I would like to thank Lenora Todaro for her faith in the poem: *Altera Torquatum cepit Leonora Poëtam.*

CONTENTS

Part One

Part Two

Part Three

CONTENTS

Commandancy of the Alamo
Bexar, Feby 24th, 1836

To the People of Texas and All Americans in the World—
FELLOW CITIZENS AND COMPATRIOTS:

I am besieged with a thousand or more of the Mexicans under Santa Anna. I have sustained a considerable Bombardment and cannonade for 24 hours and have not lost a man. The enemy has demanded surrender at discretion, otherwise the garrison is to be put to the sword, if the fort is taken. I have answered the demand with a cannon shot, and our flag still waves proudly from the wall. *I shall never surrender or retreat.* Then, I call on you in the name of Liberty, of patriotism, and everything dear to the American character, to come to our aid with all dispatch. The enemy is receiving reinforcements daily and will no doubt increase to three or four thousand in four or five days. If this call is neglected I am determined to sustain myself as long as possible and die like a soldier who never forgets what is due his honor and that of his country.

VICTORY OR DEATH

William Barret Travis
Lt. Col. Commanding

Compañeros de armas:

Estos restos que hemos tenido el honor de conducir en nuestros hombros son los de los valientes héroes que murieron en el Alamo. Sí, mis amigos, ellos preferieron morir mil veces a servir el yugo del tirano. Qué ejemplo tan brillante, digno de anotarse en las páginas de la historia. El genio de la libertad parece estar viendo en su elevado trono de donde con semblante halagüeño nos senala diciendo: "Ahí tenéis a vuestros hermanos, Travis, Bowie, Crockett y otros varios a quienes su valor coloca en el número de mis héroes." Yo os pido a que poniendo por testigo a los venerables restos de nuestros dignos compañeros digamos al mundo entero. Texas será libre, independiente o pereceremos con gloria en los combates.

Brothers in arms:

We have had the honor of carrying on our shoulders the remains of the brave heroes who died at the Alamo. Yes, my friends, they preferred dying a thousand deaths to wearing the yoke of tyranny. Such a shining example will surely be noted in the pages of history. It seems the spirit of liberty is watching from its throne on high where, with a bright countenance, it tells us: "There you have your brothers, Travis, Bowie, Crockett, and many others whose bravery places them in the ranks of my heroes." I ask you, as the venerable remains of our worthy companions bear witness, to tell the world of these deeds. Texas will be free and independent or we will perish with glory in combat.

Speech of Colonel Juan Seguin
at the interment of the ashes of the defenders of the Alamo,
San Antonio, February 25, 1837

The Muse, disgusted at an age and clime
    Barren of every glorious theme,
In distant lands now waits a better time,
    Producing subjects worthy fame . . .

There shall be sung another golden age,
    The rise of empire and of arts,
The good and great inspiring epic rage,
    The wisest heads and noblest hearts.

Not such as Europe breeds in her decay,
    Such as she bred when fresh and young,
When heavenly flame did animate her clay,
    By future poets shall be sung . . .

Bishop George Berkeley, "Verses on
the Prospect of Planting Arts
and Learning in America," 1752

PART ONE

BOOK ONE

SHIPWRECK

THE ARGUMENT

Eighteen Thirty-Five. Once more
in Mexico, a civil war.
The military chieftain, cruel
Santa Anna, wars to impose his rule
on liberal Zacatecas in
the north. Anglo-American
Texans, the majority,
now fear for their security.
One faction seeks only to appease
Santa Anna; others hope to seize
control and then to separate
Texas from the Mexican state.
Sam Houston and his allies plan
secession as soon as their man,
young Travis, wages an attack
upon the fort at Anahuac.
The plot to start a war rebounds
when frightened colonists denounce
the War Dogs. Travis soon has fled,
a bounty on his hunted head.

BOOK ONE

Confusion. All around is churning smoke,   1
    a supernova's planet-flensing shroud,
an embryonic solar system's yolk.
    No shapes, but for the shadows in the cloud
    that swell and sway and pulsate to the loud
oceanic throb, a thunder to convulse
a cosmos, the percussion of a pulse.

The fog unravels. But this is no fog,   2
    this blear amalgam of a scumbled dust
and stinging fumes. An isolated leg,
    wrapped like a maize ear in a tattered husk
    of trouser cotton, glows in noonday dusk.
A headless soldier bows; the freckling paint
has made his gulping pal a stigmaed saint.

Across the fuming field, the dying stir   3
    among the dead. Their moaning and their throes
alert the splendid cavalry, who spur
    their horses and parade amid their foes.
    Wielding their spears as bargemen would use
their staffs to lever flatboats, lancers pole
from man to man and spare no pleading soul.

4   Beyond, more butchery. The rebel town
        is bleeding streams of black into the skies,
the way a seal, when sharks have dragged it down,
        will stain a turquoise current as it dies.
        Across the splintered barricades with cries
of "Death to traitors!" grimy conscripts vault.
The breastworks tumble under their assault.

5   With bayonets, daggers, and naked hands,
        the stormers hack and chop and stab and slash.
The slow notes of *Deguello* from the band's
        emplacement drone through cannon croak and crash;
        the melody that Spain learned in its clash
with Muslim arms, "No Quarter," starts to swell
as Zacatecas is annexed by hell.

6   These scenes a spyglass frames within its lens;
        lowering the lorgnette, the architect
who drafted this methodic violence
        gives rage a voice: "Serrano's almost wrecked
        my strategy! I told him to connect
with Rivas at the square . . . They've let some go!
Where are the lancers? Why are they so slow?"

7   He gnaws plug-opium, although in truth
        he's grown already giddy with the aid
of hot twelve-pounders. Still a handsome youth
        in aspect, this commander, in his braid
        and bicorne, might be marshal of a parade;
the frills may be a fop's, the soul within
belongs to a practiced puppeteer of men.

Santa Anna scowls, barks, paces like a coach   *8*
   upon the sidelines in a frantic game,
only to fall silent, as horsemen approach,
   shepherding gentry diminished by shame.
   A captain gives one prisoner a name:
"This one is the *alcalde* . . ." "Excellency,"
the mayor begins, "for all of us I plea —"

"Where is Zavala?" Santa Anna snarls.   *9*
   "Where is he? Where's the traitor? Has he flown?"
The *alcalde* murmurs something, then he curls
   in pain around a stock, emits a groan
   as soldiers warp his arm. "Zavala's gone
to Texas —" "When?" The President wants to know.
"He left a day . . . perhaps two days ago . . ."

"Gone to Texas." The young *caudillo* swears.   *10*
   "The man is now a traitor to his race,
and not just to his country. Damn it, where's
   Almonte?" The adjutant assumes his place
   beside the general, trying to keep pace
with Santa Anna's stride (his master, bred
of Creoles, tops Almonte by a head).

"Almonte — a dispatch to General Cos   *11*
   up in Coahuila. Tell him to prepare
to reinforce all the presidios
   along the Texas coast — and the one at Bexar —
   what is it? Alamo. I once fought there,
with Arredondo. Fifteen years ago
we crushed seditious San Antonio."

12 "That was a day like this —" A cannon thud,
        succeeded by a whistle, punctuates
Santa Anna's reminiscence. "So much blood,
        such slaughter! Every old *Tejano* hates
        the name of Arredondo. Still, the gates
have been secure a while on that frontier,
thanks not to loyalty, but thanks to fear."

13 "What that old butcher taught me, I'll remind
        the *yanquis* up in Texas, if they dare
to join the rebels here. They have designed
        for years to sever Texas; if they tear
        that province off, then powers everywhere
will join them in their plundering — Britain, France,
and Spain, they'll rush to amputate our lands."

14 The autocrat watches his conscripts prod
        the men of Zacatecas into groups,
forcing them to strip and kneel, to be shot
        or bayoneted. Nearby, inside loops
        of hooting, waiting comrades, other troops
rock atop stunned women. "See the fate
seditious towns in Texas can await."

15 The rebel leader and the forlorn hope
        who won the war for Texas in defeat
I aim to recollect. The lonely troop
        who spurned alike surrender and retreat
        to stand with stubborn Travis will repeat
their vigil on the consecrated wall
of Alamo and with it once more fall.

That legion yet stands watch on the frontier   16
    between imagination and the tract
of memory, where echoed speech rings clear
    as poetry, the truth's own dialect.
    The dame of that domain, if lore be fact,
embodied in blue light will sometimes prowl
a hollow lane or glide through a corral;

more often, she's a woman in a cloak   17
    on horseback, face occulted by a hood,
no sooner glimpsed than blent with wind and smoke —
    the Weeper, whose half-lost, half-understood
    lament will swell through cactus clump and wood
as she hunts for new children who, when found,
can take the place of those whom she has drowned.

Our Lady of the dolorous frontier,   18
    search for your brood no more. Tomorrow we
as well must follow you through bend and tier
    to melt in eddies of infinity.
    Those who precede us, Lady, let us see;
restore what the assimilating flow
absorbed, two armies at the Alamo.

From Zacatecas orders galloped forth.   19
    Before the month had ended (it was June
of Eighteen Thirty-Five) a pair rode north
    from occupied Coahuila through the moon-
    like craters of the Texas road. By noon
the second day, the couriers vaguely knew
their shrinking shadows had grown shadows too.

20   Swerving as one, the soldiers left the trail,
        spurs pumping the felt bellows of each beast.
    They did not slow in answer to the hail
        of masked pursuers — three of them, at least.
        Just when the riders thought the chase had ceased,
    they saw the fourth one waiting. Summer sun
    flexed like quicksilver on his leveled gun.

21   Morosely the two messengers looked on
        as captors skinned the bags. Though kerchiefs masked
    their features, their accented tones belonged
        to North Americans. Their leader tasked
        his men to hurry, though not one had basked.
    Above his silk bandanna, turquoise eyes,
    scanning a dispatch, widened in surprise.

22   That night, in the informal capital
        of Texas, the crude cabin colony
    of San Felipe de Austin, in the full
        town-council chamber, settlers mobbed to see
        the civil war's most famous refugee,
    lately ambassador of Mexico
    in Paris, now his former master's foe.

23   "This tyrant never tires," Zavala told
        the Texans jostling in the lamplit room.
    "The blood of Zacatecas makes him bold,
        that vampire bat. Now equal horrors loom
        for sad Coahuila, sentenced to its doom;
    its Governor, Viesca, has been seized
    by General Cos. No doubt Santa Anna's pleased."

"Before the Governor was overthrown,   24
    he moved the seat of government to Bexar;
the net Santa Anna's weaving will be sewn
    completely, if he plants an army there.
    I dread to think how Texas then will fare."
The dapper rebel daubed a somber face
belonging to his nation's ruling race.

"The choice is yours, my countrymen, my friends.   25
    Let Texas thunder 'No!' to tyranny,
and here this Caesar's dream of empire ends.
    If San Antonio is not to be
    our Philippi, we must prove liberty
is not the creed of cowards. 'Cicero!'
must be our cry. Let Roman daggers glow!"

Zavala's answer came from J. B. Miller,   26
    the town's boss: "Don Lorenzo, shouldn't we
be fretting more about this Meskin feller
    than all them Romans?" The raucous glee
    had to be gaveled down insistently.
"Now, folks, I have a letter, signed by Cos,
addressed to 'countrymen' — that's us, I suppose."

"Now General Cos, he tells us he's restored   27
    lost 'order' to Coahuila — that's his phrase,
in Spanish. He goes on to give his word
    that from now on our customary ways
    will be respected. Oh — in a few days,
as part of Santa Anna's amnesty,
our good friend Stephen Austin will be free."

28 His later words were lost beneath a cheer
    no gavel could restrain. There was no man
  respected more in Texas than the austere
    successor to the Moses of this land.
    His skill in parley with those in command
  had won Stephen Austin fame — till his arrest
  in Mexico, as warning to the rest.

29 If even Austin, peacefulest of all
    the Texan leaders, could be seized and penned
  without a hearing, what fate might befall
    those fellow Texans aching to defend
    their chartered rights with more than ink and wind?
  The news of the impresario's release,
  to this, added an argument for peace:

30 "We have to wait, till Austin has returned
    unharmed." The voice was that of Lemuel Wright,
  a farmer, but the thought, it would be learned,
    was common property. "This ain't our fight.
    Forgive me, Don Lorenzo, but we might
  just have to dicker with this latest corps
  of Generals, as we did with them before."

31 To shouts of "Yellow-belly!" Wright replied,
    "You call me what you want, but I have seen
  these revolutions come in like the tide
    and go out the next day. What do they mean
    for us up here in Texas? We'll just lean
  toward Santa Anna as we did before
  toward Bustamante; our peace, and their war."

"You do not understand!" Zavala cried.   *32*
　　"I know Santa Anna well. This amnesty
for Austin, it's a ploy meant to divide . . ."
　　The voices medleyed, their cacophony
　　too fit a symbol of their polity.
Like ants within a hall a twig has wrecked,
the settlers were convulsed to no effect.

Debate declined when, through the crowd, with slow,   *33*
　　majestic strides, a graying giant lumbered
whom none in hall or country did not know.
　　This white-skinned Cherokee had often slumbered
　　upon the robe in which he was encumbered;
his hat was Mexican; like souvenirs,
accoutrements evoked the man's careers.

Before the grave Sam Houston could begin,   *34*
　　Lem Wright assailed him. "Houston, you and all
your War Dog friends want to stampede us in
　　a war with Mexico. That's been your goal
　　since you arrived. And as for us — to hell
with us old settlers, who came here in peace!"
Sam Houston faced the crowd, and spoke with ease:

"You've heard me called a 'War Dog' here tonight;   *35*
　　a 'War Dog'! That's not rhetoric, it's rant.
A warrior, I'll own to; if a fight
　　is justified, I'll add my strength, I grant.
　　To hint, though, that we blooded soldiers pant
for slaughter, just because we plan and spar,
proves ignorance of warriors and war.

36　　"Each morning I am wakened by the wound
　　　　　I've worn since, with my brother Cherokee,
　　　I rushed the barricade at Horseshoe Bend
　　　　　for General Jackson. No one need tell me
　　　　　about the costs of war's ferocity;
　　　the orphaned child, the bride both newly wed
　　　and widowed I have seen; and I have bled.

37　　"There's nothing in the world that's worse than war,
　　　　　with one exception, and that is defeat.
　　　To win a clash, and at the same time spare
　　　　　the ready warrior, that is a feat
　　　　　to match a sack or siege. Those who can treat
　　　successfully need never peel the steel;
　　　a diplomatic triumph's triumph still."

38　　His face conveyed no secrets with its flex,
　　　　　no more than does the mask upon the snapper
　　　that broods beneath the Mississippi's dregs,
　　　　　invisible but for the fleshy clapper
　　　　　inside the beak's dark bell. The patient trapper
　　　bemuses prey with its tongue's wagging pink,
　　　then gulps down the hovering fish in a wink.

39　　"We've learned tonight that General Cos has vowed
　　　　　to treat our chartered freedoms with respect,
　　　and I believe a man should be allowed
　　　　　to prove he's honest. Some folks might suspect
　　　　　an oath made by the officer who sacked
　　　Coahuila's legislature — but we've heard
　　　that General Cos has given us his word.

"Now General Cos is brother, through his wife,   *40*
   to General Santa Anna. Some might doubt
a man so placed would risk his rank or life
   rather than lie in a decree sent out
   to foreign settlers. Still, only a lout
would hide the policy that he preferred;
and General Cos has given us his word."

As Houston paused, the murmur in the place   *41*
   grew deeper. Through the doorway in the back
a figure eased. The tall latecomer's face
   was hidden by a brim and silk cravat.
   As if by accident, he touched his hat,
and Houston just as casually replied
by nodding, negligently, and unspied.

"The question, then," the Tennessean resolved,   *42*
   "is whether we are willing to believe
the claims of a commander who dissolved
   a Congress before turning to relieve
   a Governor of freedom. Our reprieve
is more than such a tyranny deferred —
for that, we have — what else? the General's word."

"The General is a liar — here's the proof!"   *43*
   The voice, cornet-crisp, came from the man
beneath the broad-brimmed hat. No more aloof,
   he sauntered forward, waving in his hand
   a lettered page. "I hold here a command
from Cos to Anahuac's presidio,
intercepted only hours ago."

44   The room convulsed, despite the gavel's clang
       and Miller's: "Mister Travis, you can wait
your turn to speak!" Sam Houston's thunder rang:
       "The floor is his. We need to hear this late
       intelligence, before there's more debate."
The hubbub ebbed, as Travis doffed his hat
and paused to place his bangs, just like a cat.

45   Four summers less than thirty he had seen,
       but Travis was far more than the absurd
young dandy neighbors knew. A mind too keen
       for one of his thin years could be inferred
       from nervous eyes the color of the bird
that haunts the jungles by the Mayan sea
and dies if forced into captivity.

46   "Your Honor, would you kindly verify
       the authenticity of this dispatch?"
When Miller gave both sheets a careful eye,
       he nodded. "Yes, the signatures do match."
       Zavala next translated, patch by patch,
the orders Cos had meant to keep covert
from all but those he wanted to alert.

47   "'Some veterans from the recent campaign
       will be arriving,'" Don Lorenzo read
to his hushed listeners. "He can only mean
       the siege that left half Zacatecas dead.
       There's more, and worse," the learned exile said.
"'With these new troops, the Texas situation
must be resolved in favor of our nation.'"

The voice of Travis carried through the cries 48
    that these last words educed. "Thus General Cos,
the friend of Texas, ventures to apprise
    his underlings of what he plans for those
    he's marked for carving — here, a fine fat roast,
and there, a steak — the feast to be delayed
till he equips the butcher with a blade."

Once more the town was tangled in debate: 49
    "We'll stop 'em in the west!" "No, seal the coast!"
"We ought to free Viesca!" "He's just bait!"
    The cautious Miller, who had been opposed
    to any provocation, saw that most
of his constituents were now agreed
upon a course too dangerous to lead;

he nominated Houston to enlist 50
    militiamen from Austin's colony.
From Houston, a recusal: "I insist
    that Travis take command. He knows the sea
    approaches to Fort Anahuac, which we
must make our own." He added, "I hear tell
that Mister Travis knows that fortress well."

Like honking geese that cease their aimless eddy 51
    and fall in, one by one, behind a bird
that rakes a wake with strokes both sure and steady,
    frontiersmen followed Travis, undeterred
    by neighbors who insisted they had erred.
The doubters shared misgivings with Lem Wright:
"Because of that young fool, we'll rue this night."

52 Beneath a canvas curve, the schooner named
    Ohio hurdled swells the next afternoon.
    A small six-pounder on a truck was aimed
        at mocking gulls; it favored a spittoon.
        The soldier-citizens brayed out of tune
    and passed a flask and wagered on the pack
    of dolphins racing them to Anahuac.

53 In sight of palisades that sentried sand,
        the schooner anchored. Soon her cannon throbbed,
    and water poled where foam besieged the land.
        Then, following the missile they had lobbed,
        a dozen raiders, in a bark that bobbed
    and bellied up, rose dripping from the suds,
    like foot-washing Baptists, dunked in their duds.

54 To half a dozen farmers and their wives,
        young Captain Travis (so he had been styled
    that morning by the crew) announced, "Your lives
        and property will never be defiled
        again by tyranny!" A staring child
    advanced and, in a flute's high piping note,
    quizzed Travis, "Hey, mister, is that your boat?"

55 "When they seen you boys coming, they cleared out,"
        explained a sideburned settler, at whose side,
    atop a gig, his bride, lipless and stout,
        was staring solemnly. When Travis tried
        to supplement his muster, none replied
    with baying to the trumpet of the hunt;
    they'd come to see, not be, the elephant.

An ancient story held that while Rome slumbered   56
    one midnight, it was menaced by the Gaul,
unheard, unseen, unconquered, till the unnumbered
    geese who dwelt there awoke the Capitol.
    A Latin goose on duty — that was all
that still remained in Mexico's stockade,
with picket pigs, and pullet enfilade.

The *presidarios* had disappeared   57
    into the motte's dim maze, the way a corps
of snuffling javelinas blend with weird
    penumbras in the forest near the shore.
    Like hunters tracking down the horrid boar,
the anxious rebels scanned the green and dun,
hearing, in every footfall's crack, a gun.

Within the gloom, a banner flapped, as pale   58
    as flags a flustered whitetail herd will raise.
"Don't shoot! I'm an American!" came the hail
    from Andrew Briscoe, wading through a haze
    of branches and mosquitoes, to embrace
the rebel leader. "Travis, who'd have reckoned
that where you caused one war, you'd start a second?"

The merchant told of how Tenorio,   59
    the garrison's new Captain, had him jailed
for smuggling. "That's his way to let you know
    the tax is going up. That man's blackmailed
    this town worse than Bradburn. And now you've bailed
us out at gunpoint. By God, it would singe
old Bradburn's beard, if he saw your revenge."

60   To this, Travis replied, with a sharp glare,
        "I haven't come for vengeance. We've been sent
  to seize the arsenal and to prepare
      to meet the reinforcements Cos has lent
      Tenorio. Now tell me where he went."
  Subdued, the trader passed along a greeting
  from the commandant, who sought a meeting.

61   The sun had sunk and stars begun to spark
        when Travis, tracked by marksmen he had picked,
  traversed a moonlit trail into the dark.
      "Tenorio! Tomorrow we expect
      our force to be increased. You can select
  a peaceful exit, or prefer a fight . . .
  I won't wait for an answer here all night."

62   A shadow that had seemed to be a tree
        abruptly moved. Startled, the rebel heard
  a Latin voice: "What is the guarantee
      that we shall not be harmed?" "You have the word
      of William Barret Travis that no hurt
  and no disgrace will be inflicted on
  your troops, if they come out unarmed at dawn."

63   The Mexican commander, in a moment,
        responded, "Travis . . . Colonel Bradburn shared
  some anecdotes of your campaign to foment
      revolt a few years back. Twice you have flared
      the tinder here. *Señor,* you should beware,
  lest General Santa Anna and his men
  ensure you never take a fort again."

At Harrisburg, a town a little way 64
    upriver, settlers watched the schooner dock
and then divulge the filibuster's prey.
    The commandant, in braid, stirred fervent talk
    beneath the bonnets that turned with his walk.
The Mayor of Harrisburg stepped forth to greet
the officer, repealing his defeat.

Infuriated, Travis told the Mayor, 65
    "Tenorio's a prisoner of war!"
The answer made the rebel clench and glare:
    "No, sir, he's not a captive anymore.
    It's you they'll fit for feathers and for tar;
the settlements are voting to condemn
your raid as one young vengeful hothead's whim."

"What's happened, Travis?" his companions pestered 66
    their bitter Captain, as he climbed the boat.
He spat out: "They've surrendered to the bastard."
    On shore, a band struck up a jaunty note
    as notables admired the fancy coat
and saber of their unexpected guest.
Men's hands he shook, and ladies' hands he kissed.

Now rumor gusted inland. Hurricanes, 67
    in carouseling, send the selfsame shock
through blinded lakes and tawny, hackling plains;
    on hearing thunder nearing, horses pock
    their pens with nervous runes, the roosters squawk,
and cattle boom in answer; so the towns
were stirred by murmur. Travis was denounced.

68   "They're saying Cos is heading toward us now!"
      a rider shouted to the startled settlers
in San Felipe's tavern. "This is how
      I told you it would be, if we let meddlers
      like Travis have their way!" A hiss like a rattler's
assented to Lem Wright's vindictive croon.
The mob dived into dusk from the saloon.

69   Like hounds whose prints erase the puma's paw
      they follow, as they drag ranchers despoiled
of goats or beeves, contemptuous of law
      and warden alike, the colonists roiled
      around the shack where Travis slept and toiled
beneath a lawyer's shingle. When they wrenched
his door, they learned their prey would not be lynched.

70   A few miles north, the prairie was at peace.
      The cattle lowed in shadow. In corrals
the horses stood like trees. The dogs had ceased
      their clamoring. The fluting of the owls
      emerged from thickets, and the bobcat's growls.
The way was lit for possum and raccoon
by a belligerent Comanche moon.

71   Two tiny riders, in that silver noon
      at midnight, made their slow uncertain way
across the chaparral. A satrap moon
      spied from the river where they chose to stay.
      Their camp was spare, in case there was a fray;
fearing a campfire's flicker would reveal
their bivouac, they gnawed a dry, cold meal.

"Remember, Joe, the night we waded through   72
    the border?" The slave shifted on the ground
beside his master. "Sure enough. Wind blew
    the fire plumb out." The pensive Travis frowned.
    "You fussed, I cussed, we nearly turned around.
Joe, tell me if I'm wrong; the old Sabine,
her eyes, they didn't glitter half as mean."

BOOK TWO

THE
FIRST REVOLT

THE ARGUMENT

In hiding, Travis tells his friend
James Bonham how he had been penned,
a prisoner, three years before,
at Anahuac, on the Gulf shore.
When Travis and an ally planned
revolt, the Colonel in command,
named Bradburn, took them hostage, and
impaled them daily on the sand.
A vigilante army swore
to rescue them — and lit a war.

BOOK TWO

A dozen dawns. Then sunrise sent its pink   *1*
transparent fingers through a musty stable
to mark an interloper. Through a chink
    the dawn light seeped, striping him in sable
    and pumpkin tones. A hayloft near the gable
erupted in a glitter of wild straw;
the intruder felt the weight, before he saw

the form, of his attacker. Down they crashed,   *2*
    the waylaid pummeled by a piston fist,
too stunned at first to fight. The two men thrashed
    through filth, like bobcats that hiss and twist
    inside a trembling thicket. Travis missed,
his foe connected. Then the stranger cried,
"For God's sake, Travis, I am on your side!"

"You *are* Buck Travis?" said a voice that rang   *3*
    with echoes. "I'm Jim Bonham. From the road
to Charleston." Travis tasted blood's tart tang.
    "From Carolina? Bonham . . . lo and behold,
    it's Jimmy Bonham. We two were — how old?"
James Bonham rubbed his jaw. "Seems you've been taught
some new tricks since the last time that we fought."

4 "Apologies," the Texan rebel said.
  "I can't afford to be the second draw,
now that I wear a price upon my head.
  You're in a land where one man's will is law."
  Freeing himself from clinging quills of straw,
Buck Travis led his visitor outside
to meet the one he sought to make his bride.

5 Alarmed, Rebecca Cummings crossed the yard
  that parted the saloon her brother ran
from stables where her lover stood on guard
  against besieging shadows. When her man
  had told of his mistake, Becky began:
"Why, Mister Bonham, let us make amends;
Lord knows that Buck has lost too many friends."

6 The lawyer, fresh from Alabama, paid
  for breakfast with a tale. During a trial
that he had argued, Bonham thought a maid
  offended by a judge. At once, with style,
  he tweaked a nose both honorable and vile.
The nose had him confined. "Belle after belle
piled up the tribute flowers in my cell.

7 "All but for one, betrothed to be my bride.
  She frowned upon my taking up the cause
of any other woman's sacred pride;
  to me, the ladies' martyr behind bars,
  milady sent her ring, fresh from her claws.
And so," Bonham smiled, "with a shattered heart
I've wandered here, to make a second start."

The servant interrupted, to report   *8*
    the gig was packed. As Becky went to bid
her brother bye, Travis helped Joe to port
    a saddle to a horse. He fixed the bit:
    "We're off to where I can be better hid;
too many know I'm here." Bonham agreed:
"I only raised your name, and you were treed."

Glancing houseward, Travis summed up his life   *9*
    before the one-man jury of his friend:
in Alabama, he had left a wife,
    he quietly explained. She would not send
    their son to him, or let their marriage end,
so he and Becky could not yet be wed.
Then Becky neared. Of this, no more was said.

Before the prairie could begin to steam   *10*
    inside the oven sky, they had begun
their trek to exile. Joe chided the team
    of mules that drew the gig; shielded from sun
    by a bonnet, Becky mused. Riding shotgun
with Travis, James Butler Bonham was told
of Anahuac, site of the first revolt.

"Two years ago — no, three, in Thirty-Two —   *11*
    it seems forever — I had just arrived
in Anahuac . . . but most of us were new
    to Texas, fresh from the States, unwived,
    undebted, or unpunished. We revived
that groggy settlement upon the coast;
it was a young man's town, all booze and boast.

33

12   "The commandant of the presidio
          was one of our own breed, a fellow named
     John Davis Bradburn. Before Mexico
          enrolled him in its ranks, he had been famed
          back home in Mississippi, where — ashamed
     though he was to admit it — his face haunted
     post office walls. At least there he was wanted.

13   "Of course we smuggled goods in from the States;
          that was the country's custom, one defied
     by no good Texan. As for tariff rates,
          those formed, at most, a rough-and-ready guide
          to calculating the commander's bribe.
     The Latin officer's less strict than sly;
     his motto: 'I obey, but don't comply.'

14   "This was the slogan that had always guided
          Dom Ugartechea, who governed Fort
     Velasco, and Piedras, who presided
          at Nacogdoches. If they tried to extort
          too much too fast, an uprising would start;
     they took care not to jerk the reins, upon
     instructions from General Mier y Teran.

15   "We thought that Mississippi's renegade
          would soon adopt the lax philosophy
     of Mexico, as he had donned its braid,
          and, like the rest, treat us indulgently.
          But Bradburn — Colonel Bradburn, pardon me —
     got drunk on office, the way white trash
     intoxicate themselves on bathtub mash.

"Like Marius, the exile was upraised   *16*
      by rabble legions — *presidarios,*
a hundred of them, men who'd been disgraced
      and sent to soldier duty, Mexico's
      debased and desperate. John Bradburn chose
the cruelest to make his Praetorian Guard,
and let the others romp, hounds in a yard.

"The Colonel drafted men, and boys as well,   *17*
      to brick two kilns inside the palisade;
like Hebrew slaves, they toiled until they fell
      for a pharaoh in a kepi and some braid.
      The ladies — there were some — were soon afraid
of those who should defend them, the police.
Thus a buckra Caesar made a Latin peace.

"Appeals to Bradburn's masters had no effect.   *18*
      The government down south had come apart.
Since Spain was ousted, this poor derelict
      has drifted, prey for pirates. From the start
      their army's auctioned office in the mart.
Now Santa Anna renounced his allegiance
to Bustamante. Both gathered their legions.

"As civil war was kindled once again,   *19*
      commanders in Coahuila and in Texas
were cautious, waiting to see who would win.
      Now masterless, John Bradburn piled new taxes
      upon us, booty for his convict Mexes;
and then he told our help that they were free;
he made our boys a colored soldiery."

20   The Southerners glanced back at strong young Joe,
          commanding the carriage. Travis resumed:
"At that point we resolved to overthrow
      the mercenary. One midnight, I boomed
      from darkness to a picket as he loomed
atop the palisade: *'Señor! Señor!*
The vigilantes mass nearby for war!'

21   "As we had hoped, the message, once relayed
          to Bradburn, goosed the rascal. He sent troops
to flush for ghosts, the way a townsman played
      for a fool will stalk the snipe. The empty coop's
      contingent could have been trapped, if our group's
determination had not failed. Instead,
like Samson we pulled ruin on our heads.

22   "The Alabaman judge who taught me law
          conveyed much wisdom when he shared his skill;
what I remember most is this old saw:
      'Don't hit a man, unless you mean to kill.'
      We'd injured Bradburn, and yet left him still
empowered to avenge his tortured pride;
and so he did, upon the next day's tide.

23   "His soldiers seized my good friend Patrick Jack,
          like me, a leader of the opposition.
They caught him at the wharf of Anahuac,
      greeting a sloop that smuggled ammunition
      from New Orleans. Bradburn charged him with sedition
and jailed him in the fort. That lunatic
commander locked him in a kiln of brick.

"I led three dozen roaring colonists   *24*
    to face down Bradburn at the fortress gate,
demanding that he cancel the arrests
    and free Pat Jack; then we'd negotiate.
    His answer was a stare of feral hate;
he gave an order, and I was enclosed
by dozens of armed *presidarios.*

"'I'll learn y'all who's in charge at Anahuac!'   *25*
    the mercenary snarled. His creatures tore
my jacket and my shirt right off my back,
    and bound my wrists till they were raw and sore.
    He laughed the louder as I spat and swore;
my friends could only watch, as Bradburn's goons
staked me, spread-eagle, on the stinging stones.

"His saber at my throat, the renegade   *26*
    replied to my companions with a sneer:
'If any of y'all try to mount a raid,
    then Jack and Travis will be buried here.'
    Frank Johnson, a veteran of this frontier,
told Bradburn he'd soon pay the penalty;
I heard him holler, 'Buck, you'll soon be free!'

"I never yet had drunk distilled despair   *27*
    until the crowd reluctantly retreated,
leaving me a helpless hostage there,
    half-naked, burning, crucified, defeated.
    The sun seared into me the way a heated
iron marks a calf; the scorch of that brand
was least, though, of the torments they had planned.

28   "With night came yet a new trial to survive.
         They sealed me in a kiln of crumbling brick,
tight as a coffin, whose load, still alive,
         can hear the hail of sod fall, fast and thick.
         The kilns — for there were two — by some cruel trick
were named for the saints of free Mexico,
the patriots Morelos and Hidalgo.

29   "The other dome of brick entombed Pat Jack,
         my partner in the plot, and now my mate
in agony. The wardens would attack
         whenever we tried to communicate,
         pounding us bloody. We learned to create
a private code of whistles, coughs, and kicks,
assuring one another through the bricks.

30   "That bastard Bradburn staked us every day
         as a warning to the settlers, crucified
us daily in a tyrannous display.
         Each sunset, we were shoved again inside
         the cramping ovens. Much as we two tried
to nurture our defiance, we were stuff
more brittle than the clay that kilns make tough.

31   "There was a man, Montera — less a man
         than animal — but animals aren't cruel,
though they can be ferocious. . . . What men can
         inflict on men, I learned, in that bleak school.
         I'd cheer on my companion, when that ghoul
afflicted him. . . . The worst torture, it seems,
is writhing helpless as your buddy screams.

"While we fought to endure at Anahuac,   *32*
    at Turtle Bayou, northward up the coast,
the volunteers, by hundreds, bivouacked.
    As its first act, that brave and righteous host
    elected our friend Johnson. He composed
defenses of the imminent revolt,
in words that echoed like a thunderbolt.

"The Turtle Bayou Resolutions told   *33*
    of Bradburn's usurpations and abuses;
the goal, they claimed, was to restore the old
    accustomed liberties and civil uses
    of Mexico. . . . If all of this confuses
your patient mind, consider this: the charter
described Santa Anna as a saintly martyr.

"Frank Johnson reasoned that the now insurgent   *34*
    commander would be pleased to have us rise
in Texas — and preoccupied by urgent
    campaigns to make the capital his prize.
    Later, the general chose to centralize —
but then, the friends of Texan liberty
were Santa Anna's Yankee cavalry.

"From Johnson's camp, riders began to depart   *35*
    with copies of the Turtle Bayou writs —
John Austin, to a town he'd helped to start,
    Brazoria, a settlement that sits
    within the 'Arms of God' — in Spanish, it's
the *Brazos de Dios* — no, this was John,
not Stephen Austin — before I go on,

36   "I'll try to tease this tangle with a tale.
          John Austin, a Connecticut Yankee
      like Stephen, after studying at Yale,
          took up a life of jetsam drift at sea.
          In New Orleans, Austin joined the conspiracy
      of Doctor James Long, who planned to win
      this country for our Saxon race of men.

37   "With Long and with another filibuster,
          Ben Milam, Austin warred, not once, but twice,
      for Texan independence, winning luster,
          but losing each campaign. Their only prize
          was prison in the south; only advice
      to Mexico from the U.S. envoy there,
      Joel Poinsett, caused the trio to be spared.

38   "It seems that Poinsett went to school at Yale
          with Austin; as they say, it's who you know.
      Though three were freed, one of the friends would fail
          to leave the capital of Mexico;
          as they were being ushered from the hoosegow,
      one of the guards — on orders, it is said —
      planted a bullet in the doctor's head.

39   "Ben Milam and John Austin had the task
          of bringing news of their companion's fate
      to Jane, his wife, his widow. She would mask
          her sorrow with the courage of the great;
          to this day, though, as though dressed for a state
      funeral, Mrs. Long wears only black;
      of late, the ash of age has matched the sack.

"They came to conquer, but they stayed to build.   40
    This trio — Austin, Milam, Mrs. Long —
planted Brazoria. Soon laughter spilled
    most nights from Jane Long's tavern, and bright song.
    The spirit of that place seemed strange among
those spirits; like Queen Circe, she used wine
to learn who were the heroes, who the swine.

"A few whom Widow Long considered fit   41
    successors to her husband and his men
would be inducted, hardly knowing it
    at first, into the cause. Guests in her den,
    we'd hear the saga of American
attempts on Texas; what James Long designed
was ours to finish. We had been assigned.

"That beautiful sad woman was presiding,   42
    it hardly need be said, within the inn
when the Brazorians were deciding
    what action they should take, and how, and when.
    John Austin, that old soldier, once again
unfurled the ragged banner of revolt;
his audience, though, kept their passion rolled.

"The farmers in these parts fear to offend   43
    the master — any master — of the legions;
they know what to expect if troops descend
    on Texas, from the wreck of neighbor regions.
    Thus tyranny wins the farmer's allegiance —
but I may be too ready to accuse;
those with the least have got the most to lose.

44   "Foremost among the brave — the reckless — few
         inspired to follow Austin was a fellow
    whom all of us Americans here knew;
         we knew him by his voice, a bullfrog's bellow,
         and by the little planet of his belly,
    and by his fringe of deerskin, and a hat
    equipped with paws, the pelt of a bobcat.

45   "Behold Strap Buckner, coon-ass Hercules,
         complete with lion skin, one of those brutes
    who claim both horse and gator pedigrees.
         'We can make jaw-music till the owl hoots,
         and write a mess of brand-new Resolutes —
    for what? Just honking like a Delta goose
    ain't gonna bust old Bradburn's calaboose.'

46   "With only a few dozen volunteers
         (Strap Buckner counted twice) to make a troop,
    John took to canvas, after many years.
         He commandeered *Brazoria,* a sloop
         whose mate remained on board, to guide the group
    and see the vessel suffered from no harm.
    Once more John Austin sailed to make a storm.

47   "The plan was hazardous. The sloop would bring
         both stores and cannon to Frank Johnson's corps
    outside of Anahuac. They had to swing
         around a fort, Velasco, on the shore,
         a cactus bristling with the spines of war,
    studding the delta where the Brazos fed
    the hungry Gulf with what the land had bled.

"Dom Ugartechea, the officer   *48*
   in charge of Fort Velasco, was well known
to Austin, who asked if he would defer
   and let the party pass, no protest shown.
   Though Ugartechea would weep like stone
if Bradburn faced a fitting punishment,
he served, not justice, but the government;

he could not let the sloop pass unopposed.   *49*
   The two men shook — add this, to Bradburn's charges,
that thanks to him such friends were forced to blows.
   Retreating up the river, next to barges
   Brazoria docked, along the grassy marges
of Eagle Island — but you must have heard
of Wharton, and of Jared Groce's hoard.

"Will Wharton, when he married Groce's daughter,   *50*
   annexed the cotton duchy the old man
had built upon his fastness in the water.
   Now Wharton's gangs carried out Austin's plan,
   refitting the *Brazoria* as a man
of war, with fascines made of wispy bales,
and cannons nosing over the gunwales.

"They tell me, who were there, that revelry   *51*
   succeeded labor. On the green parquet
of Eagle Island, Texans, slave and free,
   shared barbecue and whiskey, while the day
   cooled into dusk. Fireflies surprised the gray,
as flickers just as silent showed the host
of thunderheads that mustered near the coast.

52 "I watched that glimmer in that welcome cloud
    from where I twisted, staked into the sand.
  John Bradburn must have seen that gales allowed
    relief for my raw flesh; he came to stand
    above me and related what he planned:
  'Well, Travis, seems your friends have hitched a wave
  to hurry here. They'll liberate your grave.'

53 "His mockery was lost, as thunder growled.
    The trees began to rattle, full of wind.
  A few miles north of where my captor scowled,
    Colonel Piedras was asked to attend
    an execution by Frank Johnson's men.
  The muskets popped, the field was filled with smoke,
  a tethered boy dropped sagging on an oak.

54 "'He killed a kid his age,' Frank told the chief
    of Nacogdoches, 'when his bullet missed
  its target: me. That Mississippi thief
    is now a gangster, paying to enlist
    assassins like that boy.' Piedras hissed:
  'No officer has ever done such harm
  to us as this Yank in our uniform.'

55 "Like Ugartechea, Piedras felt
    compassion for us, and yet could not draw
  his sword against a man who wore the pelt
    of Mexico. What followed was a draw,
    a 'Meskin standoff,' as the force of law
  from Nacogdoches and the rebel force
  retired to twilit tents with shared remorse.

"Some distance to the south, the schooner called   *56*
    Brazoria soon dropped anchor, where its spars
could not be seen by pickets who patrolled.
    At night, the dune hills there are marked by scars
    when hopping mice dance underneath the stars,
the prey of the coyote; where those mice
cavort, grim gunmen jogged, alert, precise.

"Earth's thunder was preempted by our own.   *57*
    Brazoria now commenced a cannonade,
the signal for the gunmen to make known
    their presence. Their diversionary raid
    allowed a second sally to be made
by Austin's party, limping from the weight
of breastworks they had made the schooner's freight.

"Unwitnessed, that team halted fifty feet   *58*
    from Fort Velasco's palisaded berm.
Like crabs in sand, they mined, swift and discreet,
    gouging out trenches and packing them firm.
    One of the volunteers, though, found the worm
in his tequila; Ed Robinson, sloshed
and swaying, lobbed a shot. The raid was botched.

"That drunken fool — he was the first to fall.   *59*
    He tippled, then he toppled to a crash.
The swivel gun atop the fortress wall
    tattooed the scrambling raiders, lancing flesh
    with lead and splinters. Men began to thrash
and rise from sand, as though on Judgment Day,
to curse, or warn, or wail, or weep, or pray.

60   "They say Strap Buckner shimmied through the dunes,
            marooned like a monster whale before the fort;
        there he was betrayed, by the rainbowed moon's
            effulgence. With a blast as his retort,
            he answered every shot, till he ran short
        of fortune, and a ricocheting ball
        pierced all his pelts. There was a mighty fall.

61   "Now Austin scanned the wreck of his design.
            The swivel gun stitched metal to the beach
        between the ship, still blasting from the brine,
            and raiders. The survivors could not reach
            the sloop that lightning vied with guns to bleach.
        Explosions, like the cubs that move a bear
        to bellow, woke deep thunder in the air.

62   "In Anahuac, Frank Johnson did not know
            that down at Fort Velasco war had flared,
        that Texan troops and troops of Mexico
            were trading lead. At dawn, as he prepared
            to fight the bluecoats, a messenger shared
        news of a decree — till then (they said) ignored —
        that made Piedras Bradburn's overlord.

63   "'Well, bless the Virgin, boys,'" Frank Johnson told
            the Mexicans. Together now, they pounded
        the road to Anahuac as rain unrolled,
            the buckskin and the bandolier compounded.
            Inside my crypt, I heard the warning sounded
        in Spanish and in English. Then the crack
        of muskets echoed through Fort Anahuac.

"Confinement had reduced me to a vile   *64*
    homunculus; Montera hauled a figure
half-human from the kiln. His checkered smile
    divulged his thought; before he pulled the trigger,
    my Joe told him to halt. 'Looky, that nigger
is shooting Travis!' Rescuers, confused
by Joe's Mex outfit, struck. While they abused

my boy, Montera vanished with a laugh.   *65*
    John Bradburn, though, was pinned by pioneers.
Pat Jack, as wobbly as a wet new calf,
    soon aimed a borrowed gun between the ears
    of Colonel John D. Bradburn. Now the sneers
belonged to Pat, hearing his captive plea:
'Piedras, I submit to custody.'

"Put down the pistol, Pat," Frank Johnson urged   *66*
    my shuddering companion. I hear tell
the rebel blood of passion pinkly surged
    in Pat's tight face. 'I'm sending him to hell.'
    In town, the church marked freedom with a knell.
Pat let the pistol sink. Piedras snapped
an order. With the crowd, the irons clapped.

"Down at Velasco, storming turned the stores   *67*
    of gunpowder to mud, forcing a lull.
The raiders dragged themselves back to the shore's
    concussions, taunted by the shrieking gull.
    They learned a cannonball had punched the hull;
the mate who, in the hold, thought he'd escaped
the battle had left little to be scraped.

68 "Into the low white sky, above the berms,
        more white ascended. Ugartechea's corps
surrendered. Wharton quickly wrote the terms
        the two commanders signed upon a shore
        piled with a dozen who would fight no more.
Chased from the bodies, gulls began to keen.
By noontime all of Texas was serene.

69 "Piedras, ruling now at Anahuac,
        had prisoners transferred to Liberty
for civil trial; there I, along with Jack,
        as that town's name might hint, were soon set free.
        Our captor, captive, rode with cavalry
to Nacogdoches. And Velasco's fort?
Disarmed, it was a place where mice could sport.

70 "The battle claimed a final casualty.
        In Coahuila, General Mier y Teran,
responsible for Texas, learned that he
        had been disgraced. The general went to don
        his full dress uniform, then prayed alone
within a ruined church. Into the ground
he set his sword, and sighed, and toppled down."

BOOK THREE

IDYLLS

THE ARGUMENT

News of the raid on Anahuac
prompts Santa Anna to strike back;
he orders the arrest of all
the rebels. Travis wins a small
reminder of his bitter past;
with family, his days are passed.
His country idyll, though, is ended
by Jane Long, the widow who tended
Travis after his release
from Anahuac. Her news: the peace
has broken down. The war they sought
for independence will be fought.

BOOK THREE

By afternoon the journey was complete.   1
Rebecca caught her breath, when she beheld
the crumbled mission that would be the seat
    of Travis in his exile. Time had felled
    the timbers that the limestone once upheld;
the sacristy, where brothers in their cowls
had softly sung, was now a court for owls.

They set to work, as shadows grew and merged,   2
    and built a lean-to round one chalky wall.
By twilight all the woodland was submerged
    in dimness. Kindred dark began to crawl,
    a seeping stain, from zenith, till the pall
of sky with earth's was blended, and below
the stars the only light was one fire's glow.

At fluctuating flicker Travis peered,   3
    a medium enrapt by clouded glass.
"I knew," he said, "back when I volunteered
    for Anahuac, things might come to this pass.
    This was a test to learn if we were a mass
or mere minority. We're overpowered
— for now, at least — by the tribe of the coward."

4   "It chafes, I know," he heard his comrade say.
         "Three years ago, I buckled on a sword
and spurs and donned a Nullifier's gray;
         I longed to send that Tennessean's horde
         of Hessians to their master, gimped and gored.
My neighbors flinched, though, when they saw the gun
old Jackson pulled on us from Washington."

5   To Bonham's words, the flames began to snap.
         "Let Texas be annexed unto the South
and we can leave a Union grown a trap.
         Just think of the potential for our growth —
         there's Cuba, Haiti, the isthmus, and the mouth
of the Amazon. Our cotton and our cane
could ring a Gulf renamed the Dixie Main."

6   Travis replied: "Sam Houston's known to speak
         of founding a new Rocky Mountain empire.
Division, though, would make the nation weak.
         Each petty state would be its neighbor's vampire,
         till Britain, France, or Russia played the umpire.
Look at the Rhineland, or at Italy;
that's what America, once split, would be.

7   "Or look round, at what's left of mighty Spain.
         No, sir, the Union's fate is to expand,
absorbing a free Texas in its train,
         New Mexico, the Oregon, the grand
         expanse of California, all the land
the British claim in Canada. One strong
dominion, with one law, one flag, one tongue."

James Butler Bonham, chuckling, shook his head: *8*
    "Depend upon it, sir, our liberties
will perish of the creeping rot that's bred
    of empire. To mere servile satrapies
    the states will be diminished, if it please
some Saxon Caesar or Yankee Bonaparte;
far better, to live freely, and apart."

To his companion Travis raised a toast: *9*
    "I give you Greece." "I give you Roman peace."
Then Travis murmured, "Here we have disposed
    of countries, when we cannot even seize
    a county." Darkness rattled sieging trees.
The friends patrolled, returning to retire
to dreaming kindled by the dwindled fire.

Far to the south, through galleries of a great   *10*
    palatial residence, an officer hurried
upon an urgent mission for the state,
    his posture stiff, pace brisk, and aspect worried.
    At his approach, gloves blizzarded and flurried,
saluting, as grand doors were opened wide.
Almonte stopped, stunned by the scene inside.

The pygmies who adopted Hercules   *11*
    had found a new protector, so it seemed,
though parrots, not cranes ranked by rookeries,
    attacked the titan as the tiny teemed.
    Almonte could have warranted he dreamed
when Mexico's commander, in his vest
and shirtsleeves, turned, hearing himself addressed.

12 The Colonel's boot heels knapped, machinelike, loud.
   "Your Excellency, the favor of a word . . . ?"
The President came wading through the crowd
  of tots, a scarlet nightmare of a bird
  riding his shoulder. The adjutant had heard
that Santa Anna had adopted scores
of children he had orphaned in his wars.

13 "What is it now? This business cannot wait?"
   the President replied, the red macaw
beside his ear, a councilor of state.
   He learned a band of Texans dared to draw
   their swords against the agents of his law:
"The colonies, though, have condemned the raid
upon Anáhuac this man Travis made.

14 "This Travis, a young lawyer, is the same
   who led a revolt there, three years ago,
against Juan Bradburn." "I recall the name
   of Bradburn . . ." Santa Anna's voice was low.
   "This Travis, he's a puppet. Our true foe
is Andrew Jackson, their 'Old Hickory,'
no stranger to subversive trickery.

15 "Twenty years ago, that general, stationed near
   the boundary of Florida, helped to guide
rebellion by the yanqui pioneers
   against the rule of Spain. Now he has tried
   to do the same with Texas — from outside,
of course, and through his proxies, like this man
named Travis. But I have perceived his plan.

"Draw up a writ that calls upon the settlers   16
    in Texas, on pain of martial occupation,
to render up all these seditious meddlers
    for trial by General Cos where he is stationed.
    I'll have this Travis shot, to teach his nation
that we are not some feeble Indian band
to be expelled by Jackson from our land."

The parrot screeched in echo, as it hopped   17
    from Santa Anna's shoulder to his wrist.
"Almonte, take him. . . . No, no, he won't drop
    my pretty bird —" This, at the bird's protest.
    The parrot pecked Almonte's medaled chest.
The Colonel had known trials, since he first
became a soldier; this, though, was the worst.

One child sat all alone upon the floor,   18
    morosely toying with the tiny crutch
that stood in for a leg lost in a war.
    He knotted up in fear, when he was clutched;
    but soon, on Santa Anna's neck, he touched
the piñata. Laughing, the orphan flailed;
from the gutted bull, like blood, the candy hailed.

In Texas, Bonham went upon his way,   19
    his old friend's secrets locked within his mind.
The exile and his servant, day by day,
    enlarged the shack from a mere hunting blind
    to something like a cabin. So, designed
by instinct's artless art, a hive expands
near flower fields patrolled by droning bands.

20   The exile practiced pistolry for hours,
             annihilating branches by the score;
        on summer nights, besieged by thundershowers,
             the lovers wound, sealed in by the downpour.
             When Becky woke at night, through the stone door
        she'd glimpse her lover, by a candle's arc,
        construing Scott, Herodotus, or Plutarch.

21   One of their rare and covert visitors
             brought news one day that Travis would not share.
        "Some business" — Becky's man was strangely terse;
             he had to go; he could not tell her where.
             Before he left, she placed the ring she wore,
        a smoky cat's-eye, on her darling's hand,
        as though to chain him with the little band.

22   One morning, at the notch on the skyline
             she knew by now as well as her own face,
        a growing seed appeared. Her hopes defined
             the image first, before her eyes could trace
             her man's familiar form. Though her heart raced,
        with measured dignity the woman strode
        to meet her man returning on the road.

23   He did not ride alone. A yellow dog
             was panting by the doubly burdened horse,
        but Becky hardly noticed. Travis dragged
             the reins; then, with the same strong, gentle force,
             he handed her an elfin boy, the source
        of her perplexity. She listened, stunned:
        "Becky, this is Charles Edward. . . . He's my son."

Buck's wife in Alabama, Becky learned,   *24*
   refused still to divorce him; but his plea
and threat and bluster finally had earned
   the father uncontested custody
   of their one boy. Thus a new family,
in the eyes of God, if not of governments,
on that unstoried prairie would commence.

The days that followed were not part of time,   *25*
   no more than oxbow lakes remain a part
of rivers with whose curves their swervings rhyme.
   A child beside his child, Buck got a start
   a second time in life. Once more, all art
and skill were wizardry, once more the world
was fragrant, frail, and recently unfurled.

Like Adam dubbing animals with words,   *26*
   the father taught his image how to name
the roadrunners and candied ladybirds,
   the snake, that molten pipe blown on a flame,
   the strafing hummingbird, the deer that frame
a hazy dawn, so faint that they will seem
to be but shadows in the silver steam.

They hunted arrowheads, and fossil shells,   *27*
   and shreds from snakes the raking flint would flay.
They gathered paintbrushes, and yucca bells,
   and thistle blooms to make Becky's bouquet.
   And when coyotes had sung the sunken day,
the boy would learn what circus figures dwell
within the slow, blue, blinking carousel.

28   By moonlight they watched coons, like small, intense
              and sad-eyed bears, sift supper's cold remains;
      by noonlight they would mark the handlike prints
              that patterned mud in ornamental chains.
              Sometimes the dog would lead them through dry rains
      of startled grasshoppers to a raccoon
      glimpsed through the boughs, a mottled, mortal moon.

29   In silver morning and in twilight gray,
              the men would wait in thickets for the deer.
      His father told Charles Edward of the day
              that he became a man in his twelfth year,
              when Pa and Uncle Alex joined to smear
      the life still bubbling from his first slain buck
      upon the cheeks and forehead of young Buck.

30   A rustle. Joe squeezed Charles, as Travis aimed.
              A crack, and spooling smoke. Weaving, the beast
      attacked the antlered shrubs. Into the maimed
              and palpitating creature, Travis eased
              his Bowie knife. The velvet pumping ceased.
      Charles Edward stared. He shrank back, when his dad
      stretched out a finger slick with shiny blood.

31   Back at the cabin, Becky sighed, dismayed,
              when Joe and Travis limped out of the brush,
      toting the sagging brute, in a parade
              Charles Edward led. The red was not a flush
              upon the boy; it glistened. "Go and wash
      your face right now" — his second mother's plea.
      To Buck she murmured: "We've got company."

Three years had passed since Travis had exchanged   *32*
   confinement in the kiln at Anahuac
for new captivity. His thoughts deranged
    by fever, he had rattled on a rack
    of cool soft linen. Every new attack
brought ministering spirits to eclipse
the candle, daub his brow and dew his lips.

His hospital, he learned, was Jane Long's tavern,   *33*
   far from the coast, upon the Brazos banks.
The room was quiet as a tomb or cavern,
    though music sometimes seeped up through the planks.
    When a muddied mind grew clear, he offered thanks
to the widow Long, and payment for his care;
of payment, though, the lady would not hear.

"You've paid already, William," Jane replied.   *34*
   She was a tone, a waterlight, a shade.
"To win our freedom, you quite nearly died.
    For that, you are the one to be repaid."
    Her soft hand cooled his brow. "How long we've prayed . . .
When some day this is chronicled, your name's
assured a place beside that of my James."

The strength the ordeal had wrung out of his flesh   *35*
   refoliated soon, the way a wood
dismasted by a fire will know a fresh
    luxuriance; where toppled columns stood,
    green saplings banner; birds prospect for food
in wet black corduroy. So Travis mended,
a broken sparrow that a girl child tended,

36   an eaglet hobbled in a queen's own mews.
          A captivated Travis learned details
of the earlier revolution from the Muse
          of Texan filibusters, from the pale
          palladium of soldiers doomed to fail.
His mind, diverted from his injury,
gazed back in time a quarter century.

37   "James warned me not to join him," Jane Long said,
          her eyes upon the painted soldier's face
and not upon the soldier in her bed.
          "I was to stay home in New Orleans, and raise
          our little girl, and abacus the days
until the arrival of our second child
 — or his return from warring in the wild.

38   "Oh, he was right — but I was just a girl,
          impetuous, determined. . . . And a war!
Compared to that, what was the gentry's whirl?
          All of my life, I'd heard how Aaron Burr
          and General Wilkinson, my kinsman, were
allied to conquer Texas — now my James,
where they had failed, would accomplish their aims.

39   "And so I sailed for Texas, with my daughter,
          then eight, and my girl Kian, and a child
nascent within me, confident that slaughter
          would be complete before Galveston isle
          with flourishes greeted the queen of the wild.
Instead, as the first winds of winter crooned,
my partial family found itself marooned.

"John Austin and Ben Milam had joined James   *40*
    to strike more deeply into Mexico;
the garrison he left there — to their shame! —
    would wait for them no more, and chose to go.
    If I'd been a mesquite, with roots that grow
a mile beneath the earth, I would have been
more easily pulled up by James's men.

"They left a month's supplies, and then they left.   *41*
    One woman and two girls now held the fort.
I smiled and sang, although I felt bereft.
    Though held to strictest rations, we fell short
    of food in a few weeks; and still, that port
remained forgot by man. I began to dread
that James was now, and we would soon be, dead.

"The gales of winter quickly laid us siege.   *42*
    The compound's toothworn timbers broke the blast,
but Kian and I had to brave the beach
    to pull the trotlines that we nightly cast —
    oh, William, those cold gusts would cut like glass!
That salt wind would make oceans of the eyes
and turn a body's very bones to ice.

"Our Bible was our comfort, and a few   *43*
    romances I had brought in my valise
from New Orleans. With their help, we exiles flew
    to lands where swains had royal pedigrees
    and girls disguised as boys braved pirate seas.
Unworthy entertainments, I must say;
and yet, those stories saved us, in a way.

44   "I still remember Kian's voice, when she
          called from the palisade, 'Miss Jane, Miss Jane!'
     She laughed and clapped, possessed by demon glee.
          At first, I joined her, when I saw the chain
          of fires across the strait. I looked again,
     and realized that friendly-seeming blaze
     was lit by savages — Karankaways.

45   "At dawn, from the beach opposing our own,
          a file of dark canoes glided to sea,
     like alligators easing, one by one,
          across a slough. Their crews were shocked to see
          a flag rise in a fort that seemed to be
     abandoned; they'd been more shocked, I suppose,
     to learn they viewed a lady's underclothes.

46   "With Kian's help — poor, terrified, sweet girl —
          I packed grapeshot down an abandoned bore,
     and lit the powder. That explosion hurled
          a warning to the barks nearest the shore.
          We watched the Indians halt and turn and oar
     back to the torchlit sands of Galveston.
     The good Lord had preserved us. We had won.

47   "From that day forth, we never dared to leave
          the palisade, except in uniforms.
     Like shepherdesses trying to deceive
          the pirates in a tale, we hid our charms,
          Kian and I, in shirts and coats whose arms
     drooped past our hands, and baggy, dragging pants,
     precautions we had learned from a romance.

"Soon, laden by James's unborn child,   48
    I could not work at all. To Kian passed
the duty to sustain us in the wild.
    A night came I was sure would be my last;
    my shrieks were blended with a blizzard's blast;
dear Kian held me, as, amid the screams,
I bore a second daughter to my James.

"The Lord's lately reclaimed her; at that hour   49
    I counted her a miracle, a sign
to reassure us, from a watching power.
    More proof that we were wards of a divine
    custodian came soon. I drew a line
to find a giant catfish at the end;
what joy could such an augury portend?

"Like Jonah we abided on that fish   50
    until one day a sail showed out at sea,
first petal of the spring, a granted wish.
    The first of Stephen Austin's colony,
    approved because of his diplomacy,
found us at Fort Defiance, waiting word
that James had conquered Texas by the sword.

"They told us the campaign had met defeat   51
    in Mexico; some filibusters fell
in combat, others vanished in retreat.
    With John and Ben, James had shared a cell
    in Mexico, a catacomb, a hell;
the instant they were pardoned and released,
my James was shot by some half-blooded beast."

52 The widow, for a while, could speak no more.
        In silence she studied the Doctor's sword
    upon the wall, a fang snapped from a war
            that fed upon its maker. "Ben brought word
            from Mexico of all that had occurred,
    some fourteen years ago . . ." Her resignation
    gave way to anger at her native nation.

53 "Damn Washington! I blame their policy,
        as much as Mexico, for our defeat.
    For years the U.S. winked at the piracy —
            as it has been misnamed — of Jean Laffite.
            I met him. James himself sent me to treat
    with that gallant corsair, at his resort
    on Galveston, not far from our own fort.

54 "Laffite had built a palace of red brick,
        La Maison Rouge, and filled it up with treasure
    from England, France, and Spain. I had my pick
            of wines to match a dinner for my pleasure.
            He was no thug, but a gentleman of leisure,
    a cavalier, I learned, in our colloquy
    in the dialect of love and policy.

55 "I won a promise from that Gallic Drake:
        while James engaged the Mexicans on land,
    Laffite would make the Gulf a Texan lake.
            If all went as we had agreed and planned,
            the Gaul, a second time, would help to plant
    a new Saxon republic in the west;
    Spain's ruins would become an eaglet's nest.

"But Washington reversed its policy,   56
    and sent the navy to harass Laffite.
When James needed his allies out at sea,
    they had been scattered, by the American fleet.
    The cannon of our mother country beat
the grand walls of La Maison Rouge to red
detritus, as their noble master fled.

"Sometimes I think of how the banquet hall   57
    where candles glimmered and the goblet swished
must look today. I wonder what might crawl
    where dancers turned. And breakers — have they washed
    where carpets were? All shattered, now, all hushed."
Jane Long fell silent, in a reverie.
From far below rose filtered revelry.

All this was sunk in memory three years deep   58
    when Travis hurried from the heat of noon
into the mission he had made his keep.
    There Kian stood, and Mrs. Long, the moon
    to Becky's tawny day, a statue hewn
of ivory and cold obsidian,
immutable as a meridian.

"Why, Jane . . . ah, Mrs. Long," Travis began.   59
    Like a tardy pupil who has dashed to school
damp from the shower, Travis ran a hand
    through tangled hair. The widow's voice was cool,
    peremptory. "I have ignored the rule
of secrecy because you have to know
your arrest has been ordered by Mexico."

60   "I'm not surprised," said Travis, though he winced.
        Becky touched him gently, and then she turned
to face their solemn visitor, incensed.
        "You might have led them here!" The lady spurned
        the protest, as if she had not discerned
the woman. "William, it's time to leave this place;
Santa Anna has redeemed you from disgrace."

61   Jane Long explained. The government's command
        that Travis be rendered up, a sacrifice,
had led the Texans, almost to a man,
        to rally round the War Dogs. In the eyes
        of Texas, Travis learned to his surprise,
he was a symbol of their resolution
to answer tyranny with revolution.

62   Only the day before, the widow Long
        had stood beside Ben Milam, Houston, Wharton,
and other friends of Travis in the throng
        in San Felipe. Stephen Austin, pardoned
        by Mexico, now feeble and disheartened
from long imprisonment, had sadly said
his hopes for a peaceful settlement were dead.

63   "It's war," Travis murmured. A slow smile spread
        across his boyish face. "It's war, it's war!"
He hugged Rebecca; growing calm, he said,
        "It's war, then." Jane sent Kian to the car;
        the girl returned with a plank or a bar
wrapped in a blanket — but no, that was wrong;
it was the sword once wielded by James Long.

A paladin charged by a somber queen,   *64*
    William Barret Travis drew the blade
in pious silence, dazzled by the sheen.
    The rebel's widow smiled. Becky, dismayed,
    touched the ring on Buck's left hand. His right hand weighed
a greater metal, as his boy, with a bough,
began to jab and flay a fancied foe.

BOOK FOUR

HORSE

SOLDIER

THE ARGUMENT

Midwinter, Eighteen Thirty-Five.
The packtrains from the south arrive
to help the troops of Mexico
endure in San Antonio
despite the Texan siege. Intent
on winning glory, Travis, sent
to stop the trains with fellow rangers,
encounters more than human dangers.

BOOK FOUR

The spirit dog. That is the name the nation   *1*
who dwelled first in our sea of grass bestowed
upon the beasts who served in the invasion
    of strangers from the east. From servitude
    a few escaped, engendering a brood
of horses that would never know the reins —
the mustangs, dogged spirits of the plains.

Those herds have melted now, like thunderheads   *2*
    resolved in rain, in river, and in sea;
reconstitute them, Lady, let slim heads
    emerge from time's avulsion, let us see
    those nomad crests held high. Let memory
restore the horde to a replenished plain,
from which the all-effacing currents drain.

They came in autumn, herded by the chill   *3*
    Canadian gale, to the margins of Bexar.
Here they would linger, where the granite hill
    commanded pastures choked by prickly pear,
    mesquite, and live oak: Brindle, a bossy mare
who requisitioned clover; and slow Trudge,
always the last of the *manada* to budge;

4   and Gnasher, calmer now she was a mother,
           her foal her wobbly shadow; knobby Blaze;
       young Flicker, and black-eared Flick, her brother.
           All told, two dozen animals would graze
           and prance and groom each other in the gaze
       of their contumelious suzerain,
       a skewbald stallion with a mottled mane.

5   This vast *manada*'s master hailed from hell,
           or so *vaqueros* claimed, who had seen his bite
       trenching his foes, or glimpsed him in a corral
           covering mares. He had been known to fight
           from Palo Duro's mazes to the bight
       of Galveston; for his fierceness, as for his
       seraglio, *Tejanos* knew him as

6   the Sultan. Now, with senses trained
           to paramount acuity, he tested
       autumnal winds, ears rotating, neck craned.
           A faint redolence held the horse arrested;
           and then, alarming quail where they had nested
       in shinnery, he rippled up a cliff.
       His nostrils filtered and distilled the whiff.

7   Some miles to the southeast, three hundred mares,
           escorted by the Mexican cavalry,
       trudged wearily beneath war's heavy wares —
           munitions, food, and feed. Then, suddenly,
           a musket's crack, and cries; a company
       of Texan rebels swept down on the train,
       as Britons once chased treasure fleets of Spain.

The cavalry, though, rallied and repelled 8
  outnumbered raiders. The Texans, defeated,
withdrew, a few men injured, no one felled.
    The herd continued north. That evening, seated
    around a fire, the Texans, feeling cheated,
derided Captain Randall Jones — among
the harshest, Travis. Hearing, Jones was stung.

But Jones deferred revenge. He led his few 9
  subordinates and fewer friends, devoid
of kudos, back to the camp that spread in view
    of San Fernando's belfry. Here, deployed
    the whole month of November, unemployed
and rusting, the rebels besieged their foe,
General Cos, who still held San Antonio.

One morning, Jones, strolling through the tents, 10
  saw Joe, the slave of Travis, bent above
his master's boots, the squire to a young prince.
    "You, boy," said Captain Jones, "you bring your stuff
    and shine my boots." Soon Travis, hearing of
the confiscation of his servant, marched
up to his Captain, frowning, shoulders arched.

"I seem, sir, to have lost some property," 11
  the Lieutenant told the Captain, who just smirked
and answered: "From now on, your boy will be
    the company's. I've seen the way he's shirked;
    it's high time, Travis, that your niggra worked
for all of us." To this Travis replied:
"I won't allow it, sir. You have no right —"

12 On hearing this, Jones leaped up to his feet;
        nearby, Joe turned from toil; a volunteer's
    harmonica fell off; the drip of meat
        sizzled on the coals. A dozen ears
        attended to a colloquy of sneers.
    Jones answered Travis, "What? I have no right?"
    He drew himself up to his utmost height.

13 "By God, sir, while I'm Captain of this corps
        I've every right — and you, sir, you have none.
    Your boy, your horse, your sword, are mine — what's more,
        Lieutenant Travis, so are you. Why, son,
        in this here company, I'm the only one
    with any rights. You'll get what you deserve,
    Lieutenant, when you've learned at last to serve."

14 The soldiers who had gathered watched the two
        contenders share a paralyzing stare,
    like pit bulls snarling at each other through
        the mesh they test, as their trainers prepare
        the arena. Then the gray November air
    was fractured by a bugle that commanded
    a meeting. The duel's audience disbanded.

15 The bugle summoned hundreds from the trees,
        excited minnows mobbing round a stone
    plopped in a creek. An officer barked, "At ease!"
        The volunteers — not one appeared to own
        a uniform — talked in a steady drone
    throughout the ceremony, just as though
    this were a fair, the rite, a minstrel show.

The voice of General Stephen Austin, weak $\qquad$ *16*
    by nature, further weakened by his stay
in Santa Anna's prison, matched his sleek
    and lawyerly attire. "Effective today,
    I have relinquished all authority
to General Burleson, whom you've elected
by secret ballots honestly collected."

Saluting his successor, Austin coughed $\qquad$ *17*
    and shuddered. Edward Burleson led the men
in three hurrahs. For months, the ranks had scoffed
    at Austin, born — they said — to wield a pen.
    As a diplomat, Austin would seek to win
support in the U.S. No more an affront
to warriors, he would serve on a second front.

The cheering faded, though, when Burleson cued $\qquad$ *18*
    a man the volunteers viewed with suspicion,
Sam Houston. Brooding in a solitude
    amid the mob, he seemed deaf to derision
    when he stepped forth, a baffling apparition
in dandy's togs and patterned Indian cloak
that robed him like a toga as he spoke:

"As Major General and commander in chief, $\qquad$ *19*
    appointed by the Consultation, I
now ratify General Austin's relief
    by General Burleson, whom I hereby
    confirm as General —" From the ranks, a cry:
"We choose our leaders here, not some committee!"
And then another: "Houston, ain't you pretty!"

20   The flyting did not ripple Houston's calm;
          grim and implastic as an Olmec head,
      a monstrous baby's face that glowers from
              its sanctum in the ferns, the General said:
              "The enemy we must above all dread
      is our disorder. We need government,
      a capital that can command the tent.

21   "To that end, the delegates who have convened
          in San Felipe have at last assumed
      the reins of this rebellion that's careened
              too long without direction in the gloom.
              What's more, they demand the country resume
      the Constitution of Eighteen Twenty-Four —
      for now, that's why we wage our legal war."

22   The graying giant waved. A color guard
          ran up a banner bearing the impress
      of their adopted country: snake and bird
              atop a prickly pear. Under that crest
              in mourning black was the date of the best
      of many charters Mexico had known,
      each one, by putsch or rising, overthrown.

23   While Houston raised his hand in a salute
          to the flag of free and federal Mexico,
      the crowd of volunteers, a snuffling brute
              inside a ring, crazed by a mantle's glow,
              burst into bellows: "You take that flag and go
      to hell!" one cried; another yelled, "We're fighting
      for independence, not for reuniting!"

So, too, was Houston; but he had prevailed 24
    upon the Consultation to delay
declaring independence for a spell,
    to win liberal support, and to allay
    Tejano fears. This, though, he would not say;
he had learned, in Washington and Tennessee,
when silence more than talk served policy.

His silence was an opportunity 25
    for General Burleson to reprove the men
he claimed to lead. "Attention! This will be
    an army, not a lynch mob!" Only when
    the ranks grew quiet did he speak again.
"We'll let the politicians talk, while we
take San Antone and set all Texas free."

At this, the Major General interjected: 26
    "I know you men are eager to attack
the city and see General Cos ejected;
    but we don't have the field arms, and we lack
    sufficient numbers. So we will hold back
and let the winter crush them by degrees,
with our best allies: hunger, cold, disease."

Dissent among the ranks had boiled and steamed 27
    beneath the surface while the General spoke;
contention geysered now. The most esteemed
    of all the older settlers, gray as smoke
    from age and battles, red with anger, broke
from the ranks. Ben Milam, veteran of Long's
attempt, pawed with his hooves, and brandished prongs.

28   "By God, sir, I thought I would never hear
         a Texan soldier counseling retreat,
     retreat, retreat. Abandon the frontier
         and run away, and make the very seat
         of government the place where we will meet
     invasion? General, we will make our stand
     right here, no matter what you may have planned."

29   Endorsement, from the chorus. Houston eyed
         Ben Milam as a duelist might a foe
     before a knot of seconds: "Some have tried
         what you are recommending — as you know;
         three times now Texans have mulched Mexico
     with rebel bones. Three times! If we repeat
     the strategy of Long, headlong we'll meet defeat."

30   Almost two decades earlier, Doctor Long
         had bled to death, twitching in Milam's arms,
     shot in a Mexican jail. The Texan throng,
         offended as one man, now raged, like swarms
         of yellowjackets, tormenting a farm's
     proprietor, whose hatchet strokes inflame
     hornets when carpentry had been his aim.

31   The chief commander — if only in title —
         soon rode from camp, ominously quiet,
     on Saracen, a steed easier to bridle
         than soldiers of fortune drunk upon a diet
         of rhetoric and rotgut. From that riot
     the General rode; Buck Travis caught his eye,
     and Houston nodded as he trotted by.

Soon General Burleson gave a field commission   *32*
    to Travis as a Captain, Cavalry,
assigning him and Jones a common mission:
    to stop the trains that with impunity
    kept Cos supplied in town. "Now we will see
who is the better ranger," Burleson winked.
"And Joe? The quartermaster's corps, I think."

Among the mustangs, murmurs. In the gray   *33*
    of early morning, mares began to snuffle
and whinny. The young foals forgot to play,
    sensing the tension. Their mothers would ruffle
    their manes, reassuring them in the shuffle.
The Sultan paced and pawed, snorted and snickered.
Along the western skyline, dawn light flickered.

The orange vortex that brought summer swelter   *34*
    belatedly to winter's balding oak
sent spokes through flaring woods. The squirrel's shelter
    capsized, boughs blending with the blinding smoke;
    the sparrows breasted breezes that would stoke
the furnace roar; coyotes chased the ash;
the cedars candled and began to crash.

As waves of gold left pools of cooling tar,   *35*
    the horsemen wove through puffs that rose to stain
a copper sun. Thus Travis waged his war
    against the very land that might sustain
    three hundred head of Mexico's packtrain.
The convoy itself eluded the ranger,
to his distress, for he ached for danger.

36   In camp, when Travis and his company
          returned without a single captured mule,
      his former chief doubled his misery
          by means of unrelenting ridicule.
          "So, Travis, didn't they teach you at school
      to cut for sign?" the rival Captain baited
      the arrogant young lawyer he so hated.

37   Discouraged, Travis offered to resign
          his field commission. Burleson instead
      gave his friend a week to make up his mind.
          Sulking in his tent, the young man read
          a borrowed almanac. The crude gazette
      was crammed with yarns and primitive cartoons
      of Mike Finks, Davy Crocketts, Daniel Boones.

38   One woodcut showed a smirking Davy Crockett,
          in coonskin cap, emerging from a bear
      with jaws like a valise. Atop a rocket
          the Canebrake's Congressman soared through the air
          on one page, on the next he dropped a pair
      of redcoats, by bowling with a cannonball:
      "I'm of a mind to find myself a brawl!"

39   This time, Travis resolved, he would not lack
          the soundest guides and allies he could find;
      he knew he needed locals, who could track
          a spoor that most would miss. One came to mind.
          Not far from camp, behind a hunter's blind
      of scraggly oaks, he watched the man he sought
      employ the skills he needed to be taught.

Jim Bowie loomed atop his mustang's saddle,   *40*
    like a circus bear balancing on a bike,
as he merged with a herd of longhorn cattle,
    cutting one bull out. He leaned to strike;
    with massive hands, he grabbed each spike
and kicked away his horse and swung around
and tried to root his boots into the ground.

The beeve hauled Bowie through the turf he trenched,   *41*
    an anchor whose black flukes would not hold fast.
Still hanging from the horns, his red face clenched,
    the barrel-armed frontiersman tried to twist
    the creature's neck. The brute could not resist
the brutal strength that forced it first to kneel,
then flipped it, as it complained with a squeal.

Soon planks of pink grew crusted on the coals.   *42*
    With Bowie and his men, Travis enjoyed
a steak with beans, tamales, cornbread rolls.
    "I'm Santa Anna's in-law," Bowie toyed
    with Travis. "For some reason, you've annoyed
my kinsman so he's ordered you should die.
You'd better watch your back when I'm nearby."

The bravo threw his head back and he bellowed,   *43*
    his cowboys joining in. Buck Travis knew
a little of Jim Bowie, the fiercest fellow
    west of the Mississippi — how he grew
    to manhood in Louisiana's slough,
how whittled foes confirmed he was the best
knife-fighter in the red and raw Southwest.

44   The older showed the younger man the blade
       that bore the Bowie name. "My brother Rezin,
he like to cut his thumb clean off and bled
       to death, gutting a deer. He started messing
       with knife designs; he kept in mind the lesson
he'd learned at such a cost. The guard's the trick;
it keeps the blood from making your hand slick."

45   Now Travis had his say. When he had made
       his offer, Bowie sawed at meat and chewed
awhile in silence. Then the bravo said:
       "I'd like to help you, Travis, but my crew
       and I, we've got our own scouting to do.
But I can recommend a local guide;
ain't rabbit-eared, but he is eagle-eyed.

46   "Deaf Smith's your man. Erastus is his name,
       but we all call him Deaf. He's nearly lost
his hearing — though some think it's all a game,
       a pretext for deciding, when he's bossed,
       what orders he'll obey." The big man paused.
"Frankly, Travis, between me and you,
he's deaf in English, and in Spanish, too."

47   The second evening of his second mission,
       a curious Travis learned his unit's guide
had found the cure for deafness: "Prohibition.
       That's what the doctor ordered." Deaf Smith sighed.
       "I tried to give up booze, I really tried;
but when I thought about it, it was clear
I'm fonder of what I drink than what I hear."

The company laughed with him. Travis rode   *48*
   with twelve handpicked companions, trusted friends;
Deaf Smith and two *Tejano* trackers showed
   the little band its way through shrubby bends
   and stubbly prairies. This would make amends
for failure on his first attempt, the proud
young rebel to himself devoutly vowed.

The third day out from camp, Travis debated   *49*
   Deaf Smith about the traces of a herd.
"This ain't our train," Smith said. Marks indicated
   another answer: "Mustangs. Mark my word."
   That night, around the fire, the cowboys purred
a ballad, a *corrido,* celebrating
a demon stallion and his midnight raiding.

The next day Mexico was reinforced   *50*
   by thunder. Travis and his cavalry,
pursued by lightning, slipped through land that coursed
   like potter's clay. A foaming, flickering sea,
   a bloated creek, barred the company
from following the melting mustang spoor.
Slumping, the saddled Texans eyed that shore.

The young commander sent his men, by teams,   *51*
   to separately hunt the Mexican train;
tomorrow they would meet here at this stream,
   successful or defeated. In the rain
   the rangers blurred. Their Captain thought with pain
of his humiliation, again resolved
he would not fail. The steaming hills dissolved.

52
    Beneath a drooling shelf of mossy chalk,
        the Texan found asylum from the squall.
    Here, like a drenched and baffled sparrow-hawk
        the clouds have exiled, Travis watched the pall
        of storm give way to the gray of nightfall.
    Tented in his serape, lulled by the sound
    of nickering, in streaming dream he drowned.

53
    He was in Alabama, he was back
        in Claiborne, in the lane behind the inn,
    that lane, again. In dream Travis would track
        that man, as once in fact; and once again
        his jealous fury would destroy his plan
    to goad his rival to a duel. Once more
    the pistol in his hand would splatter gore.

54
    The county courthouse caged him, in his mind;
        he was on trial for murder. From his seat
    Judge Dellet, his dear mentor, his face lined
        by grief, looked down. The parlor and the street
        had filled the pews, the petty and elite
    of all the county; Travis saw his wife
    beside that man, somehow restored to life.

55
    The young attorney, in his nightmare, pleaded
        the case for the defense, for his defense;
    Sam Houston, by dream's logic, now succeeded
        Judge Dellet on the bench. And then a fence
        appeared within the courthouse — no, the immense
    blond framework was a scaffold in the square,
    and Travis, at the rope's end, hung in air.

He lived, but could not move. Though he could hear   56
    himself cry out, nobody in the throng
could hear him, as they clustered there to peer.
    His wife gazed up at him; Mrs. Long
    was in the crowd, and Becky — it was wrong,
yet right. The murdered man was there, of course,
although at times he seemed to be a horse.

He woke in panic. He was all alone   57
    somewhere in Central Texas. Where the rain
had runneled was the beaded dew of dawn.
    The images were fading in his brain,
    like stars absorbed into the milky stain
of morning. He shook dew from chevroned folds
and mounted up — and felt a sharper cold.

What seemed like Spanish moss, clotting the branches   58
    of a humongous oak, as Travis neared,
became a warrior of the Comanches,
    suspended over Texas in a bier.
    His flesh had shriveled, but his braided hair
was black and young. His vest of brittle bone
was molting its components, one by one.

The soldier backed away. He heard the rasp   59
    of buzzards grounded by the morning chill.
The gargoyles eyed him, grinning as they clasped
    the boughs with reptile hands. Another kill,
    they sensed with a premonitory thrill
as Travis passed. His horse beneath him tensed,
but it was not the scavengers she sensed.

60   Screened by mesquite, the rebel ranger gazed
                into a gully, where the mares he stalked
        before their wardens jostled, flounced, and grazed.
                Each tier of curving silhouettes was blocked
                by other horses when they bobbed and rocked,
        the way that boats in rows will gently sway,
        eclipsing one another in a bay.

61   Surrender was repaid by clemency,
                when Captain Travis, master of the mares,
        allowed the conquered Mexican soldiery
                to keep small arms. The troops would be prepared,
                while riding south, to meet the foes they feared
        more than the Texans: Lipans and Comanches,
        the terror of two nations on the ranches.

62   The fire was high that night, the talk was higher;
                the whiskey splashed, the kettle brimmed with stew
        and barbecue. "Y'all mark me for a liar,"
                said Smith, "if Travis didn't holler, 'You
                arrest me!' to that rascal in the blue!"
        The Captain smiled; before he could reply,
        one of the pickets raised an urgent cry.

63   A Mexican attack? A Lipan raid?
                The rangers stared and swore, when they beheld
        their enemy. A speckled stallion swayed,
                rearing, above a man its kick had felled.
                The Sultan whinnied, and the mares all belled
        in answer. Yellow teeth had gnawed the hide
        holding half a dozen horses tied.

The creature snickered, snorted, sniffed the scent   64
    the scorched earth lately taught him to despise:
the stink of burning brands. The hateful glint
    traced comet trails across his liquid eyes.
    He flinched and thrashed in anger and surprise
as grassy loops slapped on his croup, his side;
soon, like a tent, the lassoed horse was guyed.

A little while the horse seemed reconciled;   65
    the stallion, though, just bowed his head to chew
his twilling bonds. And then he dervished wild
    once more, a hub to snapping ropes that flew
    like cables in a hurricane's wet flaw.
From his saddle Travis was reeled, entwined,
a hunter now the trophy of his find.

He rolled upright in time to stop a ranger   66
    who held a musket leveled. "Let him go!"
roared Travis. Dancing free of further danger,
    the Sultan boxed and whinnied. From the glow
    of torches he withdrew, a craggy floe
varnished by auroras with green light
that drifts past startled sailors in the night.

Outside of Bexar, the Texan volunteers   67
    awoke in their tent suburb to a rumble.
Framed by his tent flaps, Randall Jones heard cheers,
    then felt the tremor. Pots began to tumble,
    and horses flinched and neighed. The Captain's grumble
was never finished. He stood still, unnerved
on seeing how the velvet torrent swerved.

68 The way a pebble warns a mountaineer,
   shrunk on a ledge, of the descent
of half a mountain, the first mares to appear
   alerted Jones by pounding past his tent.
   Too late the horseman ran from imminent
immersion in the swaying, drumming swarms;
his tent collapsed amid the flashing forms.

69 The riders Travis led regrouped the herd
   within a field. Deaf Smith brought up the rear.
The army jubilated, when they heard
   the verdict of Ed Burleson: "I declare.
   Why, Travis, you just might have won the war."
From a barrel that the mares had spun around,
the cautious Jones emerged, a rodeo clown.

70 December's air was clean and metal-cold
   when Travis came to Jane Long's inn beside
the Brazos. She did not stir as he told
   what he had heard of how Ben Milam died.
   "November twenty-sixth I left to ride
for San Felipe, to raise a regiment.
The siege of Bexar, it seemed, would never end.

71 "In town, the troops of Cos had been weakening,
   ever since we cut their pontoon bridge
of horses. Soon they would be ripe for reckoning.
   But Ben, Ben was not suited for a siege.
   One morning, I am told, in epic rage
he climbed atop a cart and waved his sombrero,
the staff that stirred a storm against the pharaoh.

"'Who'll go with old Ben Milam into San   72
     Antonio?' His bellow woke the tents.
He took his musket stock and traced a line
     through Texan soil and challenged all his friends
     to join him. And they did; though the regiments
erased it as they shuffled to his side,
we'll always look upon that line with pride.

"The army was not Houston's, nor did it   73
     belong to General Burleson: it was Ben's.
Three hundred men long weary of the bit
     he freed to charge. He and his ardent friends
     blew like a hurricane right through the fence
of pickets. As though drilling into rock
they took the town, block by barricaded block.

"They say that Ben was standing in the yard   74
     of the Veramendi house, of Bowie's kin,
all boarded up. There he stood, and roared:
     'Let's get 'em, boys!' A sniper, though, had been
     assessing him. The men all swear that Ben
felt nothing. Jane, he did not die before
he knew that we — that *he* had won the war."

Three times Jane had been widowed — when her James   75
     had fallen to a jailer's musket shot
in Mexico; when John Austin fell to flames
     of fever a few years back, having fought
     at Fort Velasco in the war that bought
the captive Travis freedom; and now when
the foe had slain the last triumvir, Ben.

76   Each of the three young men who joined the plot
              in her New Orleans parlor to annex
      all Texas to themselves had found a plot
              of Texas by which he had been annexed.
              Who of her paladins would be the next?
      She turned from Travis. To the silent room
      rose laughter through the floor from the saloon.

77   "What you have sought so long has been achieved,"
              Travis suggested to the somber beauty.
      "Tonight — though it still seems hard to believe —
              there's not one Mexican soldier on duty
              on Texan soil. All of us who have rooted
      ourselves in this vast country now are free,
      thanks to you, and to the immortal three."

78   The painted ghost of Doctor Long looked down
              as Travis murmured, "The giant race
      that dwelled upon this earth have all been drowned."
              "Not all of them," said Jane. Through mourning lace
              and tears she condescended now to face
      her final knight. The young man bowed to give
      her hand a kiss. He had four months to live.

PART TWO

BOOK FIVE

*THE BATTLE
FOR COMMAND*

THE ARGUMENT

Santa Anna's troops have been expelled
from Texas. The Alamo is held
by a depleted garrison.
The rebels think the war is won.
Jim Bowie, in a drunken spree,
sets friends in Bexar's hoosegow free;
his act attracts a reprimand
from Travis, who claims the command.
Defeated, Travis leaves with troops
who take his side. While he regroups
his men on the Medina River,
thousands march and sink and shiver
in winter mountains. To surprise
the Texans, Santa Anna plies.

BOOK FIVE

Infuriated officers dividing   *1*
    the garrison at Bexar before the legions
arrived — of these, and reinforcements riding
        to their destruction, of confused allegiance
        and war consuming all the country's regions,
Llorona, help me tell. A tale that fame
has hallowed I make mine, a greater theme.

Twice Travis fell at Bexar, as twice before   *2*
    he fell at Anahuac. Two months had passed
since Cos gave up the Alamo. The war,
        it seemed, was won. But concord did not last
        among the Texans; while their foes amassed
to wreak revenge on the rebels they hated,
the victors dithered, bickered, and debated.

"Whose orders?" asked the jailer once again,   *3*
    eyes narrow, musket ready, resolute,
a javelina hackling as the men
        and dogs close all around. A blond-haired brute
        in buckskins answered, "Friend, you'd better scoot,
on orders of Jim Bowie." The lawman eyed
the jeering North Americans outside.

4   "And Bowie, who gave him the right to pardon
          convicted criminals?" Somebody lobbed
     a bottle that crashed near the flinching warden;
          he raised his gun, fearing he would be mobbed.
          Above the churning crowd a pink face bobbed,
     framed by thick sideburns, nodding into jowls
     just like a bulldog's. The whoops and the howls

5   now ebbed away. Above the warden towered
          the bravo in a black, expensive jacket
     that barely bound his bulk. Jim Bowie glowered,
          his voice a growl that cut right through the racket:
          "I'd rather use the key, but I can crack it
     wide open if I have to, friend. You choose."
     The warden wilted in the fumes of booze.

6   "Don Santiago!" "Jaime!" "Mister Jim!"
          The inmates cheered and whooped, as Bowie passed
     their cages with the jailer. All the dim
          gray shadows peopling the cellblock pressed
          the icy bars. "It was a false arrest,"
     one prisoner proclaimed, "I was set up."
     The verdict on the man's appeal: "Shut up."

7   Now Bowie stopped before the cage that held,
          among a dozen, a wiry young man,
     Antonio Fuentes. "I hear you were jailed
          for pilfering a horse . . ." Bowie began.
          Fuentes replied, "You have to understand,
     I thought it was an orphan. Like a kitten,
     all pitiful and hungry. I was smitten."

That cavern rang with laughter. Bowie told   *8*
   the frowning jailer, "Well, sir? Set him loose!
Hell, turn 'em all out. They're hereby paroled.
   With Santa Anna coming, I could use
   some reinforcements." From the calaboose
they sashayed, blinking as they left the shade
and joined their patron's men in a parade.

"Fuentes," said Jim Bowie, as he passed   *9*
   a bulbous jug, "I know a very pretty
young *señorita* who has pined and missed
   you something terrible. Her name's Black Betty."
   The crowd guffawed, as, one by one, the city
jail's emancipated took a swig:
Antonio Fuentes, then a mate from the brig,

Guerrero, called Brigido, a cattle thief   *10*
   who requisitioned, he said, for the cause;
and Bill Malone, who shivered with relief
   while guzzling. Gripping the jug in his paws,
   Jim Bowie swayed. "I think we ought to pause
to honor Betty for this lunar cure
she makes from bottled moonlight, sweet and pure."

The laughter rolled from Military Square   *11*
   across the river — if this winding creek
deserved the title — to the fortress, where
   three dozen regulars had camped a week,
   settlers from the colonies with a stake
and kin in Texas. Travis, now Lieutenant
Colonel, commanded these newest tenants,

12   and several others whom their Colonel, Neill,
             called home by family illness, had surrendered.
      The little unit labored now to seal
             the limestone gaps where cannonballs had entered
             during December's siege. Against a splintered
      palisade of crumbly logs that patched the north
      facade, the men were packing poultice earth.

13   Their young commander labored at their side,
             sweating, despite the February chill.
      He helped three others roll a log upright
             to plant it in the post hole dirt would fill
             instead of mortar. Soon the timber grill
      was finished. Travis stepped back and assessed
      the work, allowing grimy troops to rest.

14   The sound of shouting drifted from the town.
             They watched a strange procession wind its way
      across the river, watched their comrades clown
             and clap and saunter. On the holiday
             devoted to Saint Anthony, burros would bray
      in ribbons, and the porkers, pertly dressed,
      would patter through the alleys to be blessed

15   by idols born to carpentry and paint.
             Now Bowie rode on shoulders, elevated
      above the festive train, a sordid saint
             borne by the roisterers as they paraded.
             Lieutenant Colonel Travis coldly waited
      for ebbing of the hubbub. Over the arch
      he stood, as though to review an ordered march.

"Colonel Bowie," Travis called, his voice ringing   *16*
    from wall to wall, "I expect an explanation
for this display." The older man, still clinging
    unsteadily to friends, in indignation
    erupted: "Sir, I command this station;
I'm senior officer; these are my men;
I don't take orders from a boy of . . . ten."

The laughter crashed in waves against the gate   *17*
    where Travis stood. The rage inside him churned.
He answered, "Colonel Neill expressly made
    me his successor. Until he has returned,
    I'm in command. It's high time you men learned
respect for hierarchy . . ." Half the corps
responded with an agitated roar.

Then Bowie waved his hand to halt the holler,   *18*
    commanded silence. "Colonel, let these men
decide which one of us they want to follow.
    Here's where democracy ought to begin.
    We'll have a vote — and may the best man win."
The garrison assented with one voice.
Despairing, Travis saw he had no choice.

The fort became a forum, an old cart   *19*
    the stage. Green Jameson, trusted by the two
contenders, flipped a coin. Travis would start.
    The young man climbed the wagon. He could view
    a few supporters in the crowd — a few.
A lawyer, teacher, newsman, he was versed
in speaking. This speech, though, felt like his first.

20   "Gentlemen, we few here will decide
      the future of a land, a continent,
perhaps the very world. Our truest guide
      is history; the shape of imminent
      futurity in some long-past event
is often found. Man's nature does not change,
from the Old World to our own contested range.

21   "In every age, in every country, men
      must fight to keep their birthright, liberty;
for since the race began, there has not been
      a generation whose ranks were free
      of Caesars or Napoleons. Here we
have seen the proof, assaulted and oppressed
as we've been by 'Napoleon of the West.'

22   "Near Corsica, the home of Bonaparte,
      in Sicily, five centuries before
the time of Christ, a tyrant with a heart
      as wicked as Santa Anna's waged a war
      against his subjects. From the distant shore
of Corinth came Timoleon with a band
to help the Syracusans free their land.

23   "In far-off Syracuse, Timoleon
      joined his Corinthians with Sicilian men
rebelling against their Napoleon,
      their Santa Anna. They went on to win
      a splendid triumph that has never been
forgotten. Dionysius, exiled,
a king deprived of subjects, died reviled.

"The men of Corinth, under one command   *24*
    with native allies, framed a constitution;
now new and native shared both laws and land.
    The great Timoleon's last contribution
    was his retirement, once the institution
of democratic government was complete;
to live by laws he made is the founder's greatest feat.

"Two and a half millenia have passed   *25*
    and still that memory's cherished by mankind.
Who knows, that history may be surpassed
    by us, today. For in Texas we find
    a Syracuse, whose tyrant has the mind
and soul of Dionysius; and here too
his foes are freemen, both native and new."

Throughout the speech, the audience had shuffled   *26*
    and murmured, like the students Travis taught
in youth in Alabama. Almost muffled
    by muttering, the young orator sought
    to make his voice prevail. Seeing he fought
in vain to gain attention, Travis ended;
he left the cart that Bowie then ascended.

The veteran duelist, with mimic modesty,   *27*
    waved down the demonstration. He began:
"I want to start, by saying I agree
    with the young Colonel here. He is a man
    born with a silver tongue, who surely can
persuade a crowd, the way that Stephen Austin
talks purses open in New York and Boston.

28   "Now me, I need an Aaron; I am halt
            of tongue and slow of speech. I'm not the sort
      who's good at speechifying. It's a fault,
            I reckon, in a politician or
            a preacher or an envoy to a court.
      If you want eloquence, your choice is clear:
      it's William Austin — I mean Travis here.

29   "I'm just a boy from out the bayou, bred
            and reared in Rapides Parish — some of y'all
      have come from New Orleans, where your neighbors said:
            'Thank God they've gone to Texas, one and all!'
            Tomfoolery aside, we learned last fall
      the only thing that really counts in war
      is who the men, not who the leaders, are.

30   "'Who'll go with old Ben Milam into San
            Antonio?' I still see Milam hold
      that hat up high — just one enlisted man
            among the others, just a mite more bold.
            We violated orders, I've been told,
      when we left camp and took this town again;
      old Cos, he wished we'd shown more discipline.

31   "I've used up most of the few words I tote.
            I won't stand here all day and bend your ear.
      You want a learned leader, why you vote
            for Stephen — I mean William Travis here.
            I'm happy with a place in front or rear,
      as long as I can kick ass with the best
      damn crew of rascals in the whole Southwest."

The cheering told the outcome of the poll.   32
    Soon thirty members of his small brigade,
each with his guns, knives, ammo, and bedroll,
    spurred solemnly with Travis through the gate
    of the Alamo to an uncertain fate.
Bowie shrugged, when Jameson pointed out the train
of riders dwindling on the wintry plain.

The February norther, as it yowled   33
    through Cordilleran hills and gaps and trails,
left every peak of every mountain cowled
    with dimpled snow. Like small, round, ivory snails,
    the trees and bushes glowed among the dales
of spongy foam. The landscape shone, enticing,
a cake with domes and cones of curly icing.

More marvels: sculpted horses made of snow,   34
    like topiary fancies, blooming bright,
and horizontal snowmen, each a floe
    encasing frozen men in rinds of light.
    A dozen Latin busts emerged from white
vacuity, like youths quilted by sand,
amusing friends upon a flashing strand.

Here, mules and men were mingled in a heap,   35
    like monsters drowned in California tar;
scaled over by the frost, the meat would keep
    for several days. The instruments of war
    as well were mangled — cannon, wheel, and car;
beside these wrecks, a pharaoh's drifting ranks,
lay soldiers half-immersed in cloud-clean banks.

36 At times the *soldaderas* gave their aid,
   troops in the female legion that escorted
 the men of Mexico. Upon the grade
   of silver-white, camp followers lay contorted
   beside the soldiers they had once supported
 with warmth and food and blankets they would find;
 in death, as life, the two ranks were combined.

37 Like seagulls wheeling round a fishing skiff,
   a dozen shrieking *soldaderas* crowded
 around one snow-mired wagon, tearing off
   the rags with which its coffers were enshrouded.
   Swords drawn, riders came trotting; they routed
 the women, who replied with pleas and curses
 spat at the cavalrymen on their horses.

38 Two members of the presidential staff
   observed the petty war. "Those blankets thrown
 on boxes warm battalions of the gaff,
   His Excellency's birds," said Castrillon,
   a Cuban-bred commander who had grown
   silver in Mexico's wars. At his side,
 Almonte watched as women begged and cried.

39 "Disgraceful," said the Colonel, who was well
   aware the general was one of a few
 high-ranking soldiers unafraid to tell
   their master he had erred. Almonte drew
   close to the soldiers, barking, "All of you
 should be ashamed!" Then angry women closed
 around the adjutant, clawing his clothes.

"The President! It's Santa Anna!" cried   *40*
    a girl whose black braids had been aged by snow.
The frightened women sought somewhere to hide.
    The man they thought the lord of Mexico
    turned to the riders. "You men there, you throw
these women your blankets; sleep in your coats."
Almonte tossed his own, through swirling motes.

He watched the women rip a quilt as clean   *41*
    and candid as the snow. The soldiers tucked
recovered rags into the cracks between
    a dozen crates. Inside, the roosters clucked,
    startled by the drafts through crack and duct.
"The President is kind," said Castrillon,
winking, and tossing a blanket of his own.

The officers rode on, passing a scattered   *42*
    battalion of young men with brows of frost.
"Surprise is no advantage, if we're shattered
    by winter on the way." Almonte crossed
    himself. The General answered, "We're not lost.
Most will survive — and it has been well said,
'Tonight in slums more soldiers will be bred.'"

Meanwhile, as Santa Anna's thousands marched,   *43*
    Lieutenant Colonel Travis and his few
rode southward, backed by wind so cold it scorched.
    Within a grassy pasture with a view
    of glittering Medina, black oaks grew,
clenching like hands. Travis identified
alarm on the face of their local guide.

44   "My God," said Travis. What at first he thought
        were chunks of chalk, he realized were bones
and hair and flesh in five degrees of rot.
        Like worming roots exposed amid the stones
        along a bank an abrupt flood hones,
the corpses lay uncovered in their bed.
The living rebels gazed upon the dead.

45   Arocha, their *Tejano* guide, was making
        the cross in air. He babbled, "This is where
they killed them, all of them . . ." The man was shaking.
        Dismounting, Travis paused before the lair
        of bony death. He seemed to see the flare
of *escopetas,* heard the butchered scream
in anguish, in the wreckage of their scheme.

46   Here, twenty years before, the rebel forces,
        the first republicans of Texas, met
the troops of Spain; here rebels on their horses
        had charged into the trap that had been set
        by General Arredondo. Like a net
the waiting regiments had closed around
secessionists whose cratered battleground

47   became their cemetery. Quietly
        Arocha told of what the old recalled:
survivors of the battle for a free
        and independent Texas, shocked and mauled
        by battle, had been captured and corralled.
While Arredondo watched, they dug long trenches
they spliced with logs like rafters or crude benches.

In small groups, herded by the bayonet,   *48*
    the Texans were compelled to strip and stack
their clothes and boots. These volunteers had met
    but recently, the few who dared attack
    the government of Spain; upon the rack
of tree trunks now two naked nations stood,
the brown and pink, condemned to blend their blood.

Some cried out, "Texas!" as the muskets popped,   *49*
    some cried for God, or mother; some just cried;
their bellies bloomed with wounds, they swayed and dropped
    and sprawled together. Those who had not died
    were killed when bayonets and sabers tried
the slimy forms. The next men to be shot
were forced to spade black earth into the slot,

before they lined up on the slippery beam   *50*
    and toppled in their turn. The killing took
an hour, maybe two. "They say the steam
    of battle hung for years." Arocha shook
    with more than winter. He tried not to look
at heralds of the hundreds who still lay
beneath their feet inside the river clay.

Travis had a preacher in his command,   *51*
    a Baptist, William Garnett, twenty-four.
When the bodies were reburied in the land
    that Arredondo sowed, Garnett implored
    his God to bless this field plowed by the sword.
There were no speeches. No more could be said.
They camped above the revolution's dead.

52 That night the Texans, huddled round a flame,
   debated destiny. "It's liberty,
that's what this is about," John Forsyth claimed;
   the Captain had supplied the company
   he raised from his own pocket. "We few free
republicans will spread democracy
along the Gulf and the Pacific sea."

53 But Garnett, the young Baptist preacher, said,
   "Wars, and rumors of wars. The end times are near;
it's written down in Scripture to be read.
   In Turkey, or in Russia, will appear
   the Antichrist. Meanwhile, we Christians here
must make a western refuge, far from the East,
protecting true religion from the Beast."

54 James Bonham, his fine features underlit
   by embers as by stage lights, rolled his eyes.
"The issue, gentlemen, is which race is fit
   to rule this land, with the Lord or otherwise.
   This war is one more chapter in the rise
of our old Saxon race, which since the dawn
has always traveled toward the setting sun."

55 Throughout, Travis had listened. Now he strolled
   through darkness to the river, lost in pondering.
The stars were washed by clouds, filmy and cold
   as frost upon a window. Travis, wandering
   along the whispering riverside, was wondering
what fate awaited him. He eyed the moon;
its rainbow warned there would be thunder soon.

In his imagination, Travis gazed   56
    across a windswept canyon on the moon.
Beneath a gibbous Earth, weird cacti raised
    their spiny pods toward an armored balloon,
    a vision from an almanac's cartoon.
Retracting wings, the ship began to drag
its anchor till the tines caught on a crag.

Now Travis, in his fantasy, watched crewmen   57
    of the Aerial Navy, in the planet light,
saluting as a ritual marked human
    appropriation of Earth's satellite.
    Sailors rigged a tower, whose electric light
in Morse code flashed the message to the world:
upon the Moon, Old Glory had been unfurled.

Beneath the roving spirit, clouds divided,   58
    leaves whirling on a creek's transparency.
Below there glowed a continent united
    from the Rio Grande up to the ice-roofed sea.
    Deterring acts of windborne piracy,
the U.S. fleet patrolled the cumuli,
its ships like calves of foam-whales floating by.

In fancy Travis soared above great ranches   59
    where buffalo had scudded in his day,
and quilted tillage where once the Comanches
    had labored to make all their neighbors prey.
    From hilltop villas, grandees could survey
their acres, nodding to the cowboy's strum
or chants the hands on their way home would hum.

60   A city twinkled, somewhere in the west,
          a second and a greater sovereign seat
of empire, the bald eagle's newer nest.
          Here obelisks and temples lined each street;
          no chimney top, no gable, was complete
without a winking light, to warn balloons
that paisleyed heaven like migrating loons.

61   The gentry promenaded in the parks
          or perched behind black drivers in strange coaches
whose clockwork motors ticked and dribbled sparks.
          Where all the boulevards and green approaches
          converged, as big as morning when it broaches
the skyline, swelled a marble pantheon,
a dome the color and the shape of dawn.

62   Within that vault, the murmuring pilgrims gazed
          upon a titan molded out of snow,
a youth adoring moonbeams had embraced.
          Atop the lictor's staves, a mantle's flow
          revealed a cap and rod, and, just below,
scales and a sword. On this ensemble, screened
by marble folds, the man in the toga leaned.

63   Beneath the negligence of his left hand,
          a sculpted scroll unrolled, with graven letters:
INIMICA TYRANNIS. On the stand
          beneath lay fragments of demolished fetters,
          and crumpled crowns, and guerdons all in tatters,
pointed out by the giant's lowered sword
so that the lesson would not be ignored.

The first of four murals showed the defeat   64
   of Santa Anna on Medina's banks;
his soldiers were scrambling in full retreat
   before young Travis, gouging his mount's flanks,
   his saber summoning his Texan ranks.
Medina had become a new Scamander,
the Granicus to a second Alexander.

From liberated Texas, Travis rode   65
   to free New Mexico. Before a mission
of brown adobe, the skillful painter showed
   the alcalde and the bishops in submission
   to Travis, reconciled to the decision
of Providence. Haloed by a ray,
the General clasped the key of Santa Fe.

Next, Travis wore a marshal's feathered crest   66
   and braided coat; he sparkled in the sun
of San Francisco, conqueror of the West.
   More world than Wolfe and Washington he had won,
   a Paulus, not a new Timoleon,
warring, not for his adopted home,
but rather for his triumph back in Rome.

A graying Travis, in the final scene,   67
   surrounded by grave statesmen ranked in rows,
was watched by multitudes thronging the green
   before the Capitol. In front of both
   his families, William Travis took the oath
as President, that second Washington,
aged fifty-two, in Eighteen Sixty-One.

68   All this, this could be his — if only he
          commanded Texan armies based in Bexar.
      Jim Bowie would not block the destiny
          of William Barret Travis. His despair
          gave way to wrath, ambition banished care.
      No man, he thought, *will take what's rightly mine.*
      He made his way back, guided by moonshine.

BOOK SIX

THE
NEARING STORM

THE ARGUMENT

*The bitter struggle to command
the Alamo comes to an end,
negotiated by a new
arrival. Holding a review
along the Rio Grande, the master
of Mexico directs disaster
toward unsuspecting rebels. While
the Texans feast and drink and dance,
Santa Anna's regiments advance.*

BOOK SIX

The welcome light of morning and the song   *1*
    of birds upon the eaves woke Judge Seguin
within his modest home. He rose to don
        his coat and boots. A pair of hound dogs, lean
        and graceful, padded with him through the clean
white chambers. The old man treated his guest
to the hospitality of the Old West.

"Good morning, Colonel Travis," said Seguin.   *2*
        "Please join me for a meal." As servants brought
a breakfast that was simple but not mean,
        the judge complained, "Colonel Bowie has fought
        with me, as well as you. A thief I thought
I'd sent to jail showed up again in court —
Antonio Fuentes — eager to report

he had Santiago's pardon, and would we   *3*
        return his confiscated clothes. The gall
of that young rascal. . . . Oh, it's sad to see
        how Bowie has declined since losing all
        his family to the plague, two years last fall.
We knew Ursula, as a little child;
she tamed him; but without her he is wild.

4 "Colonel, you are a better officer
   than Santiago Bowie is, by far,"
old Don Erasmo said. "I would prefer
   to see you in charge here during this war.
   I wish I could do more. Comanches are
a threat to all my ranches north of here;
my forces must patrol my own frontier.

5 "But several dozen cowboys who have wintered
   on my estates agree to volunteer
as soldiers or as scouts . . ." A servant entered,
   whispered to Don Erasmo. "They are here,"
   the judge told Travis. They left the austere
old ranch house and reviewed seraped men
on horseback, ranked with perfect discipline.

6 Their commander was Don Erasmo's son,
   the scion of this Texan dynasty,
himself a man of influence in San
   Antonio, a champion of a free
   constitution and of local sovereignty.
Seeing Travis, Captain Juan Seguin saluted,
and then so did the men he had recruited.

7 Just then, a few hundred miles south of town,
   the armies Santa Anna led to maim
the Texans had begun to ford the brown
   and shallow Rio Grande. Hillsides will flame
   sometimes, when mobs of orange pennons jam
together, flimsy cymbals silently
percussing in a summer symphony,

a smokeless, heatless lava. Birds will scream 8
 above the tender flames, drop from the skies,
and learn too late the meaning of the gleam:
 whatever tastes the monarch butterfly's
 emblazoned wings inevitably dies.
A myriad monarchs fluttered on the banks
of Rio Grande, unfurled above the ranks.

First came the troops of the Vanguard Brigade, 9
 Ramírez y Sesma, a general
of cavalry, commanding. This was made
 of three battalions; two of them were full
 of blank recruits whose military school
would be the war itself. Fully one half
of the San Luis Battalion came from the draft

or lottery, men yanked from silver mines 10
 or textile mills, from fields of whispering maize,
cantinas, markets. Scattered through the lines
 of another battalion, this one raised
 in Matamoros, were others gangs had seized,
one conscript for two veterans. Here they marched,
these ragged Indians, wobbly, dusty, parched.

They looked forlorn, beside the infantry 11
 battalion named Jiménez, fourteenscore
who had endured without complaint or plea.
 At Zacatecas many had met war,
 which now held no surprises, only fear
diminished by familiarity.
Their bayonet blades glittered like the sea.

12 Next came a regiment of cavalry,
   the Dolores Regiment, three hundred men
 in gleaming crested helms. Artillery
   rolled after them, three score assigned to tend
   eight pieces — two four-pounders that could send
 a message, two six-pounders and two eight-
 pounders that could flatten a wall or gate;

13 they also had two howitzers, designed
   for catapulting grimly hissing charges
 over a wall or hill when firing blind;
   across the river these were hauled on barges,
   then tugged by men and mules up muddy marges.
 In all, fourteen hundred soldiers manned
 the vanguard in Ramírez's command.

14 Beyond, aglitter like the filmy leaves
   of spring, the Second Division was arrayed
 in three brigades, led by three fighting chiefs:
   Gaona, Tolsa, Andrade. The First Brigade
   of General Antonio Gaona, on parade
 led off with the Aldama infantry,
 four hundred, with recruits as one in three;

15 beside them, in neat rows, were veterans
   who filled the First Toluca Infantry
 Battalion. Here, too, were the soldier sons
   of Querétaro, where, in a mountain lea,
   an aqueduct worthy of Rome built on three-
 score arches cooled the town; and here, as well,
 a battalion who had marched to this hell

from Guanajuato, where houses roofed   16
    with emerald grass would shame the stepcase yards
of Babylon, a sight that always moved
    the traveler in the pass to hunt for words.
    Beyond them, sixty with shakos and swords
made up the presidial company that gleamed
like the grand river for which they were named.

The sappers were one hundred eighty-five   17
    in their battalion, Mexico's elite
each known by scarlet jacket, ivory glove
    and black-furred helmet, commanding a fleet
    strong Arab mare. Each sapper on his seat
of leather sat grandly, like an antique
Achaean underneath a ship's black beak.

They did not seek preeminence, it was theirs,   18
    they were the blue jays swaggering above
the sparrows in a yard. Now came three pairs
    of cannon that artillerists had to shove
    and shoulder from the banks; theirs was a rough
frustrating task; these sixty men begrudged
the sprightliness of sappers as they trudged.

This, then, was the brigade Gaona led,   19
    one thousand seven hundred fifty men
and half a dozen guns. The next brigade
    was led by General Tolsa — seventeen
    hundred men and six cannon. His machine
of men and metal was made up of three
dozen soldiers assigned to artillery,

20 and five brigades: Morelos and Guerrero
   were first to ford the stream, each unit named
in honor of a hallowed homeland hero;
   then one called Mexico; the others claimed
   their ties to Guadalajara, back then famed
for well-swept streets, and Tres Villas, which lent
two hundred new to musket and to tent.

21 And after them, the Cavalry Brigade
   of Juan José Andrade, twenty-two-score,
divided in two regiments, arrayed
   together and caparisoned for war:
   one from Tampico, where the hot rains pour
discomfort in the summer; and the horse
contingent Guanajuato gave the force.

22 Their master gazed upon them, satisfied,
   a shepherd numbering his gathered stock.
Some dozens had deserted; more had died
   upon the mountain trails, meat for the flock
   of buzzards that had shadowed them through rock
abysses; many lay preserved in snow
deposited a whirling week ago.

23 But most who had begun the trek were here.
   For all their weariness, they felt a thrill
on realizing that the goal was near.
   Beyond the next hill, or beyond the hill
   behind it, were some rebels they could kill.
The hate they had felt for Santa Anna turned
to hate for Texans, hate these men had earned.

The troops began to chant, the way that geese,   24
    their necks grown long with song, will join in harsh
polyphony, banking on the same breeze
    that brings them echoes from the delta's marsh
    and Mississippi's bank. Ceasing to march,
the men presented arms; their voices, though,
preserved the cadence: *"Viva Mexico!"*

And: *"Viva el Presidente!"* From his mare,   25
    the lord of half the continent surveyed
his legions, felt the chorus shake the air.
    Once more he scanned his soldiery, he weighed
    the strength of each battalion, each brigade;
at length, his voice echoing, he addressed
his thousands, the Napoleon of the West:

"Soldiers of Mexico! The battlefield   26
    of Texas lies before you. Pray no more;
by your own strength your fate will be revealed,
    my destiny as well — for you, my corps,
    will determine whether ages will deplore
the name of Santa Anna or revere
that proxy for the names of you men here.

"My own desire is merely to retire,   27
    to don a rancher's mantle, hang my sword;
but so long as the foreigners conspire
    to steal our patrimony I will ford
    whatever river, strike whatever horde,
not from ambition — mine's a kindly fate,
I've got my land — I fight for your estate.

28   "Each one of you shall win his rightful share
            of country you will scrape clean with the blade;
      the farms the *gringo* settlers make their lair
            shall soon be yours, for joining this crusade.
            Your title shall be *yanqui* rebels laid
      within the land they thought to make their own;
      they'll die a second time, when your plows break the bone.

29   "Nor should you fear too great a cost in blood;
            you go to battle North Americans,
      pale braggarts who have never battled good
            opponents. Some few might have emptied guns
            into poor, naked, starving Indians,
      or triumphed over Negro serving girls;
      most of them, though, have only shot at squirrels.

30   "Their numbers have been swollen by the filth
            of ports and trading posts, unmarried men
      rejected by their countries. Our land's wealth
            they covet — when they learn they cannot win
            it easily, they'll flutter off again,
      their flag of convenience conveniently furled.
      Cutting them down, you'll slaughter half the world.

31   "If I do not know you, I know your chief;
            and many of you men I recognize
      from Zacatecas, where we shared our grief
            at our reluctant duty; but our eyes
            in Texas shall be dry. When metal flies
      to flay the rebels, I will know whose hand
      strikes bravely, whose brigade, and whose command.

"Soldiers of Mexico! I beg you, forgive 32
    this soldier for delaying your campaign.
My wonder has perturbed me; if I live
    a hundred years, I'll never see so plain
    a target as our foes. I will not rein
you further, I'll no longer hold you back.
The Texans taunt you, Mexicans. Attack!"

Four thousand soldiers answered with a roar. 33
    Their voices blent in thunder, bayonets
and spears dripped lightning in a storm before
    the great commander. Helmets bobbed on heads,
    a black armada; like a vast tank's treads,
the feet and hooves and wheels made Texas quake.
This was a force that force alone could brake.

In San Antonio, beside the creek 34
    they called San Pedro, tiers of tombstones rose,
and timber crosses. Following antique
    prescription, here the mourners had disposed
    of what the treasured dead had treasured most:
a shattered pipe, a broken plate, a token,
useless to thieves, of life now likewise broken.

Fresh rectangles of earth pasteled the yard, 35
    roofing the victims of December's battle.
Here, too, mementos: a Bowie's blue shard,
    a powder horn, the stirrup from a saddle.
    The winter wind rasped like a serpent's rattle
as Travis crossed the charnel yard to join
a man who, waiting, flipped and flipped a coin.

36   "Colonel Bowie," Travis coldly met his rival.
          "I have a note inviting . . ." Bowie sneered,
      "I know. You were informed of the arrival
              of David Crockett with the volunteers
              of Harrison, or some such. It appears
      that we have both been. . . . Well, what have we here?"
      They saw a dozen riders drawing near.

37   Among them was a young man, tall and strong,
          in buckskin and a furry, brindled dome
      from which his black locks flowed, uncombed and long.
              Travis called out, "Colonel Crockett, I presume?"
              Another said, "I'm Crockett, sir. And whom
      am I addressing?" Travis, as he eyed
      the Tennessean Congressman, replied.

38   A well-dressed gentleman of fifty years,
          with graying hair beneath a round felt hat,
      the kind that farmers wore, the wild frontier's
              most celebrated son was far from that
              cartoon in almanacs, the half bobcat,
      half alligator brute who loved a fight.
      The man was quiet, courtly and polite.

39   He introduced the Mounted Volunteers
          of Tennessee; their Captain was a man
      of twenty-five, Bill Harrison, two years
              younger than Travis. On their way to San
              Antonio, the group had picked up men
      in Nacogdoches. Their link with Tennessee,
      General Houston, had assigned the company

to bolster Bexar's garrison — divided, *40*
    they now discovered, by a bitter feud.
At private distance, Crockett now provided
    the rivals with gifts from a glossy-hued
    and felt-lined box. The Texan Colonels viewed
twin pistols of a curious design,
both demonstration pieces, fancy, fine.

"A fellow name of Samuel Colt designed *41*
    these beauts," said Crockett. "They're revolvers — see?
Six shots without reloading. Colt was kind
    enough to send these models down to me
    from Maryland. I don't think these will be
much more than toys. Still, think what might be done
by armies with a cheap, repeating gun."

Each Texan weighed and turned a sample Colt. *42*
    Each mint revolver had a bayonet,
a serpent's tongue, a frozen lightning bolt.
    Upon the cylinder were faint, inset
    engravings, murals framed within a fret
of scrollwork. The trigger's clicking spun
a little world enclosed within a gun.

The artisan had etched a civil tumult, *43*
    defenders holed up in a palisade,
besieged by countrymen. The two sides pummeled
    each other with volley and cannonade.
    Nearby on the band, the craftsman portrayed
election day. The factions of a nation
eyed one another at a polling station.

44   With equal cunning, the engraver showed
        some riders cornering a mustang herd,
   appropriating what no law bestowed;
        they glanced round in anxiety, alert
        for rivals. Next upon the band occurred
   an auction; as the cylinder was rolled,
   to babbling scat the branded herd was sold.

45   Two lovers and a swing beneath a bough
        the artist then portrayed, a private revel
   within a wood. The craftsman also showed
        a man and woman bonded in the civil
        sacrament of marriage by a gavel-
   wielding justice of the peace. Around
   his porch stood witnesses, the couple's town.

46   "Remarkable," said Travis. On the grip
        were two reliefs. As in a cameo,
   a dying General Wolfe began to slip
        from life, as watching soldiers mimed their woe;
        before he faded, his men let him know
   he had defeated Montcalm on the Plains
   of Abraham and won grand green domains

47   for British North America. Soon France
        avenged itself, aiding the man who rode
   across the grip, seeming to move with the glance
        of shadow, the stern soldier who bestowed
        his name on Washington. The engraver showed,
   along with these commanders, on the base
   of the pistol's stock, a desolated place,

a capital of empire tilted down   *48*
    beneath the breakers. Fractured pediments
were crusted thick with coral; through the drowned
    arcades flowed sharks and stingrays. Sediments
    had suffocated plazas and immense
eroded galleries where fish would veer,
each flashing school a living chandelier.

Now Crockett said, "You gentlemen are free   *49*
    to keep those guns — on one condition, please;
this argument about authority
    has got to end, or else our company's
    departing for a post where unity's
not threatened. Duel or deal, this split must end;
shoot at, or with, each other, gentlemen."

Jim Bowie, in a low and angry tone,   *50*
    rebuked the Tennessean: "Congressman,
I think how we resolve this is our own
    concern." "Beg pardon, Colonel, if I've done
    offended you. These boys rode to join one
united garrison. I recommend
you gentlemen consider joint command."

"Ridiculous," snapped Travis. "Two in charge?   *51*
    That's monstrous as a double-headed calf."
Beneath his visor, Crockett wore a large
    and friendly smile, enjoyed a little laugh.
    "Why, sir, that's a mistake, a downright gaffe.
I used to court a fine two-headed girl:
to port she was named Sue, to starboard Pearl.

52   "Her Pa, he let us stay out twice as late;
       each sister, you see, acted chaperone
when I was with the other on a date.
       When one dozed off, we two were all alone.
       Those twins were very different. Pearl had grown
up liking reels, while Sue preferred the jig;
Pearl was a Democrat, and Sue a Whig.

53   "Now Sue, she was a Methodist, but Pearl,
       she was a Baptist, the foot-washing breed.
You should have seen Pearl baptized; how that girl
       protested when the preacher dunked her braid
       while Pearl was praying — oh, how Suzy brayed!
They both were baptized, thus, by Brother Lou,
who had three noggins: Christian, papist, Jew."

54   Despite themselves, the Texans had to smile
       as Crockett spun his yarn. "Well, tell me, sir,"
said Bowie, "why didn't you walk the aisle?"
       The answer: "I was forced to choose 'twixt her
       and her. Which one of them did I prefer?
Well, Sue and I, we wanted to be wed,
but Pearl complained to Pa, who vowed to have my head."

55   In laughter all the tension was dissolved,
       the way a soggy drought will suddenly
explode in cleansing rain. The foes resolved
       their bitter battle for supremacy;
       each order that was issued now would be
approved by both commanders, who would share
authority. Travis returned to Bexar.

That afternoon, beneath a rising ring   *56*
    of gun-dark storm clouds, Crockett showed his skill.
His Tennessee Long Rifle's crack could bring
    a squirrel down at a hundred yards; his kill
    bounced from a far-off oak, plunging to thrill
the watching town, the way a drop's survivor
in Acapulco does, a daring diver.

The soldiers laughed and whooped. Then Judge Seguin   *57*
    addressed the jocund crowd. "Allies and friends,
you are invited to help me convene
    tonight's fiesta. Each one who attends
    is welcome at the feast until it ends.
My home is yours. You're welcome, one and all,
to dine with me tonight within my hall."

The offer was rewarded with applause.   *58*
    Soon Crockett, walking with the old grandee,
was learning of the land and lore and laws
    of Mexico. "This wilderness you see,"
    said Don Erasmo, "was the property
of savages, who were as ignorant
and untamed as the creatures they would hunt.

"And then, they claim, Quetzalcoatl came   *59*
    from beyond the sea, a monarch and a sage
who coaxed the natives forth and sought to tame
    their passions. His reign was a golden age;
    but Toltecs and later Mexicas waged
long, brutal wars. At last the Aztecs rose
to power on red mountains of their foes.

60   "The Aztec kings sent forth their feathered knights
          to herd the human levies to their Crete
      for sacrifice on artificial heights,
          on pyramids above their island seat
          within their lake of blood. At last, defeat
      was visited on them for all their sins
      by Cortés, come to free the Mexicans.

61   "Against the rule of Spain, in turn, we fought;
          no sooner had we torn away than brutal
      new Aztecs rose — Iturbide sought
          an empire's crown, that bauble of a feudal
          and superstitious age; next was the futile
      reign of Bustamante on the throne
      that Santa Anna's lately made his own."

62   To Crockett, the grand Creole pointed out
          the old house of the Spanish magistrate,
      and San Fernando's tower, a redoubt
          for birds fleeing from clouds the shade of slate.
          Fat drops were slanting when they neared the great
      stone house of the Seguins. The cattle cropped
      the riverside, where now the matrons shop.

63   Meanwhile, in a cantina near the quarter
          called La Villita, Bowie told his rival
      of Major General Houston's direct order
          to raze the Alamo before the arrival
          of Santa Anna. "Damn it, our survival
      depends on stopping Santa Anna here,"
      insisted Bowie, "right on the frontier."

For once Travis endorsed the older man. 64
 "Though I respect the General, I'm inclined
to agree. We need our own, offensive plan."
  He did not say, though it was in his mind,
  that only by attacking could they find
perpetual fame. A tactical retreat
would be almost as shameful as defeat.

Soon the two Texan Colonels sat beside 65
Erasmo Seguin, as he proposed a toast.
"My friends, it is with pleasure and with pride
  that I discharge the duties of your host,
  and join with you to celebrate the most
propitious birthday, the greatest event
since our own Lord's miraculous Advent:

the birthday of George Washington, a saint 66
  not only to your people, but mankind.
Without corruption and without complaint
  he served in war and peace; but we must find
  true greatness in his choice, when he declined
the office of dictator. With disdain
he answered officers who offered him a reign.

"Your young republic was anchored in its berth 67
  by the example of George Washington;
he chained the floating island to the earth.
  My drifting country, though, resembles one
  of those apparent islands that will stun
the shipwrecked when it wakens from its sleep
— a Kraken, dragging all into the deep."

68　A crack of thunder followed. Then the rain
　　　came rattling downward, besieging the town.
　　Implicated like the links in a chain,
　　　Tejanos and new Texans gathered round
　　　the laden tables, to a fiddle's sound.
　　Men passed the fiddle, demanding an air
　　from Crockett. He climbed up atop his chair.

69　"You'd better watch out, Travis," Bowie smirked
　　　to his young colleague, as they drank and viewed
　　the spectacle. "You saw the way he worked
　　　that crowd this afternoon. He may act crude,
　　　but, damn, he's sly." His former rival chewed
　　and wiped his lips. "Sir, we'll have no more votes
　　for leaders. He would have our tender throats."

70　The Tennessean, with a weary smile,
　　　held up the violin. But first, a tale:
　　"On our way here, after many a mile
　　　in barren wilderness, we heard the wail
　　　of a nearby fiddle like a friendly hail.
　　We hadn't met but possums for a week,
　　and here's somebody sawing 'Cripple Creek.'

71　"We came down to a clearing, by a stream,
　　　a Cripple Creek it was — for in his gig
　　there sat a preacher man and his mule team,
　　　marooned. His wheel was broken, and his rig
　　　was chawed by waves, the way a momma pig
　　is tugged by piglets. I said: 'Why in heck
　　you fiddling, parson, in a sinking wreck?'

"He sets his fiddle down; his eyes, they grow   72
    like popcorn in a fire, and he replies,
'Why, Brother, I could be stuck in this flow
    till Judgment Day, and my pathetic cries
    would be ignored by every soul who plies
this wilderness. Nary a backslider would
appear to rescue me from this here flood.

"'I prayed until a voice spake, loud and clear: 73
    Take up thy fiddle, scrape that dreadful wire;
if there be sinners near, they'll rush to hear
    the sinful sawing of the devil's lyre.'"
    The laughter masked the norther's steady fire,
as Crockett, winking, said, "I think his tune
went just like this . . ." The strings began to croon.

"Don Santiago!" From his reverie,   74
    Louisiana's fiercest son was roused
and pointed to the chamber's door, where three
    of Juan Seguin's scouts huddled, slicked and soused
    by rainfall. Bowie, in the door, was doused
himself by silver waves, as he tried hard
to focus on the intelligence he heard.

Soon Bowie bellowed, "Travis!" Through the hall   75
    his huge voice rang. The younger Colonel's glance
was mocking, as he swayed amid the ball,
    a *señorita* guided by his hands.
    "Can't you see I'm in the middle of a dance,"
called Travis, "with the fairest bloom to grow
in the desert soil of San Antonio?"

76 But Bowie's swearing cut the waltzing short.
    The merriment of Travis slowly faded,
  when he heard the *Tejano* scout's report
    that Santa Anna himself had invaded,
    that four, five thousand soldiers had paraded
  by the Rio Grande. Apart from the scouts,
  Bowie acquainted Travis with his doubts.

77 "I know these men," said Bowie, "and I trust
    their judgment, with respect to what they've seen;
  but what they've heard. . . . No army could have crossed
    the mountains. Santa Anna'd be insane
    to march men through a blizzard." Though Seguin
  demurred, the chiefs ignored the scouts' alarm.
  The party thundered on, as did the storm.

78 A few short leagues away, the mounted scouts
    of Mexico could hear a torrent splash
  between the town and punishment. For routes
    across the rush they hunted, till a crash
    resounded all too soon after the flash.
  Their commander, Ramírez y Sesma, gazed
  on churning currents that the lightning glazed.

79 "We'll wait till dawn," the general directed,
    shouting to be heard above the thunder.
  He spurred along the slurry that protected
    the rebels from paying now for their blunder.
    The ranks of shadowy horsemen bowing under
  the whipping rain at times could hear the brittle
  reverberations of a festive fiddle.

BOOK SEVEN

BESIEGED

THE ARGUMENT

Bexar's townsfolk flee Santa Anna's troops.
The Texan garrison regroups
in panic in the Alamo.
Defiant, Travis sends the foe
a message with a blast. Seguin,
riding as a courier, makes a clean
escape through hostile lines. That night,
while Mexicans observe a fight,
two Texans undertake a raid.
A transfer of command is made.

BOOK SEVEN

The bell of San Fernando wakened San   *1*
Antonio early on the twenty-third
of February. Colonel Travis ran
      out of his fortress chamber when he heard
      the clamor. From the little village, blurred
and dim before the dawn light, trains were rolling.
The snap of whips blent with the belfry's tolling.

An inlet's crescent, scabbed by films of oil,   *2*
      becomes a trap for seabirds. Sticky pitch
welds useless feathers, gulls and herons toil
      to free their claws from slime. So in the ditch
      their weight created, carts would sink and pitch
their contents — children, furniture, or coops
of clucking birds. Against the sinking hoops

men rammed their shoulders, while the oxen suffered   *3*
      and neighbors passed, in too much of a hurry
to render help. Abandoned items covered
      the molten road, a shipwreck's inventory,
      each thing a cue for some poor exile's story:
a smashed wardrobe, a pipe, a trampled hat,
a lonely shoe, a muddy, mewing cat.

4   An *aguador*, a water seller, lurched
        on brown columnar legs. Upon his back,
    clinging to his neck, an old man perched.
        Once, bent beneath the yoke that held the rack
        of sloshing clay, the youth would trace his track
    from door to wealthy door. Today he bore
    his widowed father from the coming war.

5   Now Travis fought to steer his skittish mount
        through fugitive *Tejanos.* "The President!"
    they cried in Spanish. Oxcarts groaned and ground
        beneath whole clans, wheels spinning to indent
        the sucking gumbo. Kicking, Travis sent
    his mare negotiating through the mire.
    The bell kept knelling, as amid a fire.

6   Atop the belfry, Travis found a young
        Kentuckian, Daniel Cloud. "I seen 'em, sir!"
    Wincing each time the mighty bell was rung,
        the Colonel could not see the slightest stir.
        Half in the belfry and half in the air
    he balanced, like an eagle on a bough
    above Lake Travis, with a mane of snow.

7   Commands rang from the belfry with the peals.
        In moments, Doctor Sutherland rode with
    John Smith, the garrison's grocer, through the hills
        due south of Bexar. When Sutherland and Smith
        topped a crest, all talking died. They caught their breath.
    Between the oaks, an army glittered, bright
    cuirassiers all in steel for standing fight.

Stunned like the first inhabitants of Bexar 8
    when armored centaurs first had crossed the prairie
shouldering lightning, the astonished pair
    spurred and rode hard. Where a violent slurry
    had melted a hill, a horse tried to scurry
but failed. Legs twisting, the shrieking brute slapped
the ground. Beneath it, Sutherland was trapped.

"Go on, go on!" the gray-haired doctor cried. 9
    His horse rolled off and wandered. Circling back,
Smith hauled his crippled comrade to his side
    upon the saddle, let the reins go slack,
    and spurred again. Warning of the attack,
the scouts came scudding back into the square:
"They're right behind us! Santa Anna's here!"

Now panic, like a twister spinning through 10
    exploding neighborhoods, sent startled men
into the streets. Travis scribbled two
    appeals for aid. Doc Sutherland again
    went galloping, in anguish. Only when
his native bride had safely joined the flood
of neighbors did Smith rocket through the mud.

Lieutenant Almeron Dickinson had hauled 11
    his wife and baby up onto the saddle.
The fifteen-month-old Angelina bawled;
    a mother's and a father's arms would straddle
    the infant, and the wail give way to prattle.
Through waves of hats and manes that family
meandered, as the bell rang frantically.

12 Three blocks away, a family was parted.
    Old Don Erasmo gripped the hand of Juan,
  who urged him, "Father, you must go. Get started."
    If the Virgin and the saints would spare his son,
    the old man vowed in prayer, there was not one
  catastrophe that he could not endure;
  if not, the father hoped to die, before

13 his ears could hear the world could yet hold worse.
    Seguin was helped to the gig by his heir,
  who bade the driver hurry. With a curse,
    the muleteer moved the team. Juan met the glare
    his wife, Gertrudis, sent him with a stare
  of calm authority. She felt betrayed
  to be thus exiled while her husband stayed.

14 "Load up! Come on!" a soldier bellowed down
    at Joe. The young man glared and told the slave
  of Captain Carey, John, "We could leave town."
    "Oh, yeah?" John grunted, as he turned and gave
    his friend a bag of flour. "You go save
  yourself. To Mexicans, we're niggers, too."
  They clambered on the wagon with the crew.

15 Two brothers, men of San Antonio.
    Francisco said, "You're talking about treason!
  This is their fight, not ours." Gregorio
    Esparza gave his brother just one reason:
    "They are our friends." That night, half a dozen —
  Gregorio, his wife, his brood — below
  blind guns would scurry to the Alamo.

The scouts of the Dolores Cavalry,   16
    the first few drops presaging flash and clatter,
came drumming into Bexar. The refugee
    contingents that they passed began to scatter
    in panic. Rebels wobbled up a ladder
into the Alamo, as others forded
the stream behind three dozen head they herded.

Between the ivory fort and silvery surge   17
    of Santa Anna's army rocked a gig,
ornate, alone. Like skiers who emerge
    before an avalanche's cloud and zig-
    zag downhill, surviving every big
collapse of shelves behind, those in the carriage
amazed those watching with their skill and courage.

The teamster was Jim Bowie. He was in;   18
    the gates swung shut. The soldiers lent a hand
to Juana, and her baby by a man
    now dead. She had wed another, in a band
    of Texans separated by this grand
surprise. Another of Jim Bowie's kin,
Gertrudis, waited for the gentlemen.

These sisters, and an old mestizo maid,   19
    were all that linked Jim Bowie to his bride,
his Ursula. The master of the blade
    had lost his sharpness when his lady died,
    with half her clan. A thing no foe had tried,
a plague accomplished. Now, a second time,
he'd learn a knife's no use in fighting slime.

20 The bravo coughed and sputtered. "Travis! Where's . . ."
   He could not end, for coughing. "Just a drink
is all I need." No answers, only stares.
   Jim Bowie took a step, started to sink,
   erupted in a retch, began to blink
through fevered tears. "Somebody help him!" cried
Gertrudis. Texans hauled their chief inside.

21 Outside the fortress wall, the trumpets blent;
   the regiments divided at the sound;
a slender horseman galloped through the rent
   and reared his horse and waved his crescent crown.
   Between the crumbling mission and the town
the roar resounded: *"Viva Mexico!*
Viva el Presidente! Mexico!"

22 Before his army the magnificent
   commander feinted. Borrowing a lance,
a javelin an obliging sapper lent,
   Santa Anna rode, unmindful of the chance
   of injury. His horse began a dance
beneath him, on the brown creek's southern shore;
hurling the lance, he now renewed the war.

23 "Wait, hold your fire," called Travis to the men
   he shared with Bowie, nowhere to be found.
A coyote prowling round a bleating pen,
   the Mexican commander rode around
   the river's curl. He bade the trumpets sound
an invitation to an embassy,
and then rejoined admiring cavalry.

Inside the barracks, Bowie, in his bed,   *24*
 with fingers trembling, scratched a note he gave
his friend Green Jameson. "Hurry, now," he said.
 "Find Colonel Juan Almonte. He might save
 us yet from Santa Anna." Then a grave
new round of spasms rang. Suspecting a ruse,
Santa Anna studied Jameson's flag of truce.

And so did Travis. Perched above the gate,   *25*
 the Colonel saw the white cloth butterfly
go bouncing through the field. It was too late
 to summon Jameson back. "It was a lie,"
 he snarled to Bonham. "Shared command! Just why
I thought I could trust Bowie I don't know."
The Colonel mustered the men of the Alamo.

His purpose was to shame his fellow chief.   *26*
 He bellowed, "Well, men? Will we cut and run?"
A murmuring arose. In the belief
 that Travis was sincere, some had begun
 to hurry toward the gate, resolve undone
by panic, rustling through the ranks, the way
a hurricane will flatten trees like hay.

The leaders of the garrison corralled   *27*
 excited soldiers, shouting to restore
dead discipline. A grizzled Frenchman howled
 when seized by Carey, Captain of the corps
 called the Invincibles. "I'm tired of war!"
growled Louis Rose. "I marched to Moscow, I
retreated in the snow. I didn't die

28   for Emperor Napoleon, that fool,
          and I ain't dying now!" The old man scrambled
      across the courtyard, over the mission wall.
          Crashing into cactus, he stumbled
          to safety. All the other men assembled
      once more and cheered on Travis, as he climbed
      beside a cannon and ordered it primed.

29   Across the river, Jameson was conferring
          with Juan Almonte when the mission's grand
      eighteen-pounder thumped, and scrap went whirring
          overhead. The parley was at an end.
          In moments, three hundred muskets were trained
      on Albert Martin, as he made his way
      beneath the second flag of truce that day.

30   The President, observing from afar,
          now chuckled. "Their two leaders can't agree.
      It seems that we have stumbled on a war."
          Both messengers returned despondently,
          depressed beneath the message: there would be
      surrender at discretion, or the sword.
      The quiet Texans eyed the glittering horde.

31   "The banner of No Quarter," Juan Seguin
          told Travis, as red lightning shimmied up
      the tower of San Fernando. He had seen
          or heard of the like, thought Travis, as the flap
          of crimson curled. . . . The fort that proved a trap
      for Jane, courageous Jane, that queen to giants.
      What was that outpost's name? Of course. Defiance.

That evening, sentries on the fortress wall   32
        cried out a warning, echoing a blast
outside the Alamo. The hissing ball
        spun in its crater, fizzling out at last.
        One of the weary soldiers who had passed
the time by betting where the next would drop
told groaning comrades, "All right, y'all, pay up."

Inside the fort's headquarters, candles blent   33
        their fumes with the cigar's. "It's settled, then,"
concluded Colonel Travis. "We will send
        a courier who can pass as one of them."
        The band he wore beneath Rebecca's gem
flashed as he spoke. Seguin agreed to choose
a rider who could slip out through the noose.

"Ah, Colonel" — Almeron Dickinson bestirred   34
        himself, uncomfortable. "You know I'm from
Gonzales, and . . . well, sir, well, if they heard
        from someone they respected, not just some . . ."
        He paused, then said, "They're likelier to come
to help if they're fired up by someone who
has standing there. Captain Seguin would do . . ."

Seguin refused. "I will not leave my men   35
        while they're endangered." Travis overrode
his fellow ranger. "A Seguin might win
        attention that would just not be bestowed
        on some unknown *Tejano*. On the road —
that's where you'd serve this garrison the best.
That's not an order, sir. It's a request."

36 Within a cave-cold chamber in the fort's
   interior, Jim Bowie spoke a tongue
that none could understand. "Ah, how it hurts
  to see the ruin of a man so strong,"
   Seguin said to the sisters as they clung
to one another. Travis, from the door,
watched as the Creole knelt upon the floor.

37 "Don Santiago," whispered Juan Seguin.
   The bravo rumbled. "Sir, I need your horse.
It's for a special mission. I'll explain . . ."
  Down Bowie's face the tears began to course.
   "Diablo . . . my Diablo . . ." Bowie's nurse,
the maid called Doña Petra, quickly pressed
cool cloth upon his brow. "He must have rest."

38 The gates soon cracked. Upon Diablo hunched
   Seguin, and close behind, Antonio Cruz
Arocha, leaning forward, tightly clenched
  upon his horse. They quickly tried to lose
   themselves in darkness. Asked for coded cues
by sentries at a crossroads, Juan Seguin
began to slow — then clattered from the scene.

39 First shouts, then shots, came after. But the two
   Tejanos, by then, were crackling through grass,
Arocha, on a mare that pumped and blew,
  Seguin, atop the mustang that could crease
   the clouds, it seemed. This blend of force and grace
was traded for Bowie's rifle by a chief
of Lipans. Now Diablo flew, a leaf

amid a twister, a flat, skipping stone   *40*
   nicking a lake of glass in glancing past.
Seguin could not know bits of ash and bone
     would be the garrison, when he at last
     returned; nor that in time he would be chased
from Texas to exile, a forlorn fate.
No easy thing it is to found a state.

A cadia had sent two volunteers.   *41*
   Charles and Blaz Despallier left the slough
for prairie, fleeing the swamp for the frontier's
     perimeterless freedom. Here the two
     had fought to take the city from the blue-
coat regiments of General Martin Cos;
here canister had sliced unlucky Blaz.

Home in Louisiana, in the Cajun   *42*
   backcountry, Blaz was regaining his power.
Young Robert Brown replaced him. On a station
     deep in a western park, a latticed tower
     above the pines, young rangers will spend hour
on hour in conversation as they scan
the hills for fire that lightning set, or man,

now joking, now confessing, now relating   *43*
   anxieties and hopes and tastes and plans,
now joined in ribald snickers, now debating
     the afterlife, the country's fate, and man's.
     So the young Yankee and the heir of France
now thought and felt as one; and now, as well,
they shared a sentry station on the wall.

44 Night. Like stars that sparkle round the moon
    some windless evening, swarming in their splendor
  above the hilltops where coyotes croon,
    the fires of Mexican soldiers, each a cinder
    within the dark when viewed by a defender
  atop the fortress wall, were burning on
  where mules and horses grazed, awaiting dawn.

45 Despallier murmured, "Pardner, do you believe
    in Fate? Or do you think it's just a name
  for what we want? I'm aching to achieve
    just one big win, to grab a little fame;
    I've got too fierce a spirit to be tame.
  Look yonder, how confident the Mexes are;
  only a few fires burning, near or far;

46 they're overcome by *pulque* or by sleep;
    their guard is down. Here's what I have in mind:
  I'm going to jump the wall, and then I'll creep
    to La Villita, where their snipers find
    their cover from our guns. That hunting blind
  has got to go, and I'm the one to burn
  those damn huts down. You cover my return."

47 His comrade, just eighteen, had been inspired
    by his best friend's ambition, as a roof
  next to a burning neighbor will be fired
    in turn. He said, "All right, you want to prove
    yourself — well, sir, you're going to have to move
  aside for me, if there's fame to be won.
  My daddy didn't raise no coward son."

Now Charles protested, "I'll need covering fire . . ." 48
    Rob answered, "You know I'll look out for you,
if you will watch my back. We'll light a pyre
      to flush the squirrels out of that chimney flue."
    His friend said, "Colonel Travis, if he knew
what we have got in mind, why, he'd be sore.
But he himself broke ranks to start this war."

The custom then in San Antonio 49
   ordained that men should gather by the tower
of San Fernando for the nightly show.
    Tonight, the crowd at the appointed hour
    was one of soldiers. Splendid in his power,
the President sat throned among his staff,
impatient for the flashing of the gaff.

While touts were taking bets, the troops were treated 50
    by *soldaderas* to a musket dance;
the women, dressed like soldiers, charged, retreated,
    and spun low to the ground. One had her chance
    when thrusting her bayonet to obtain a glance.
An aide said, "Juana Gallo, she is called."
That night the ruler's tent would not be cold.

In cages, roosters lunged. The dancers soon 51
    were followed by a singing competition
between two dueling soldiers who would croon
    to win a silver bowl. "With your permission,"
    the first said, "from our glorious tradition
I'll sing a noble ballad of a war."
The fellow winked, his hand stroked his guitar.

52　　*"To love a girl who does not love you back*
　　　　　is to find a comb when you are bald.
　　　A married woman's silver in the sack,
　　　　　a widow's copper, and a virgin's gold;
　　　　　but women turn to tin when they are old.
　　　The cockroach, the cockroach, she's gone far enough
　　　without some marijuana she can puff."

53　　The street echoed with hooting and with jeers.
　　　　　The President chewed opium, and drummed
　　　his fingers, talked with aides. To boos and cheers
　　　　　the rival songster took his place and strummed
　　　　　an overture of chords. He gently hummed
　　　until the noise diminished, then intoned
　　　a song, a song less sung than sighed and moaned.

54　　*"My Adelita, now the trumpet's calling.*
　　　　　That I will not forget, you must believe.
　　　I'll think of you, though round me shots are falling.
　　　　　If I should die in battle, if they leave
　　　　　my body on the field, then do not grieve;
　　　Adelita dear, my prayer you must hear:
　　　for this dead trooper shed a single tear."

55　　The raucous crowd was silent. Soldiers squeezed
　　　　　their women. Men alone were lonesome now.
　　　The generals saw Santa Anna was displeased.
　　　　　He stood, and clapped his hands, and shouted, "How
　　　　　depressing. You, there, you — come take a bow."
　　　The man who sang "La Cucaracha" claimed
　　　the silver bowl. And now, at last, they gamed.

The champions flew forth, beneath the tower 56
    of San Fernando, near their wicker tents,
a trickle their Scamander. Neither would cower,
    each rammed into his foe. The jagged splints
    cut flesh and feather. Whirring, then a rinse
of blood on dirt, a wink of gaffs. The victor
stood pecking at his foe, crowed over Hector.

A roar of relief erupted from the muster. 57
    "Attention!" Several hundred boots now clicked.
By lantern light, the soldiers watched their master
    stride forth and kneel. The winning rooster pecked
    at medals; as it did so, scarlet specked
the perfect ivory of the uniform.
Anointed thus, Santa Anna told the swarm:

"Tomorrow, or the next day, or the next 58
    you men will go to battle, like this stag.
Look at this creature, let the sight be fixed
    within your mind. This warrior has no flag,
    the land it fights for is a pile of slag,
and yet it scorns its life. You men defend
no dung heap, but your precious native land."

A rattle, in the distance. Voices cried. 59
    A horseman reined nearby. "It's an attack!"
Cursing, Santa Anna thrust the bird aside,
    and bellowed at his aides. "Well, don't stare back
    at me, I want a horse!" Mounted, he took
a shortcut down a lane, his blowing horse
bearing him swiftly to the shooting's source.

60　In La Villita, gobs of liquid light
　　　　were dripping from the brand Despallier held.
　　First whispers; then the wattles would ignite
　　　　　and gild the driftwood hut. His partner yelled,
　　　　　"Come on! Let's go!" The trellis flicker swelled,
　　and blades of flimsy flame began to gut
　　Antonio Cruz Arocha's wicker hut.

61　Like fireflies orbiting through pillared lawns
　　　　when June prolongs the dusk, the pair of glows
　　traced fading wakes between the little dawns
　　　　　their tapping made. Atop the Alamo's
　　　　　stockade, Travis exploded: "Who are those
　　damned idiots?" He told artillery
　　to warn the horsemen of the enemy.

62　The thunder of cascading bonfires hid
　　　　the hoofbeats. Then a horseman's silhouette
　　eclipsed an orange hut. Brown pivoted,
　　　　　evading saber swings. The ground he set
　　　　　his foot on vanished, then it rose and met
　　his body, hard. He shuddered as a hand
　　contracted — it belonged, though, to his friend.

63　"I've got you," said Despallier, as he hauled
　　　　his comrade limping from the booming blaze.
　　Reaching the small canal, they waded, crawled
　　　　　and rolled through icy water in a haze
　　　　　that stank of powder. To the firelit space
　　before the fort, men of the garrison
　　were plunging from the walls, goats from a pen.

Above the two companions, shivering, drenched,   64
    compressed within the ditch, the bullets hissed
from every side. Through the canal they inched,
    flinching and cursing at every near miss.
    "Don't shoot! It's us! Despallier! Brown! It's us!"
In moments, stooping shadows made them tall
enough to grab the hands atop the wall.

Once dried and dressed, the two companions joined   65
    the garrison's commander in his quarters.
The Colonel — scarcely older — made his point
    with crisp precision. "I do not want martyrs
    or heroes on my team defying orders.
Nobody acts, without consulting me.
I ought to have you strung for mutiny."

Exchanging glances, the two soldiers trailed   66
    the stern young Colonel back into the court.
A wall of backs divided and revealed
    Jim Bowie on his bed, borne through the fort
    as if upon a litter. With a snort,
he rumbled to his bearers, "Set me down."
His rival looked on Bowie with a frown.

"These men should be attending to their posts,"   67
    snapped Travis, eyeing his adversary.
The bravo coughed and shook; he seemed a ghost's
    impersonation. "You will get to bury
    me soon enough now, Travis. I've a very
important statement I must give these men."
His rival shifted. "Well, sir. Give it, then."

68 A fit of sputtering, then Bowie said,
   "You men have done me proud. My spirit shares
 your vigil on the walls. But a half-dead
   commander's worse than none. I'm past repairs.
   The best release I can get from my cares
 is knowing you're led by a steady hand;
 and that I know, with Travis in command."

69 "This latest feint, this sortie that he sent,
   it showed the cunning of a strategist."
 A choking gasp. "Men, I am confident
   that Colonel Travis is among our best
   commanders. Therefore . . . therefore I divest
 myself, from here on, of authority.
 Now on, when Travis speaks, he speaks for me."

BOOK EIGHT

COUNCILS
OF WAR

THE ARGUMENT

The news of the invasion stuns
the rest of Texas. Grabbing guns,
the menfolk of Gonzales ride
to the Alamo, leaving bride
and brood behind. There will be no
more reinforcements, Travis learns,
when Bonham finally returns
from Goliad. Two councils of war
and then, as Mexicans prepare
to storm the fortress, Travis makes
his final rounds. To war he wakes.

BOOK EIGHT

In Philadelphia, threescore years before,   *1*
    ambassadors of twelve seceding states
had signed the declaration of their war
        in a grand gallery. Now delegates
        from two great settler nations heard debates
inside a hall, not much more than a shack,
in Washington-on-Brazos. Word of attack

on the garrison at San Antonio   *2*
    arrived with Houston. "Santa Anna's trapped
Travis and his men at the Alamo!"
        the thunder of the giant's bellow clapped.
        The suited men fell silent, listened rapt
as Major General Houston took the floor
and told the story of the embattled corps.

"My orders were to blow up the Alamo,   *3*
    and leave no stone on stone. They disobeyed.
Their valiant resistance now may slow
        Santa Anna's movement. He won't be delayed
        for long, though. Gentlemen, the time for debate
has passed. Our sovereignty must be declared,
government framed, and defenses repaired."

4   Commotion broke the silence. "Gentlemen,"
        roared Houston, "we have suffered a surprise,
perhaps disaster. We've a chance to win —
        no more, though, than a chance. We must all rise
        above our jealousies, and sacrifice
ourselves, or else expose this entire land
to what's befallen Travis and his band."

5   Just then, a day's ride westward from the crude
        convention hall, within the muddy square
of old Gonzales, stood another crowd
        in silence. Only women gathered there;
        they watched the prairie's western skyline, where
the hoof-stirred haze marked men who chose to go
rescue their neighbors at the Alamo.

6   "Where's Daddy going, Momma?" Prudence Kimbell
        caressed her two young children, as her smile
betrayed anxiety with a slight tremble.
        The shop on Water Street, where George, with Al
        Dickinson, sold hats of every style,
was still. The Dickinsons, partners and friends,
were trapped; George had to ride to their defense.

7   Upon a porch, two somber women stood
        embracing — Louise Cottle Jackson, mother
of Thomas Jackson's children, a large brood,
        and Nancy, who had wed Louise's brother
        George Cottle. The twins to whom he was the father
would both be orphans when they were born
to a fleeing widow with no time to mourn.

A shutter's bang, resounding like a shot,   *8*
    made Margaret, widowed Jake Darst's second wife,
flinch in alarm. Her nervous fingers sought
    two silky scalps. Her neighbor Liz, the wife
    of Andrew Kent, stood with her family
upon a rough sidewalk of corduroy.
Two of her babies squabbled for a toy.

Elizabeth Kent was blinking back the tears   *9*
    that she had hidden while she watched the man
she wed back in Kentucky, all those years
    ago, diminishing with that small band.
    This, this was not the future they had planned
back in Missouri. First their eldest son
had left with rangers, now Andrew was gone.

The other children of the Kents were tugging   *10*
    at Liz's skirts, while she, distracted, peered
westward. She assured them with her hugging.
    Across the square, aloof Sidney appeared,
    the beauty at whom all the county leered;
she had been rich Tom Miller's doll and bride,
until their baby and their marriage died.

To Johnny Kellogg, half Tom Miller's age   *11*
    at swaggering nineteen, the girl had fled,
inspiring the town's womenfolk to rage
    even when law legitimized their bed.
    Upon her shoulder she reclined her head,
her finger spooling hair, studying where
two husbands and a brother turned to air.

12   Off in the distance now, new motion stirred;
            the women of Gonzales watched the carriage
      of Evaline Dewitt as she returned.
            From cloth her daughter had worn at her marriage
            last fall, the white Naomi planned to cherish,
      the widow had sewn the small town's battle flag —
      a gun, with C O M E   A N D   T A K E   I T on a rag.

13   When Kimbell and his ranger volunteers
            had left, Mrs. Dewitt had given chase,
      whip searing from her gig, followed by cheers
            from watching wives. Catching up in the race,
            the widow warned the men not to disgrace
      the ladies of Gonzales. Rangers rode
      to Bexar now with the banner she had sewed.

14   One woman of Gonzales did not see
            the menfolk leaving for the Alamo;
      the wife of Isaac Millsaps counted three,
            then four, then seven squirming heads below
            her fingers. Nor would Mary see the glow
      of cabins burning, though she'd hear the creaks
      of laden wagons fleeing, in two weeks.

15   In Mexico sometimes a field of maize
            gives up a yield of flame and fizzing steam
      before it bursts; a village starts to blaze
            as meteors arc downward with a scream
            around the babbling farmers. So a stream
      of shot and shells had showered for a week
      into the Alamo. A shell would streak

into the yard and blow a hole in mud,   16
    or roll awhile, fuse hissing like a snake,
before it cooled. The old stone fort withstood
    the steady pounding, though the chalk would shake
    with each impact. When splintered rock would flake
into a sizzling skillet at a hit,
one cook was fond of saying, "Grits with grit."

The members of the garrison endured   17
    the boom of day and cannon croak of night
inside the rooms, meat slowly being cured
    in hollow gloom. To keep men fit to fight,
    their captains set assignments. In upright
containers made of hide, the men would pour
soft dirt, creating sandbags in each door.

At other times, the soldiers hammered nails   18
    and horseshoes and such bits of metal scrap
as they could find, their substitute for hails
    of grape and canister. They dug to tap
    the groundwater, when their foes tried to stop
the small canal that ran beneath the wall;
daring the missiles, Texans dug a well.

The women, meanwhile, cooked and hung up flags   19
    of laundry half outside the doors, half in.
Anna Esparza, tearing a shirt to rags,
    complained to Juana and Gertrudis when
    Susannah Dickinson tried once again
to win a private room. "My family
is bigger — you won't hear complaints from me."

20   The sisters of Jim Bowie's wife kept kneading
      tamales on the floor, while Anna said,
"She can't work, she has a baby needing
      attention. I've got four myself, and yet
      I do my part. I ought to stay in bed.
They're all like that, they are a lazy race."
Distressed, Juana stood up and left the place.

21   "See what you've done?" Gertrudis angrily
      gave Anna a rebuke. "Did you forget
her *yanqui* husband?" Horace Alsbury
      was out of town when his in-laws had fled
      the approaching army. Whether he was dead
or safe somewhere, poor Juana did not know,
marooned with her infant in the Alamo.

22   A clamor in the courtyard. Like a wad
      of hornets, men were wrestling in the mud,
and not in play. Now Captain Carey's squad
      of artillery, who in such cases would
      double as police, pried free the blood-
burnoosed combatants. Travis joined the scene,
hearing English and Spanish, both obscene.

23   "Two more deserters, sir," Carey explained.
      "Losoya's mother and his brother elected
the jump the wall last night." Travis was pained
      to learn that more *Tejanos* had defected.
      If only Juan Seguin were here, respected
by native volunteers. "Half rations for
the brawlers," Travis told the watching corps.

Upon the wall, guns popped; a cry; then cheers.   *24*
    "They're reinforcements!" Forgetting the brawl,
the garrison grouped round the volunteers
    defenders helped to lower from the wall.
    Travis saluted Kimbell. "How many in all
have come with you?" When Captain Kimbell bragged
"Two dozen," the young Colonel slightly sagged.

Steaks bled on hissing coals by sizzling cobs.   *25*
    Men swayed with laughing ladies, or alone
stomped out a musical tattoo. The mob's
    delirium was heightened, by the moan
    of bagpipes and the catgut's screechy groan.
Loud music at ten paces was the rule:
McGregor challenged Crockett to a duel.

That evening saw reunions. Kimbell found   *26*
    his partner in the hat shop, Dickinson,
and Sue, and Angelina. Robert Brown
    nudged Charles Despallier, who had made the run
    as courier to Gonzales, and was one
of those who led the volunteers through foe-
infested fields into the Alamo.

Alone amid the many, Travis brooded.   *27*
    The sounds were tinny, distant, and the blaze
a dying star. Had he just been deluded
    in thinking that, within a span of days,
    the Texan army would appear to raise
Santa Anna's siege? He sipped his drink and eyed
the folks for whom he had chosen suicide.

28   Through March's third gray dawn, a horseman veered
       across the prairie, slowing on a swell
of shrubby earth. The Alamo appeared
       past sawtooth tents. Horse and rider could smell
       the breakfast fires. Above the fort, the pale
blue flag brought from New Orleans gave no doubt
that Travis and his garrison held out.

29   Within the mission, the distant pop and rattle
       made sentries stir. "The gate! Open the gate!"
The oak began to groan, as sounds of battle
       were answered from the walls. With one last great
       exertion, the small pony bore its freight
over the lunette spikes, with all the grace
of a champion at a fence in steeplechase.

30   The cheers died when the courier closed the door
       to Travis's headquarters. It was cold,
like its one occupant. "A ranger corps
       has joined us, from Gonzales," Travis told
       James Bonham. "Thirty men, no more." His old
companion did not speak. "I take it, then,
that Fannin will be sending us no men."

31   The Carolinian lit a flaring smoke;
       the burst, in that room's darkness, made his face
a gargoyle's mask highlighted by a stroke
       of storm light. "Fannin will not leave that place,
       and I can't blame him. It was quite a chase,
when I got through the lines. Four hundred men
might help us die. They cannot help us win."

"I sent for reinforcements, not regrets,"   *32*
    snapped Travis. Then he ran a weary hand
through tangled bangs. "Why am I wasting threats
    on you? I just . . . I have a whole command
    depending on me. It's not what I planned,
it's not at all . . ." His old friend offered him
one of two glasses filled up to the brim.

While Travis rubbed his too-young face in pain,   *33*
    Bonham told of the sad and haggard men
who staggered back to Goliad, insane
    with horror. "Johnson's regiment had been
    completely slaughtered by the Mexican
commander. They killed unarmed men, and japed
about it. Johnson, three others, escaped."

In silence Travis brooded, then he said,   *34*
    "I know Frank Johnson well. When I was held
at Anahuac by Bradburn, Johnson led
    the posse that delivered me from hell."
    The Colonel grew stern. "When his soldiers fell,
he should have fallen with them. To outlive
your troops is a disgrace none can forgive."

Outside, the soldiers mobbed atop the wall,   *35*
    like gulls along a pier. "What's going on?"
yelled Travis. "It looks like a festival."
    Off in the distance could be heard a song.
    Ascending, Colonel Travis saw the long
and glittering line of infantry and horse,
a rattlesnake uncoiling beaded force.

36 "Santa Anna has arrived," James Bonham guessed,
    erring. General Gaona, long delayed,
now marched the dusty troops he had impressed
    through San Antonio in a parade.
    Across the creek, the jaunty music played,
an echo of the Texans' impromptu
fandango, of a feeling fled like dew.

37 His force complete, the President now made
    his final plans. Upon the afternoon
of March the fourth, he gathered every aide
    and general, and he told them, "Soon, quite soon,
    we will attack. Urrea will maroon
the rebel forces at Fort Goliad;
they were the only hope these rebels had.

38 "Defectors have supplied us with a list
    of women, children, Negroes, in the fort,"
Santa Anna told his staff. "It will be passed
    among the officers. No one will hurt
    those innocents. As for the rest — the sword."
His generals shifted round the young commander.
"Well, speak!" he said. "You know I credit candor."

39 The only one to speak was Castrillon:
    "The rules of war, Your Excellency, prevent
the massacre of soldiers who have thrown
    their weapons down. Recall, these rebels sent
    our soldiers home unharmed" — at this, a squint
at General Cos, who feigned he did not hear,
touching a jewel that dangled from his ear.

"My orders are No Quarter. Anyone   *40*
   whose conscience is too tender can resign."
No one replied. The President went on.
   "To acquaint us with the Alamo's design,
   I give you General Cos. He did so fine
a job of reinforcing the Alamo,
it's rather sad he gave it to our foe."

At sunset on the fifth of March two weeks   *41*
   of thumping cannonade abruptly stopped.
Around the guns, as ripples warp a creek's
   transparency around a pebble dropped
   smack on its roof, the silence spread and lapped
the mission walls. A distant barking drifted
on winds across the quiet grass they sifted.

Inside the fort's headquarters, below   *42*
   the shadows that the candles animated,
sat all but two chiefs of the Alamo.
   Captain John Baugh, the adjutant, waited
   by Amos Pollard, surgeon of the ill-fated
contingent. Colonel Bonham made a wager
with Hiram Williamson, a sergeant major.

Elial Melton, quartermaster, paced   *43*
   with nervous energy around the room.
Green Jameson sat and whittled. Blazeby chased
   one drink with another, fighting the gloom,
   the New Orleans Greys' commander. Still as doom
sat Captain Robert White, of the Bexar Guards.
Beside him, Captain Baker shuffled cards.

44   Bill Harrison, the captain of the troop
          from Tennessee, pulled a watch from his pocket;
      the one "high private" found within his group
          shared murmurs with him, Colonel David Crockett.
          George Kimbell of Gonzales squeezed a locket
      that held his painted Prudence. Captain Carey
      sat pert by Major Evans, slumped and weary.

45   The man whom they awaited paused alone
          in his monastic cell. From that to this
      alternative his glancing thoughts were thrown,
          reflections from a watch a moving wrist
          will flick across a room. He was depressed,
      he was exhilarated with despair;
      he brimmed with tenderness; he did not care.

46   Till now, somehow, he had known a cavalry
          would sweep down and then sweep away the foe,
      the way that gulls, appearing far from sea,
          miraculous as a midsummer snow,
          would sometimes plummet through a planted row,
      saving a farm from locusts. Now he knew
      that there would be no gulls. The crunching grew.

47   "Gentlemen." Chairs scraped, as officers rose.
          "At ease." With fluency, the young commander
      had spoken once. He paused now, as he chose
          each word. "When we received the initial tender
          of terms, I chose — we chose — not to surrender,
      knowing that the alternative would be the sword
      if the enemy should take the fort.

"Until the last few days, I still believed   *48*
    that reinforcements, sent from Goliad
to Bexar by Colonel Fannin, might have relieved
    this fortress. Gentlemen, it is my sad
    and bitter duty to report the bad
news that most of you already know:
there is no rescue for the Alamo.

"The massacre of Johnson's captured men   *49*
    by Santa Anna's troops only a few days
ago near Goliad is proof again
    our enemy is willing to disgrace
    his uniform by murder. Now the face
of tyranny is seen behind the mask.
Why Texas fights, no one henceforth need ask.

"The silence of his guns may indicate   *50*
    that Santa Anna's ordered an attack
tonight, or tomorrow. The hour of our fate
    is his to choose. We can't survive a sack;
    before we fall, however, we can make
his victory far worse than a retreat,
and his advance a progress to defeat."

The men were silent. Travis took a breath,   *51*
    resumed. "Our purpose, gentlemen, is clear.
Our enemies right now prepare our death;
    our task's to make that death a death we share,
    leaving Santa Anna with few troops to spare."
He acted confident, though deeply pained;
a virtue feigned can be a virtue gained.

52   The fort's commander asked now for advice
          on turning the old mission to a clamp
      gouging the predator, a cruel device.
              What salients were likely from the camp
              of Mexico? What teams should man each ramp?
      Sharing like women at a quilting bee,
      they wove their suicidal strategy.

53   Concluding the war council, Travis addressed
          the somber men. "Each of us who has kin
      in Texas has a reason to resist:
              keeping this vicious tyrant and his men
              from savaging his family in his den."
      He heard Charles Edward shriek, saw soldiers press
      his Becky to the ground, seizing her dress.

54   "Those of you without family or land
          to rescue have your honor. That's enough.
      Why else is it we officers command
              such deference? We choose the finest of
              the dinner portions, and we sleep above
      the ground on beds. All this, so on the day
      that battle finally comes our men will say:

55   "'That officer who leads us is no coward;
          he may have dined on beef and costly wine,
      not moldy hardtack and milk that has soured;
              but still, this officer of ours is fine;
              why, look at how he stands before the line.'"
      More than one set of eyes began to mist
      as Colonel Travis told his friends, "Dismissed."

Four human columns Santa Anna built   *56*
    to stave in mission walls — the strongest, those
called First and Second, aimed to sink to the hilt
    into the north. The Third would channel blows
    against the eastern chapel, while the rows
of soldiers in the column dubbed the Fourth,
striking the south, would siphon from the north.

Quietly, the columns began to assemble.   *57*
    Inside the fortress corral, Robert Brown
reached out to clasp Despallier's hand. A tremble
    communicated more than feeble sound.
    Brown saddled up, and spurred the horse to bound,
bearing the final plea Travis would send.
Despallier watched the dark absorb his friend.

While ghostly ranks, with quiet industry,   *58*
    were bearing ladders, crowbars, cartridge packs,
and flints and axes, Travis checked to see
    that posts upon the wall had ample stacks
    of ammunition, muskets, pistols, sacks
of powder safely shielded from the dew.
He traded jokes or smokes with every crew.

Morales mustered the Fourth Column's men,   *59*
    most veterans of the Zacatecan war.
Upon the palisade they sought to win
    at dawn stood Travis, lighting a cigar
    for Crockett. The ember glimmered like a star.
"I'd rather die out in the open, friend,
than holed up like a skunk inside his den."

60   The cavalry, with muffled scuff, assumed
          position on the prairie to the east,
      as Travis strolled with Bonham. Cannon loomed
          around them in the chapel, where the priest
          had once blessed Indians. "Well, sir, at least,"
      said Bonham, "we'll be free of this hotel,
      though I would just as soon not pay the bill."

61   Two thousand hearts were knelling in the grass
          around the Alamo when Travis knelt
      beside his rival. Whispering, he pressed
          one Colt revolver in his hand, and felt
          a trace of strength that plague alone could melt.
      "Travis?" Sense renewed, and then eluded
      the dying man. A man soon dead saluted.

62   Just blocks away, Santa Anna fingered maps
          once more with anxious aides, as Travis strode
      into the sacristy, beside the apse
          a cannon's ramp now filled. Amid a node
          of candles, pools of warping crimson showed
      Enrique Esparza, with his parents and
      his siblings. The boy raised his tiny hand

63   in a salute, which was sharply returned.
          The Colonel joined the Dickinsons and smiled
      at gurgling Angelina. His eyes burned
          as he thought of his son, and of the child
          he'd never share with Becky. He beguiled
      Susannah's baby with the sparkling ring
      that Becky gave him. "Do you have a string?"

The thousands waiting outside in the gloom   *64*
   maintained strict silence as the enemy
commander joined his slave inside their room.
   "Joe, if I fall, you tell my family
   what happened . . ." "Yes, sir. I can tell Aunt Bea,
with Mister Johnson. She'll tell cousin Joan . . ."
That Joe had kin, his master had not known.

The Texan pickets, poised on the cool ground   *65*
   beyond the fortress walls, gazed up in wonder
at armies of the stars. There was no sound
   in all the dark and dormant planet under
   those glimmers, bright as rainbows after thunder.
The prairie wind, an intermittent breeze,
blew from the effervescing galaxies.

Above the silhouette of Bexar's church,   *66*
   the tranquil blue stars of Centaurus gleamed;
beyond that glint, stormers began to surge
   across a log stockade. Onward they streamed,
   two-legged reptile warriors, redeemed
in battle, when they rendered up their lives
as tributes to their queen and all her hives.

Another war was starting, in a void   *67*
   a million galaxies away, due east
of Bexar through Boötes. Strikes destroyed
   a satellite, but not till it released
   a swarm of missiles, black and smooth. They teased
their rivals by a gas globe's amber glow,
some cratering an ice moon's rigid snow,

68   some thistling soundlessly. While robots fought
         three worlds away, in bunkers far below
their polities their masters watched as dot
         chased phantom dot. Their agitation showed;
         on leopard-colored slugs the tendrils glowed
red with anxiety. Which rival side
would own the homeworld, proxies would decide.

69   At just that moment, on a fissured moon
         beneath a crescent knotted by faint storms,
a stone-walled city by a farmed lagoon
         was taken. Standards wobbled as the swarms
         advanced down ramps of glass. The trilled alarms
of nurses were too late; by axes held
in mandibles, the squeaking grubs were felled.

70   That massacre continued, fifty times
         the Milky Way's diameter away
from earth, through Draco. Where the ecliptic climbs
         from Taurus through the Twins, the death of day
         brought an armistice in another fray,
permitting flight by exiles, quadrupeds
whose fingered antlers grew from mouthless heads.

71   The frightened calves were clicking, soothed by strokes
         from pliant horns. Most here were cows, or bulls
too old to fight. A crowded wagon's spokes
         sank mired in mud; the slaves tucked in their gills
         and hoisted. Clicks of panic greeted hulls
of sleek dirigibles, soft antlers bristled
and clenched as volleys flashed and rockets whistled —

all this, west of the sleeping Alamo,   72
 above the skyline's fringe of sable brake.
The starlit Texan sentries could not know
 that war balloons were veering round to rake
 those refugees, just then; the light would take
a billion years to reach earth from that star.
That morning, half of heaven was at war.

"It sure looks peaceful, don't it?" said Warnell.   73
 James Stewart did not answer; he had crashed,
his throat cut wide. Two Mexicans now fell
 upon the living picket; Warnell, slashed
 and bleeding, scrambled to the creek and splashed
to shuddering safety. Wounded, he would see,
before he died in June, all Texas free.

Still undetected, through the reefs of dark   74
 the human tide was gliding. But the cries
of *"Viva Mexico,"* the bugle's bark,
 would forfeit the advantage of surprise.
 Across the walls, alarms began to rise.
As Texan guns commenced to crack and boom,
Travis, trailed by Joe, dashed from his room.

The way a great stallion, bolstered by oats,   75
 will jump a fenced corral and leap in sport
down to a creek, shaking a mane that floats
 above his shoulder, Travis crossed a fort
 lit up by guns and rung by their report.
His voice knelled through the courtyard like a bell:
"The Mexicans are on us! Give 'em hell!"

PART THREE

BOOK NINE

DEATH
AT DAWN

THE ARGUMENT

The sixth of March at dawn. From all
directions, columns strike the wall
of the Alamo. The garrison's
replies of grapeshot from its guns
rip through attacking ranks, repelling
wave after wave. Regrouped and swelling
when the reserves at last surge forth,
commingled units breach the north.
The fort is now Santa Anna's prize.
The walls are vaulted. Travis dies.

BOOK NINE

The battle of the Alamo began.   *1*
    Deep in the muffled galleries of green
roofing the hollows and the hills that span
        the two Americas, a filtered sheen
        will sometimes light a tantalizing scene,
a spectacle to stun the wanderer
whom chance allows to watch the rite recur.

The twittering of antbirds, as they wrangle   *2*
        above the jungle's carpet, will precede
the whine of flies. Then butterflies will spangle
        the murk with sudden color, panoplied
        regatta fleets; they, too, have come to feed.
Marauders all, these rob the creeping train
that flees before the all-absorbing stain.

It sends out probing pods, this rug of mail,   *3*
        this ooze, this percolating forest floor.
Each army ant is just another scale
        upon this dragon that foregoes a roar
        for seething sizzle. Just like a shore
that fizzing suds ingest, the ground will slide
to nourish that assimilating tide.

4   The dread implanted by that apparition
        cannot match what the Texans on the wall
now felt, as stormers poured around the mission.
        The drumming crunch of boots, the bugle's call,
        the peal of Spanish somewhere in the pall
enveloping the fort were just as dire.
The garrison heard Travis: "Hold your fire!"

5   Our lady of annihilation, show
        the seed of good within the pulp of pain,
the weal to grow from healing of this woe.
        The arms of rival armies on the plain
        of Rhodes, transmuted, rose above the main;
so may a new colossus stand and glow
beside the warless Gulf of Mexico,

6   saying: *Let others, Yank, debase the proud,*
        and dominate the destitute and weak.
Your fate's to touch the planets, pierce the cloud
        of secret nature, teach the tongue you speak
        to sing with all the flair of the antique,
and make, with mongrel bronze, a blended race
matching its metal model in its grace.

7   Northwest of the Alamo, four hundred men,
        the Aldama Battalion, made their charge
through moats of dark that looped the fortress in.
        Each panting gasp, each footfall, seemed to enlarge
        a wall as blackly massive as a barge
grounded atop a sandbar. General Cos,
their master, urged the troops against his foes.

Back in December, he had held this fort   *8*
　　against the rebel ranks, only to lose
his honor with the cannon in that court
　　when he surrendered. Months had made the hues
　　grow pale, but still he felt the purple bruise
upon his soul, still felt disgrace's twinge.
This morning Cos would relish his revenge.

Now Travis gave the order: "Fire at will!"   *9*
　　Along the north facade a dozen bores
erupted. Each cry recorded a kill
　　or mauling in the moving dark. The force
　　continued to advance, without remorse
for comrades who had fallen. But the first
reply from the Alamo was not the worst.

A lifeless comet's coal begins to wake   *10*
　　still distant from the sun. Its cinder crust,
though long since petrified, begins to quake
　　and fissure. All at once, a fan of dust
　　spurts geysering; then others feed the gust
that veils the crumbling lump in atmosphere.
The halo, the translucent wake, appear.

As suddenly, the Alamo exploded.   *11*
　　The cannon on the northern wall spewed out
tornado flame and thunder and corroded
　　scrap metal that streaked through the shrieking crowd
　　of infantry. The courage that endowed
the bravest melted in that hellish hail
of superheated horseshoe, pellet, nail.

12   One storm of grapeshot downed a dozen brave
         attackcrs. Juan Bautista Peña fell,
an Indian who thought his cross would save
         his poll from peril and his soul from hell.
         He sipped his blood, realized he could smell
the cooking of his metal-ruined flesh.
In horror, he began to blurt and thresh.

13   Hipolito Canales wriggled on
         the dirt, a dandy drafted at a dance
by a press gang, pawns who made a fellow pawn.
         Once, with a wink, he knew how to entrance
         the married and the maid. He fouled his pants,
and felt ashamed, and then he did not feel
at all forever. He ceased to be real.

14   The troops whom arcing metal did not rob
         of skin or life were stripped of discipline.
The men of Aldama became a mob.
         Instinctively, like beeves that seek the pen
         when nearby thunder booms, the panicked men
careened away from the dragon breath
of Alamo's north face, away from death.

15   "Hurrah, my boys! We've got 'em on the run!"
         exulted Travis. Through a sooty haze
that seared his nostrils he saw Forsyth's gun
         above the northwest corner bloom and blaze.
         Pacing, he mingled orders with his praise.
"Let's send Santa Anna" — Travis took a dram
from a canteen — "a Texas telegram."

Across the fort, the Tennessean team   *16*
 behind the spike rows of the palisade
was reaping, for each bullet sown, a scream.
"Fire low, fire low!" The riflemen obeyed
 Crockett's counsel. Their Long Rifles sprayed
 the unlucky soldiers of the Fourth, assigned
to take the frail stockade the stakes had tined.

A syncopated volley from the row   *17*
 of rifles met a column daring peril
with reckless bravado. Flame seemed to flow
 like lightning, jumping from barrel to barrel.
 Invisible assaulters howled with feral
abandon. Thus Carlito Rivas brayed;
from his bayonet, a slug had ricocheted.

Morales, their commander, bellowed through   *18*
 the clatter and the wail: "Keep moving! Go!
The left! Move to the left!" Their drifting drew
 a salvo from the gate of the Alamo.
 The Mexicans fired back. Lit by the glow
of curling smoke and sparks, they rammed the haze
with ladders just like firemen at a blaze.

Bill Harrison, the Tennessean chief,   *19*
 dispatched young Archer Thomas with a plea
for reinforcements. "Tell him I believe
 the attack on the stockade is meant to be
 a feint," yelled Captain Carey. He would free
a Private Ewing, though, from crews impressed
to feed the gun commanding the Southwest.

20 Now Carey's eighteen-pounder funneled fumes
   and devastation where the south wall met
 the western side. The meteoric spumes
   arced harmless over men Morales led
   to crouch beneath the wall. At this beachhead
 the Fourth's assembled remnant bivouacked,
 like doves that crowd a bluff when clouds have cracked.

21 Back on the northern side, Cos stamped and swore
  as his disordered soldiers pummeled past.
 The Second Column took their place, a roar
   of *"Viva Mexico!"* meeting each blast
   from Texan guns. Across the rocks and grass
 Toluca Battalion streamed, tasked to invade
 the fort through the frail northern palisade.

22 Amid the vanguard Colonel Duque jogged,
   unmindful of the hazard. "Mexico!"
 he bellowed, till the sleeting metal flogged
   his frying flesh. His charge gave way to slow
   contortions on the grass. Another glow,
 another boom, and his troops, as they scrambled
 in aimless terror, left their Colonel trampled.

23 Again, the deadly wind. How many branches
   of families were pruned there on that day,
 how many souls in villages and ranches
   would never be conceived because a spray
   of lead or iron drilled a brain's plush gray
 or sliced an artery. The destiny
 of earth was altered with each casualty.

Tomás Gallardo fell, a virgin, though   *24*
    he'd sworn to have a girl before he died.
Throughout the two-week siege, the Alamo
    had made him think of aqueducts beside
    the mills of Querétaro, with their wide
round Roman arches. He spat out the teeth
the bullet shattered when it ripped his cheek.

Just nineteen years had passed, since Julio   *25*
    Menéndez had been taken to the great
Cordero hacienda, for a slow
    inspection by his godmother. His fate,
    predicted the grand mistress of the estate
his kinsmen served, would be to found a long
succession with a lovely wife. How wrong

that solemn dame had been. Her godson dodged   *26*
    and wound his way through knots of men in fear,
still clinging to his ladder, metal lodged
    inside his burning arm. When, in their sheer
    confusion, his companions in the tier
behind discharged their muskets, pins of pain
drilled through him as he struck the pebbly plain.

He was the first to fall to friendly fire,   *27*
    the first of dozens. Thinking silhouettes
they saw were charging Texans, an entire
    contingent shot courageously at sets
    of their own comrades. Bluely winking jets
were all that could be seen within the clouds
of powder smoke that choked the baffled crowds.

28   When woolen air had flecked the frozen pass,
        Ignacio Padillo had been wrapped
securely as a common soldier's lass
        in Captain Mora's arms. Now the boy tapped
        his fallen comrade, then, in panic, clapped
beloved shoulders and began to shake.
The runaway's protector would not wake.

29   A fleeing soldier paused, and tried to pry
        a boot from Mora's leg. Ignacio
attacked him with a hardly human cry
        and drove him off. Marooned within the flow
        retreating from the flashing Alamo,
above the corpse the youth stood sentry now,
a calf complaining by a crumpled cow.

30   The Second Column stumbled in retreat
        beneath new fusillades of pelting coals.
They left their lost behind, the way a sheet
        of doilied surf leaves stranded, as it rolls
        back down into the surge, deflating bowls
of glassy slime, and flouncing fish, and bits
of ragged shell. So they escaped that blitz.

31   Amid the flow of shadows in retreat,
        one figure stood unswerving, like an oak
that parts a flood, a statue in a street.
        Long afterward, the gray survivors spoke
        of how a form condensed amid the smoke,
an angel tendering her tender care,
with slender arms and spun obsidian hair.

There was an angel at the Alamo   *32*
    that morning, but her stubby legs were lame,
her squashed face ugly, and her braids of coal.
    María de Jesús — this was the name
    she gave when questioned — hobbled through the flame
and clotting smoke, now tilting a canteen,
now cooling down a brow she polished clean.

To Santa Anna, studying the battle   *33*
    at his northeastern post, came word the Second
had been repulsed, stampeded just like cattle.
    "Four hundred with Amat . . ." The President reckoned,
    murmuring. Decisively he beckoned
to General Castrillon. "Go, try to rally
Toluca's cowards for another sally."

Spurring his horse, the silver general came   *34*
    on dozens fleeing from artillery.
"The war's that way!" He gestured toward the lame.
    "The hurt will stay. The rest will follow me.
    In forty years, I've let nobody see
my back — and I have lived to be this old!"
His courage taught his soldiers to be bold.

Around the Alamo the columns veered,   *35*
    adhesive coils of a colossal squid
smothering a whale caught in its weird
    embrace. When powder flared, the shadows slid
    across the fading stone, a rocky lid
atop a pit from which the leather wings
pour out by thousands when the cricket sings.

36 Within the church, the mothers tried to hush
   their babbling children, chicks that blink and peep
 inside a tree as flames begin to gush
   across the scaly surface of their keep.
   In the Low Barracks, Bowie squirmed in a heap
 of twisted sheets. He called unheard, alone
 but for the tortured Christ hung on the stone.

37 His dead wife's kin were stumbling through the dim
   interior, Juana with her infant son,
 Gertrudis with her rosary. The rim
   above was outlined, as a fortress gun
   unfurled its ragged bloom. "Oh, hurry! Run!"
 Within a chamber on the western wall,
 the three found safety, shuttered from the squall.

38 Limping across the courtyard, Robert Moore,
   at fifty-five one of the oldest men,
 was mumbling to the bleeding man he bore,
   his nephew Willis: "You were nine or ten,
   you sprained your ankle. Boy, I thought back then
 you learned to be more careful," Robert said.
 His nephew did not hear him; he was dead.

39 Inside the roofless chapel of the old
  stone mission, earlier troops had built a ramp
 and platform of earth, strong enough to hold
   a trinity of cannon. In the damp
   before the dawn, the gunners grouped, to stamp
 and shiver — Evans, Bonham, Dickinson,
 and others, warmed soon by their metal sun.

They cupped their ears. After the thunderclap   *40*
    the crew returned to work. Again the team
collaborated in the dark to tap
    out measured powder, or to stomp a gleam
    that lit some vagrant wadding, or to ream
the cylinder and swab it, or to put
more grapeshot in the stove-hot cannon's gut.

"Fire in the hole!" cried Evans — but the fuse   *41*
    was dwindled by the wind, a candle on
bright birthday sugar, one less year to lose.
    The two companion cannon lurched upon
    their trucks. Each one convened a mimic dawn.
When Evans and his crew produced a third,
above the boom their raucous cheers were heard.

North, south, and east — all compass points but one   *42*
    the chapel's guns saluted, hailing harm
onto the eastern column. Veteran
    and tyro there surrendered to alarm,
    the tiered battalion turned into a swarm.
Of four hundred men in the unit named
for Matamoros, a full third were maimed.

The lucky died. The luckless, left among   *43*
    the orphaned ladders, whimpered for the aid
that would not be. Pierced in a pulsing lung,
    Mariano Chavez burbled, as he prayed,
    a thief and rapist. Near him, with a flayed
meat-tender face, Varela stroked the mud,
a saddler's young apprentice, hawking blood.

44   Antonio Paredes, cratered, crashed;
           his *soldadera,* sifting through the field,
      would find him later, his eye socket smashed
         by flying nails. Gonzago Pico's shield,
         a lucky coin, failed to slow what peeled
      the sunburned skin from the old muleteer's arms
      and leather from his face — so much for charms.

45   Two brothers named Herrera, born and reared
           in Querétaro, joined Santa Anna's force
      to earn some land. The land Travis had seared
         last winter had starved infantry and horse
         alike upon the trek. Carlos, grown hoarse
      during the blizzard, died; his corpse was bedded
      a hundred leagues south of where Juan was shredded.

46   Ambrosio Anaya once had planned
           to serve the church he loved. His mother grieved
      when he signed up instead to fight for land
         in Texas. Metal-stigmaed, he believed,
         in his confusion, he had been reprieved,
      that he was back in church, a bleeding Lord
      beside him, not a comrade flak had scored.

47   Among the troops who charged the Alamo
           across the darkened eastern plain were four
      young miners from Catorce. Months ago,
         while toiling naked in a mountain's core,
         they had devised a plan to smuggle ore
      using the pups that followed them when they
      descended into hell and rose each day.

The mascots, killed below, were tossed atop   *48*
    a nearby offal heap. The cunning crew
would wait six months or so, then dig them up.
    Three fell to Texan fire. The fourth now knew
    the silver hoard was his. The cannon blew.
He slumped atop the rack of human logs,
his guts as full of metal as his dog's.

Atop the rubbled chapel, Bonham lit   *49*
    another smoke. Beside him, Dickinson
was leaning on the stone that ringed the pit.
    "By God, sir, we have sent them on the run."
    James Bonham took a toke. "We may have won
the war for Santa Anna," he replied.
"We've chased them to the north — the weakest side."

The smoking crater of the Alamo   *50*
    was ringed by hundreds, crawling mauled, or still,
like trunks denuded by the blasts that blow
    concentric sheets of flame beyond the frill
    a meteor's splash creates; the timber will
compose neat rings of pillars round a dish
of glassy blisters bubbled by the crash.

Repelled by whistling volleys from the church   *51*
    and from the north facade, those who survived
from three defeated teams began to lurch
    and limp toward the northeast. Here they were hived
    with General Amat's reserve, when they arrived.
Untested troops and blooded merged, like creeks
confused in a composite flood that seeks

52   to carve a novel curve. Santa Anna watched
      the ruin of his careful strategy,
knew all his orchestration had been botched.
      From many wars, though, he had learned to see,
      in every failure, opportunity.
For just such a contingency he'd planned.
"Send the reserves!" He bellowed the command.

53   The bugle's urgent bleating stirred a rush
      among the shifting ranks of the reserve
battalion. As a norther's front will push
      gold screens of dust before its blue-black curve,
      the fresh combatants made survivors swerve
back toward the sparking hulk of the Alamo.
The battle would be won for Mexico.

54   With troops the gunlit prairie was aswirl
      suddenly, as in a snowstorm, when the flakes
come tumbling fat and welded by the whirl.
      The way that doves will flicker from the brakes
      fringing a stock tank, till the gray sky shakes
with flutter's thunder, shadow legions turned
and banked around the fortress as it burned.

55   Atop the emplacement, Travis felt the sound
      of dozens underneath him in the ditch,
a sublimated tremor in the ground.
      Firing in darkness, he turned to watch
      the streaming shadows pile around the swatch
of mud and logs that patched the fissured wall.
It rocked, a pier collapsing in a squall.

Like hornets squeezing through a paper cell   56
    and taking flight, the first few phantoms vaulted
the crumbling palisade. All eyes now fell
    on Travis. The defenders round him halted,
    to see if their commander had defaulted
or kept his vow. A cougar that a hound
has cornered, hackling, Travis stood his ground.

The Colonel hollered to his soldiers: "Fellows,   57
    you're wasting bravery. There's no mistaking
what that commotion yonder has to tell us.
    It's plain for all to see. The Lord's forsaken
    the Alamo. The fort's as good as taken.
We've just got time for one good rush. Come on!
A forlorn hope's reprieve is hope for none."

The young commander fired, and then he tossed   58
    the empty Colt. In moments he had drawn
the sword of Doctor Long. The metal crossed
    a bayonet, then bit through flesh to bone.
    Now something knocked his forehead, like a stone.
Baffled, the Texan tasted his own blood.
He staggered, sagged, and slanted to the mud.

Confusion. All around is churning smoke,   59
    a supernova's planet-flensing shroud,
an embryonic solar system's yolk.
    No shapes, but for the shadows in the cloud
    that swell and sway and pulsate to the loud
oceanic throb, a thunder to convulse
a cosmos, the percussion of a pulse.

60   Round Travis bullets hissed and ricocheted,
        unheard by him. No one remained to stoke
  the twelve-pounder whose fountain flame had flayed
        so many. Bayonet met dagger stroke,
        men fought around his form. In swirling smoke
  he sprawled, his cavalryman's skills all scoured
  from memory, his power overpowered.

BOOK TEN

WAR IN
THE WALLS

THE ARGUMENT

Through north and south into the fort
the stormers pour. Inside the court
rise piles of dead. Some Texans make
their way to barracks, where they rake
the adversary. There is no
asylum in the low barracks, though,
where Bowie's butchered. Texans try
to flee on open ground, and die.
Before the old stone church, the band
from Tennessee now makes its stand.
Here Crockett battles to defend
his station, fighting to the end.

BOOK TEN

The battle in the Alamo began.   1
    Across the northeast palisade they came,
the barbed and bristling shapes, and overran
    the terrified defenders. Muskets flamed
    and metal swished through flesh. Moaning and maimed,
Bill Blazeby, Captain of the New Orleans Greys,
rolled down the cold dirt rampart in a daze;

his forty-one-year journey from his home   2
    in England through New York and then the port
of New Orleans brought him here, to soak the loam
    of Bexar with puddling blood. John Jones, his short
    Lieutenant, a New Yorker, tried to exhort
their men to join him on the parapet;
his ribs were widened by a bayonet.

Like dolphins that a trawler's web has jumbled   3
    with flopping sharks, the New Orleans volunteers
were spun among the stormers. Garrand stumbled
    across the corpse of Travis; then, like spears,
    the bayonet blades punched him. To the tiers
of dead and dying, Samuel Holloway
was added when a saber found its prey.

4 Missouri-born Charles Clark had come to fight
   twice at the Alamo, as victor in
 December, when the rebel forces pried
   out Cos's force — and on this dawn, again;
   but this time he was vanquished. Through his chin
 a bullet drilled; he tasted sour cud,
 his knees went flaccid, and he slapped the mud.

5 John Harris, too, fought here, when Texas won.
   Furloughed in Gonzales, he had returned
 with Kimbell's force to join the garrison
   by dark five days before. Now luck had spurned
   the young Kentucky native. His cheek burned
 with saber cuts. He swatted with his gun,
 but he had been outnumbered and outrun.

6 Atop the barracks roof, a handful of
   New Orleans Greys were crouching, cut off, trapped.
 Like bison stampeded over a bluff
   by Indians, the panicked soldiers dropped
   over the outer wall. George Butler flopped,
 his right leg splintered, slaughtered where he crashed
 among chasseurs. Robert Musselman dashed

7 past startled shadows through the smoky haze,
   lungs pumping. When the U.S. Army fought
 to conquer Florida, he had given chase
   to Seminoles and slaves through raftered rot
   and cypress steam. The terror he had wrought
 he learned at last, when foemen knocked him down,
 impaling him upon the spongy ground.

Not far away Bill Linn fell, tackled by   *8*
    a shouting *zapador,* who held him fast
while comrades hacked. Dick Starr's attempt to fly
    was ended by a horseman's stinging blast;
    bleeding, the English soldier of fortune passed
a few yards more, then sank, to the surprise
of infantry, an unexpected prize.

Inside the Alamo, the spreading surge   *9*
    of conquest lapped in waves at the northwest.
John Baugh, the second in command, now urged,
    "Fall back!" Most of the figures he addressed
    were Mexicans. Trapped like a sailor pressed
upon a slanting deck above the fin
and fluke a shipwreck's drawn, Baugh fought to fend

off probing steel. Too late to save that proud   *10*
    Virginian, Joshua Smith arrived
atop the rampart, scattering a crowd
    of Latins with a swinging gun, till knifed.
    The mobbing bayonets then swerved and hived
round Sergeant Juan Badillo of Seguin's
Tejano cavalry. With a machine's

precision, like a harvester beheading   *11*
    the tremored wheat, the bayonet-quilled mass
mowed down defiant Captain Forsyth, shredding
    his costly tailcoat, popping buttons of brass,
    and shattering his pocket watch's glass.
Ximenes, a widower, paid the price
for treason now; his son was orphaned twice.

12 Four days before — though none of Alamo's
    defenders knew — Texas had been declared
  an independent country. Among those
    at Washington-on-Brazos who had shared
    in that event had been one of a pair
  of Goodrich boys. The other brother, John,
  was fighting for survival now upon

13 the northwest wall. His flailing knife cut bone
    and carved a shriek from darkness. In his side
  a point was delving. He let out a moan.
    His legs went loose. The Tennessean died
    beside a teenage Georgian, Grimes, the pride
  of a father who had signed the declaration
  that Texas was the planet's newest nation.

14 Artilleryman Zanco now stood trapped
    between two fuming cannon. The young Dane
  had decorated the banner that had flapped
    above the Lynchburg volunteers; its plain
    inscription, I N D E P E N D E N C E , had contained
  a solitary star. Deft hands now swung
  a musket, smashed a climber on a rung.

15 A musket blast, and Zanco's sooty thatch
    exploded, spewing brains. He did not see
  the dirt outside the walls rush up to crash.
    With him, his father had crossed the sea
    two years before, mourning his recently
  dead wife. And now his son, his Charles, was gone,
  and the old man in this new land was alone.

Far off, the Alamo looked like a sports   16
   arena, like a stadium by night,
where scores are marked by cheering and reports
      of harmless cannon; those on the outside
      cannot know who is winning. Briefly bright,
the walls relayed, across the meadow's breadth,
diminuendo echoings of death.

Juan Amador, a general, had made   17
   a path through rocks and corpses; now he squatted
beside the slaughtered Travis and surveyed
      the fort's interior. Black doorways slotted
      blue barracks to the left; a body-clotted
gun platform to the right. Into the murk
before him shadows dived, like fish that lurk

just past transparent shallows. "Get them! Fire!"   18
   the general commanded. Soldiers knelt
and blazed into the bluish gloom. A choir
      of shrieks pleased Amador, who had just dealt
      hot whizzing death to his own men, debelled
among their fallen foes. The fog of war
hung thick as haze upon a valley floor.

Down in that dark, Despallier was sprinting   19
   to warn the southern posts. "They're in the walls!"
The drainage ditch was suddenly upending
      the panting runner. Down he went, to sprawl
      in icy water, hand hurt by his fall.
He could not stop. He hauled himself upright
and staggered toward the bursts of cannon light.

20   "They're in the walls!" the Cajun yelled to warn
        the troops atop the platform that surmounted
the southwest wall. Arriving at the warm
        and fuming eighteen-pounder, he recounted
        what he had seen to Carey: "I . . . I counted
a couple dozen. . . . They kept pouring through.
Colonel Travis is dead. And Captain Blazeby, too."

21   "Turn her around!" the hoarse young Captain roared
        to his Invincibles. The cannon squeaked,
the gunners groaned and swore. They heard the horde
        but could not see it through a smoke that reeked
        of sizzling pain and death. Their panic peaked
when guns began to clatter — then came cries
of anguish from the dark that mocked their eyes.

22   "Y'all hear that, boys? That's enfilading fire!"
        cried Carey, jubilant. His soldiers whooped,
to see the flashes glint, as the entire
        courtyard's perimeter began to erupt.
        From barracks east and west where they holed up
after the north had fallen, Texans laid
invaders low with every burst they sprayed.

23   On sticky summer evenings, June bugs dive
        and slalom round the light above a porch,
gold ricocheting bullets; some revive
        to buzz again in frenzy round the scorch
        and dazzle, others roast beside the torch.
The Mexicans careened as crazily
past twinkling barracks as they tried to flee.

Meanwhile, though, underneath the southwest wall 24
    Morales had regrouped his frightened men.
He boomed, "I know you men, I know you all,
    I know you are not cowards. Come on, then!
    Let's go! If now is not the time, then when?
If people back home ask you what you did
in Bexar, what will you tell them, that you hid?"

He patted soldiers, as they scrambled by, 25
    as though he were a coach, sending his boys
to play a game, not to win wounds or die.
    Now ladders clacked, joined by aggressive noise —
    "No quarter!" Huffing comrades tried to hoist
each other up. A few would howl and drop;
then soldiers of Morales held the top.

In moments, Mexicans were everywhere 26
    around the eighteen-pounder. There a son
of Ireland, Burke Trammel, knocked a pair
    of stormers from the edge, fought for a gun
    with yet a third. The battle, though, was won
by numbers, not by brawn — one bayonet,
a second, and the giant was no threat.

Tom Waters fell, and Rutherford, as well, 27
    Invincibles, beside their battling chief.
His sword struck metal, with a somber knell.
    Now Carey knew there would be no relief,
    no rescue for him; still, he would not leave
the grandest gun in Texas. By that bore
he roared and swiped, just like a grizzly bear

28   above its booty, a dead elk, in snow
        far to the north; encompassed by a pack
  of yapping wolves, the monster seems to grow
       in tottering upright; its mittens smack
       a shaggy-shouldered wolf, but more attack,
 teeth dripping in black lips, ears flattened, eyes
 shrunken with hate and hunger for the prize.

29   Around the corpse of Carey, foemen streamed,
       and down the ramp of logs across the ditch.
  They knocked Despallier down. The young man screamed
       in shock, as bayonets began to stitch
       his side, his throat. He wilted with a twitch,
 the slack, slow way a bluebonnet will slump
 when rain leaks from each velvet-petaled clump.

30   Inside the sacristy, the women clutched
      the shrunken children, shuddering with each
  concussion, rabbits huddled in a hutch.
       Lieutenant Dickinson rushed in to reach
       for his child-wife, his child. His frantic speech
 came tumbling: "Great God, Sue, they're in the walls.
 Now, listen, darling, if the fortress falls,

31   you raise our baby well, you hear? Be brave,
       my darling." Then he kissed his teenage wife,
  his squirming baby, and rejoined his grave
       companions in the hurricane of strife,
       already in his brief sad afterlife.
 Susannah whined a prayer, as she squeezed
 her little angel, *Please, God, please, oh, please.*

The Texans in the chapel carried out 32
    the plan of Colonel Travis. On the ramp
they wheeled the hot twelve-pounder about,
      to face the entry. Comrades rushed to clamp
      the great doors shut. Bolts clattered to a thump.
One silent thought was shared by all the men:
they would not walk out through that arch again.

From the southwestern corner of the fort, 33
   Morales urged his troops on toward the gate,
the southern barracks, and the little court
      the chapel front commanded. The long wait
      was over for the Texians whose fate
marooned them there, survivors of a flood
stuck on a roof in cataracts of mud.

Some leapt and ran for doorways, others fought 34
    and perished at their posts. Bill Lightfoot sprang
for safety, sprained his ankle; he was caught
      while rising by a bayonet's black fang.
      Wood cracked on bone, guns rattled, metal rang,
and down fell bandaged Ed McAfferty,
and young Will Mills, far from his Tennessee.

Two sons of a U.S. General named Kerr 35
    had come with Louisiana volunteers
to Texas. One, Nathaniel, was interred
      four days before Santa Anna's ranks appeared
      in Bexar, by Joe, twenty-two, who had feared
a kindred wasting death. Now, unlike Nate,
Joe Kerr fell fighting at the fortress gate.

36   That gateway now belonged to Mexico.
        Outside, in the lunette, a hunting blind,
a desperate team of Texans hovered low,
     firing at shadow legions. From behind,
     from in the fort, they were surprised to find
themselves attacked. A rat upon a rake's
black tines, Jon Lindley drooped across the stakes.

37   Mial Scurlock folded round a bayonet;
     his hand groped his own guts. A bullet flayed
McGregor, then a sword. Mumbling the scat
     of pain Dan Bourne, another Briton, swayed
     beside James Gwynne, an Englishman who made
a last kill as he capsized. Samuel Burns
fought like one of his native Eire's old kerns.

38   Nearby, within the wedge the log stockade
     framed with the hospital and the old church,
some Tennessee Long Rifles, now arrayed
     along a second front, began to search
     for targets in the mission. From their perch
behind the low stone wall, defenders cropped
the enemy; their comrades also dropped.

39   Hawkins fell, and M. B. Clark fell, too,
     to friendly fire, and Lewis Dewall tumbled.
Across them, in their turn, collapsed a few
     attackers, screaming, faces scarred and scumbled
     by Tennessean lead. After them stumbled
their own companions, who began to hack,
each thinking that he pierced a rebel's back;

these fell, shrieking, when new grapeshot rained.   *40*
   Smack in the courtyard's middle, on a mound
with two twelve-pounders, were all that remained
   of Carey's artillerymen. Another round
   blew outward with a great granitic sound
like mountains cracking. In the cannon light
each cusping face glowed like a satellite,

then embered down to dim. The mock sunset   *41*
   brought night again and foemen by the score
to deadly scrimmaging. A bayonet
   gouged John, but still he managed, with a roar,
   to hilt his knife in a hostile heart's core.
The slave, freed when Carey, his master, died,
was one more Texan to the other side.

One rebel, then another, fought to hold   *42*
   that twelver — though without a team of men
it was as useless as a lump of gold.
   Their rivals, too, fought on without a plan,
   as frenzied as coyotes in a pen;
though hunger has been sated, in their play
they maul, then leave uneaten bleating prey.

Green Jameson died there, trying to regain   *43*
   the cannon for a cause already lost;
he slumped atop a sapper he had slain.
   There Tapley Holland fell, to a saber thrust,
   blood worming from his outline through the dust;
his family had settled here, way back
when Texas had not been a bivouac

44   for rival armies, like the ones that clashed
        around this patch of mud. Here sank George Brown,
from Mississippi, English-born; here, smashed
        like melons, lay two soldiers from the town,
        Gonzales, where war started with a round
of grapeshot — Fishbaugh, Summers. For this hill
of inches, armies were prepared to kill.

45   An adolescent boy got drunk and feared
        his father's anger — a familiar plot
in all times. But few boys have disappeared
        as Bill Malone did, when he drank and fought
        from Alabama down to moist and hot
New Orleans, where his family lost the trail.
The rebel found a home in Bexar's jail,

46   cast there by Carey, his own unit's chief,
        till freed by Bowie in his bacchanal.
He was the last to struggle — with a thief,
        and a schoolteacher — in that dark corral-
        like space for that twelve-pounder. With a growl
he bit the startled teacher's hand and scraped
the burglar's jaw. A man who might have raped

47   and robbed his way to death by noose or gun
        by virtue of a cause became a martyr,
a country's father and nobody's son,
        an icon of self-sacrificing ardor,
        safely irrelevant, like an old charter.
They say the only letter that he sent
his mother would wear everywhere she went.

No longer hazarding a grapeshot gust,   *48*
  the soldiers of Morales pushed their way
into the Low Barracks. The smell of dust,
    of mildew; darkened doors where once a Fray
    Luis or Marco would retire to pray;
then clamor — English, Spanish — and the chink
of lead on stone, black powder's searing stink.

"Go, go!" The officers forced wary troops   *49*
    to herd their bayonets through mine-dark flumes
to glacier caves. Some stormers died, the dupes
    of fake surrenders, dropped by pistol plumes
    or knifing hands unweaving them like looms
in other hollow sockets, Texans begged
for mercy, then like butterflies were pegged.

Courageous, cowardly — none got away.   *50*
    McKinney ended here, and Nelson, too,
and Patrick Henry Herndon, Freeman Day.
    In cavern blackness, infantrymen slew
    Bexar's Carlos Espalier, just a few
months over seventeen, and Robert White.
The gunbursts glowed like a spelunker's light.

The bayonets probed on, through stinging haze,   *51*
    surprising three within the neighbor cell —
George Pagan, William Baker, John M. Hays.
    The fourth, upon his pad, was just a shell
    force had evacuated, like a frail
cicada skin. In legend, he would die
with pistols blazing, and a clear cold eye

52   that paralyzed his killers in the door;
        in truth, it happened quickly, just a flame
that painted brains across the wall and floor.
      None of the troops had ever heard the name
      of Bowie; none knew of the bravo's fame.
They orbited the corpse, like flies that wail
in springtime, when milk rattles in the pail.

53   Outside, the square was conquered. To a fort
    within the fort the rebels now withdrew,
all but the few who sniped into the court
      from barracks to be tombs. Within the blue
      of powder smoke and dawn white X's grew,
the crisscross straps of charging grenadiers;
the Tennessean Mounted Volunteers

54   made these their targets, as they knelt behind
        the ulcered inner wall, as though to shoot
deer nibbling at a feeder from a blind.
      The din made Captain Harrison a mute;
      his men did not need urging, though, to root
themselves before the chapel doors, mesquite
with secret roots sunk down a dozen feet.

55   Their gunlit space, no bigger than a stage,
        projected into peril, like a home
teetering on a sinkhole, seeming to age
      miraculously fast — walls glide like foam,
      a tile roof molts into the inverted dome.
They knew; and yet no warning could prepare
defenders for what was to happen there.

The armies locked. Propelled by howling hate,   *56*
    contingents from the court rolled through the wall;
when rebels peeled off from the palisade
    to help their friends, their foes began to crawl
    across the gap-tooth stakes. In one vast brawl
a dozen fights converged, within a dark
lit only by an intermittent spark.

Micajah Autry, veteran of the War   *57*
    of Eighteen Twelve, had lived again and again
in his two score, as master of a store,
    teacher, soldier, lawyer, owner of men
    and planter. Poetry poured from his pen;
he sketched, could hold a tune, and cure a frown.
With others died a man, with him a town.

A friendship war created war destroyed.   *58*
    Last fall in Nacogdoches, Harrison
had sworn recruits to service — Fauntleroy,
    Bailey, Cloud, Thomas, and Washington.
    Together they had ridden here; each one
alone on that cold morning would confront
a separate death, hot, whistling, sharp, or blunt.

Upon the palisade, John Reynolds seized   *59*
    a frightened Mexican private's bayonet
and shoved him back. A whistling bullet creased
    his forehead; suddenly his face was wet.
    A swoop — but Will McDowell's musket met
the saber meant for Reynolds. From the green
placidity of Mifflin County in

60   their native Pennsylvania, both had moved,
          to found a new town, Mifflin, Tennessee;
      there would be no Mifflin, Texas. Sabers grooved
          McDowell's neck, his arms. He could not see
          his old friend in the darkness. Plaintively
      he called out, "John!" Beside the log stockade
      he found, not his compatriot, but a blade.

61   Some Texans chose to vault the shaven stakes.
          Elial Melton, the fort's quartermaster,
      went wading through the little ditch that snaked
          around the mission, dashed from the disaster
          past startled enemies. He pounded faster,
      faster, as the hooves of cavalry
      came crackling after. But he could not flee;

62   a rider's nine-foot lance knocked Melton down
          onto the oily grass, and when he rose
      another horseman gashed him. Round and round
          he staggered, circled by his whooping foes,
          a drunk man on a carousel that glows
      and grinds within a midway, carven manes
      ascending to the hammering refrains.

63   Like hatchling turtles oaring down a beach
          on flimsy fins, through circuits of the gulls,
      convulsing toward a freedom few will reach,
          more Texans fled the mission's blistered walls
          to meadows curtained by the powder's palls.
      Tom Roberts rolled in cactus, tackled by
      a fusilier, whose knife cut short his try.

The Dolores Cavalry chased Manson Shied,   *64*
    the Georgia carpenter, pincushioned him
with lances. Richard Stockton, briefly freed,
    swerved through the startled specters in the dim
    dilution of the night, as quick and slim
and palpitating as a knobby faun.
His dozen wounds would warm the wintry lawn.

John Thomson fell outside the walls, and so   *65*
    did Robert Campbell. John E. Gaston tried
to grab an orphaned horse, but was too slow;
    like hatcheting upon a mountainside,
    the sound of stocks that drummed him till he died.
Another fugitive was screened by sparks
when he crashed in a campfire, William Parks.

A quarter century had passed, since Bexar   *66*
    had sent an envoy up to Washington,
soliciting the north's help in the war
    against the Spanish Crown. James Madison,
    then president, met the republican,
Bernardo Gutiérrez, in a great
and glittering and glassy hall of state.

That revolution failed to found a new   *67*
    republic here in Texas that the young
republic to the north might welcome to
    its growing domain; the wars of Doctor Long
    had failed as well. This mutiny among
the colonists, though, would detach this land,
as Madison, Monroe, and Jackson planned —

68   but at a price. At Crockett's side James Rose
        had come from Arkansas to join the fight
and start anew at thirty. One of those
        who jumped the palisade, attempting flight,
        he splashed through the canal, panting in fright.
Where girls in peace brought laundry to be wrung,
this nephew of James Madison was flung.

69   The trumpet theme, "No quarter," went unheard
        in the corral, above the gun's report,
the screams of men and animals. The yard
        became a coliseum for cruel sport,
        as Mexicans fired from inside the fort
at Texan mules and Texan men. The stream
of conscripts had already downed the team

70   assigned to guard this post: John Ballentine,
        Richardson Perry, dead now at nineteen,
and two friends from Gonzales, Johnny Cain
        and comical Squire Daymon, always keen
        to pull a prank. Their bodies lay unseen
among the murdered horses, tripping up
the Texians attempting to escape:

71   Charles Heiskell, one of Bowie's volunteers,
        James Kenny, Isaac Ryan. Prisoners
in Rome's dank coliseum, dodging spears
        and swords, then set upon by cats and curs,
        the few survivors lurched among the blurs
that snorted there and reared. A volley's rattle
drew gurgling shrieks from horses, men, and cattle.

Two years before, a Philadelphia throng   *72*
    on Independence Day impatiently
had listened to a gun salute, a song,
    and Daniel Webster. Most had come to see
    the representative from Tennessee;
he praised the Founding Fathers, who, though haltered
by monarchy, had never flinched nor faltered.

He had not known he soon would be enrolled   *73*
    into another bid for sovereignty
by Yankee colonists. His barrel tolled
    against a bayonet; he could hardly see
    the lunging figure of his enemy,
whose jabs the rifle parried, with a smack
the equal of its celebrated crack.

He fenced, he bunted, as a puffing buck,   *74*
    the oldest in a valley, will defend
his mastery against young strength and pluck;
    hooves gouge the mud, necks bristle as they bend,
    black nostrils sneeze, and massive antlers grind
together, interlocked, deploying torque
from pursing muscles through each whittled fork.

Past Harrison he staggered — Harrison,   *75*
    the fierce young Tennessean who had led
the Mounted Volunteers; another son
    to Crockett, he lay bleeding, not yet dead,
    next to the crushed felt hat from Crockett's head.
More shadows mobbed the Canebrake's Congressman,
too many to be parried by his gun.

76
A saber scraped his temple, metal caught
   his shoulder, sewing in hot agony.
Instinctively, he raised his arms, he sought
   to shield his stinging face, permitting three
   more bayonets to bite. Strength fled his knee,
then darkness fell before the old stone arch
at dawn on Sunday on the sixth of March.

BOOK ELEVEN

HAND TO HAND

THE ARGUMENT

The fighting now is hand to hand,
in barracks rooms, as Travis planned.
Through darkened doors the Mexican
assaulters charge, to meet a gun
or knife. But numbers soon prevail.
The chapel door, beneath the hail
a captured cannon spews, collapses.
Up the ramp and into the apse's
emplacement stormers run. The last
defenders fall to blade and blast.
Through courts surrendered to the dead,
the few survivors soon are led.

BOOK ELEVEN

The sky was now the color of a bruise.   *1*
    Within the Alamo's black silhouette
the gunfire splashed, the way the curlicues
    of wax light from a grinning pumpkin head
    will wobble on a darkened porch beset
by small battalions. Tensely pacing back
and forth, General Santa Anna watched the sack.

The day was his, although the morning's job   *2*
    of slaughter was beginning. To the black
interior of the hospital, a mob
    of Texan volunteers had fallen back;
    here they now made their stand, amid the slack
contorted forms of comrades lying ill.
Here Joseph Bayliss managed to fill

a trooper with hot lead, before he sprawled   *3*
    on Robert Crossman, crippled in the fight
for Bexar back in December. Shadows brawled
    across the doorway. Bursts of blinding light
    imprinted fading cameos on the sight:
Andrew Duvalt, Missouri Irishman,
pinned to the wall; the Scotsman Robinson,

4 astonished by a bullet; James McGee,
   propped up, old bandages now freshly stained;
 John Blair and Lemuel Crawford heartlessly
   cut open where they lay; Miles Andross brained
   by pummeling muskets. Delirious with pain,
 Ed Mitchasson, half-murdered by a shot
 last winter, died completely on his cot.

5 Before they died, the doctors, with hands taught
   to heal, first vivisected shrieking foes
 with surgical finesse. Doc Pollard caught
   a charging teenage conscript as he rose
   from crouching, then fell victim to the rows
 of troops. The surgeon of the New Orleans Greys,
 William Howell, kept sawing in the haze

6 of stinking smoke that swirled in from the yard
   or spilled from scorching pans. Just like the fog
 that suffocates a burning house's charred
   interior, the fumes began to clog
   the blinking hospital, a poison smog
 in which the deadly musket light would flare
 the way a fireman's torch will probe the air.

7 More flickering, more moans. A hundred screens,
   a hundred cameras could not convey
 the horror in that room, the hundred scenes
   of agony. Blue steel began to flay
   James Nowlan, as the mattress where he lay
 gorged like a leech. George Nelson, bullet-gored
 last winter, felt a body-heated sword.

The cobbler from Gonzales, Marcus Sewell, *8*
   died in that howling hospital, his eye
exploded by hot lead. A death as cruel
   awaited William Hersee, forced to lie
   here shivering since he had nearly died
of wounds from winter's war. A bayonet
divided his frail body from his head.

Another soldier died upon his cot, *9*
   George Washington Main, confined here since winter;
when Texans stormed the fort, he had been shot,
   one lung half-shredded by a metal splinter.
   The other burst, as blades began to enter
through rib and flesh. Virginia's son endured
one final hurt, and then his pain was cured.

Here William Jackson fell, but not before *10*
   his pistol's single shot blew out a skull,
spackling him with his opponent's gore.
   John Garvin flailed, a maddened, streaming bull
   beneath a crowded stadium's howling hull.
The blades found Robert Cochran. Each of the three
had served in Captain Carey's company.

Ed Mitchell sank, and Gordon Jennings, gray *11*
   at fifty-six, and Henry Courtman, bred
in Germany, now a New Orleans Grey;
   inside the Alamo, all three lay dead.
   Each left a living brother who would tread
the road from Goliad and fall in turn
with twentyscore when guns began to burn.

12 The last to sink within that ringing hall
     was William Lewis. Visiting a friend
  in Carolina, he had heard the call
     of glory, not dreaming that his life would end
     in tomblike darkness where a blade would rend
  his collarbone. His mother, Mary, four
  years later, published letters, begging for

13 some relic, some memento of the son
     she raised for Santa Anna's scythes to reap.
  Moved by her plea, Bexar's citizens, from one
     corroded stone in the Alamo's heap,
     commissioned a mason to carve a keep-
  sake they then sent the proud and grieving mother,
  a modest monument. These stanzas are another.

14 On the west barracks roof, before the doors,
     like leaves a shower pastes onto the pane
  and patio, lay Texians whose wars
     had ended: William Smith, isled by the stain
     his blood had made; the preacher Northcross, plain
  in death as in his life, laid out with grace;
  and Lewis Johnson, missing half his face.

15 Beside the cannon, Captain Samuel Blair
     had knotted; his contortions showed the route
  of what had killed him. The infrequent flare
     of muskets and big guns lit the redoubt
     where the west wall's survivors now hid out,
  surrounded by bodies as pale in the gloom
  as sculpted sentries on a marble tomb.

The remnants of the units of Seguin   *16*
    and Forsyth through a western barracks door
now studied darkness. Like a submarine
    alighting on a sea mount, or the floor
    of some deep dayless trench, a balding shore
long flooded, their small building sank amid
careening shades like schools of fish or squid.

The first assault they countered, adding slain   *17*
    and mauled attackers to the crescent mound
between the barracks door and courtyard drain;
    that human half-moon mocked the crescent found
    inside the bunker's entryway. Around
the sandbags, teeth within a jaw of stone,
each Texan waited, crowded yet alone.

Some joked, some brooded. William Garnett prayed;   *18*
    the Baptist minister met the next wave
of infantry with blessings, not a blade,
    of no use to his cause — better to save
    your country than your soul. Beside him, brave
Juan Abamillo killed before he fell,
like Robert Allen heralded to hell.

The room became a lamprey's mouth, a purse   *19*
    of knives and bayonets, mulching both teams
impartially. John Thurston snarled a curse
    and blindly swung his Bowie, culling screams
    from foe and friend alike. A musket's flames
etched Andres Nava's shadow on the stone
as that *Tejano* melted with a moan.

20 No Texan walked out of that fuming den.
        Next door, however, bayonets that snouted
    a mattress pile flushed half a dozen men
        like flustered quail. A Latin Colonel shouted,
        commanding clemency for the routed,
    despite Santa Anna's orders. Hands held high,
    the mute, stunned prisoners went dragging by.

21 The Colonel cried, "You! Negro!" Muskets swung
        to mark the corner, where a table made
    a small redoubt. Joe Travis, standing, flung
        his shotgun down, and left his barricade.
        An *escopeta* cracked, a bullet flayed
    the Texan's arm. The Colonel angrily
    rebuked his troops. Joe bent in agony.

22 One room remained, along the western wall.
        The first troops through the doorway found no fight
    from the occupants. A child began to squall,
        the infant Juana Alsbury clutched tight.
        Gertrudis clutched her sister in her fright.
    "Your money! Pay up, and you won't be hurt!"
    A leering conscript grasped at Juana's skirt,

23 then toppled, tackled by a flying shape —
        Napoleon Mitchell, of Carey's corps
    of proud Invincibles, averted rape.
        He rolled with his opponent on the floor,
        fists drumming, till a bayonet blade tore
    his shoulder blade, his lung. His innards gleamed
    on bayonets. The shrunken women screamed.

The last of the Invincibles sank dead   24
    atop his adversary with a twitch.
A pause — and then a sooty soldier said
    to Juana, "Who will help you now, you bitch?"
    The answer was a chilling battle screech,
like that raised by Comanches, when revealed
atop a ridge that let them wait concealed.

Toribio Losoya, with his wife,   25
    parents, and siblings for years had dwelt
within these very rooms, until the strife
    last fall. When General Cos had been expelled,
    Losoya, serving with Seguin, had dealt
defeat to the occupiers. He had roamed
in wonder through the ruins of his home.

Where womenfolk had knelt upon the floor,   26
    grinding tamales, while the children dashed,
Losoya fought a private civil war.
    Against his bayonet, another crashed;
    it was as though tremendous eagles clashed,
their yellow talons clicking from the force
that tumbles them above a river's source.

A dozen bayonets and musket stocks   27
    beat down the Texan, to the choral wail
of women he had rescued. Soon the shocks
    made him relax within the gruesome trail
    his crawling left, the slime wake of a snail.
A sergeant helped the women from the room,
Toribio Losoya's home and tomb.

28   Holed up in the Long Barracks, what was left
of Blazeby's New Orleans Greys sat glumly awaiting
catastrophe, like pigeons in a cleft
    beneath an overpass; the road's vibrating
    becomes their shudder. The men were prating
in several tongues — mere mercenaries, these,
who had fought to win a ranch, a life of ease,

29   not to spend their blood to buy another's land,
    to fall with strangers, conquered conquerors.
Steve Dennison, who had come from Ireland,
    dreaming of acres and a hefty purse,
    was trapped beside a soldier from a worse
nation than Mexico, an Englishman
named James R. Dimkins; fate had made them one

30   with Henry Thomas, born in Germany,
    a soldier of fortune fortune disavowed.
Each in his language hurled obscenity
    into besieging darkness, prompting loud
    insults in Spanish. Soon the motley crowd,
experiencing a kind of Pentecost,
could understand the slurs their rivals tossed;

31   the Texans — or perhaps the other side —
    began to bleat and low. The door hinge squeal
of swine was heard, when enemies replied.
    Abruptly the black court began to peal
    with barnyard babbling. The two sides could feel
a sympathy that transcended the dark
where turkeys gulped and dogs began to bark.

The shivaree was brief. The cannon near   *32*
    the fallen Travis had been turned around
and aimed at the Long Barracks. With a cheer,
    the Mexicans lit the touch hole; then the sound
    of planetoids colliding. Grapeshot downed
the Texans in their darkness, turtles racked
atop a log that topple as a stack.

The infantry now rushed the barracks door,   *33*
    carving the foes the cannon's flak had skinned;
they charged the way that purple martins soar
    down to a birdhouse swaying in the wind,
    where sparrows crowd inside the chambers meant
for martin nests, rooms they fight to usurp;
above the yard, wings flutter, rivals chirp.

Will Marshall jumped a grenadier, as bold   *34*
    as a hummingbird that strafes a chattering squirrel;
a pistol scorched his face, he limply rolled.
    Behind a sandbag, in a rattler's curl,
    Jesse McCoy waited to unfurl
his full six feet, guns flaming. With a yell,
the sheriff of Gonzales rose and fell.

Three brothers from the town of Liberty   *35*
    squatted behind a sandbag barrier.
To Texas they had come from Tennessee,
    to work on Dorsett's farm, until the war
    had flared. Now Edward Taylor, twenty-four,
the oldest, was the first in death, as life;
his lungs, cut open, whistled like a fife.

36   The youngest, George, protected big slow Jim,
          blocking a bayonet with his own gun,
      before another bayonet left him
              impaled and gurgling, like a fish upon
              a boat's deck, flopping shiny in the sun,
      a hook right through its gills. Jim Taylor drilled
      his brother's killer before he was killed.

37   The frightened Mexicans found darkness squirmed
          around them. A few charged into a shower
      of lead from Jimmy Garrett, safely bermed,
              for now. Cleve Simmons tried to overpower
              a startled foe; like weevils in the flour,
      they wriggled in the dirt the bags had bled,
      until, throat opened, Simmons lay dead.

38   One room in the Long Barracks still held out,
          repelling the first wave with popping fire.
      The infantry rolled back. From their redoubt
              the Texans gazed, like plump fish that retire
              to brush, from which they stare into the gyre.
      The Mexicans could not know they would spar
      here with the settlers who had launched the war.

39   Six months before, when General Cos ruled Bexar,
          the army that he sent to claim the old
      six-pounder at Gonzales met the stare
              of insurrection, resolute and bold.
              COME AND TAKE IT read the flag that was unrolled
      above the cannon by the Old Eighteen,
      outnumbered by the army on the green.

The hail of nails and horseshoes that dispersed   *40*
    Santa Anna's soldiers in the morning mist
last autumn was answered now by a burst
    of searing shrapnel. Bits of grapeshot hissed,
    deflected in the darkness. Not all missed;
hot metal nicked the youngest, Billy King,
and Jacob Darst, one of the Old Eighteen.

Their neighbors from Gonzales ripped a shirt   *41*
    for bandages. Lieutenant Kimbell asked
if any of his other men were hurt.
    Five days before, he had led these neighbors, masked
    by night, into the encircled fort, then tasked
them strictly through the siege. His volunteers
had proven they could be a veteran's peers.

"When I get out of here," Tom Miller said,   *42*
    "I'm going to smoke the biggest damn cigar
you ever seen." George Neggan shook his head.
    "When I get out of here, I'm shopping for
    a *señorita* — maybe three or four."
"They cost too much for you," Dolph Floyd retorted.
"A heifer, maybe — if you could afford it."

"Y'all hush," hissed Albert Martin. He believed   *43*
    that he heard allies' voices drawing near.
In minutes, the trapped men would be relieved.
    Intently silent, others leaned to peer
    across the barricade into the smear
of blue in black that was the barracks door.
"It's English!" They erupted in a roar

44 of jubilation — but the men had fooled
  themselves; the cries were Spanish, from the crew
reloading the twelve-pounder. Smoke unspooled,
  the gun rocked on its carriage as it threw
  hot metal through the predawn black and blue.
This time, a dozen Texans cringed in pain
beneath the pelting of that hurricane.

45 Back in the fall, when brave Gonzales fought
  to keep its gun, James George had done his part,
tendering the oxen team that brought
  the cannon to the field where war would start.
  Another cannon, on another cart,
annihilated him, beside another
veteran, William Dearduff, his wife's brother.

46 More kinsmen perished there, from shot and steel.
  George Cottle was the uncle of the four
young whelps of Thomas Jackson; they would squeal
  delighted when they glimpsed him. As before,
  the two men stood against a Mexican corps;
born after their defeat at the Alamo
would be twin sons whom George would never know.

47 The name of Kimble County celebrates
  George Kimbell's daring, far from Water Street
in old Gonzales, where on shaggy pates
  of any size he once could fit a hat.
  That factory had since been shuttered shut;
its owners — Kimbell, Dickinson — had gone
to San Antonio to die at dawn.

"No quarter!" Through the slot attackers poured,   48
    slipping on sand that trickled from the hide
containers gusts of sizzling shot had scored.
    George Neggan killed a foe before he died,
    as did Ike Baker. Sabered in the side,
Claiborne Wright mustered the strength to slay
the Mexican who gutted Jerry Day.

"I'm hit," John Davis told his newest friend,   49
    a Pennsylvanian who had showed up in
the winter in Gonzales. To defend
    the colonies from Indians had been
    the greenhorn's dream. John Davis had again
refought his battles with the nomad nation
for David Cummings, rapt with admiration.

The two would never gallop through mesquite   50
    together, chasing Lipan or Comanch.
Subsiding from lost blood, Davis would cheat
    the testing bayonet that found a flinch
    beneath his carcass. Sickened by the stench
and terror, Cummings squirmed, but proved too slow,
a rat hacked in a basement by a hoe.

John Flanders, Massachusetts Yankee, swore,   51
    contesting a bayonet. When his father,
his business partner, opted to ignore
    a widow's debt, young Flanders did not bother
    to say goodbye. He never said another
word to his far-off folks. In cold and shadow
he died in Texas now; he left no widow.

52   His head now turbaned in a bloody band,
          Jake Darst — a farmer, back in warless days —
      now carried out a death that he had planned
              by priming several pistols. Through the haze
              he emptied each, dodging the lead that grazed
      the sandbags, like a prairie dog that pops
      up, down, up, till the rancher's bullet lops.

53   Darst, bayoneted, left a family
          headless in Gonzales. So did Kent,
      who had exchanged a Missouri spread for fee
              simple in Texas. George Tumlinson, sent
              as well from Missouri, died a bachelor gent.
      When Isaac Millsaps fell, he left behind
      seven children and a widow who was blind.

54   A scuffle in the murk pitted Dolph Floyd
          against a young draftee who shared his fear
      and desperation. Trying to avoid
              his rival's jabs, Dolph backed into a spear,
              began to bellow like a butchered steer.
      His thirty-second birthday had arrived.
      By Ester, widowed twice, he was survived.

55   The rich man of Gonzales was among
          his neighbors — Thomas Miller. His young bride,
      eye-baiting Sidney Gaston, once had sung
              caged in his parlor. When their child had died,
              their marriage had as well, and Miller's pride;
      divorcing him, his Sidney shared the bed
      of Johnny Kellogg, nineteen, whom she wed.

The men who had shared Sidney shared perhaps   56
    a dozen words during the past few years.
They fought together now, as thunderclaps
    lit up the few Gonzales volunteers
    still struggling. Sidney would ration her tears,
not knowing one of her men gave his life
protecting one to whom he lost his wife.

The day that Kimbell and his little band   57
    of neighbors rode to help the men besieged
in San Antonio, they passed the land
    of John G. King. Billy, his son, beseeched
    his folks. Riding hard, the young man reached
the startled horsemen, holding up the gun
the father of nine had lent his firstborn son.

That empty shotgun Billy learned to wield   58
    to sweep back clustered spikes. A bobcat bristling
before coyotes, he refused to yield,
    until a pistol sent a hot drop whistling
    into his throat. He smelled his own flesh sizzling.
At fifteen, of the Gonzales volunteers
he was the slightest only in his years.

The broken day now leaked its golden yolk   59
    above the kindled skyline. Brindled deer
were filtering through filigrees of oak.
    The does and fauns looked upward. They could hear
    the thunder from a city that was near
and yet so alien; a poison stew
was morning mist there, blood and tripe the dew.

60   The cannon boomed again. The chapel door
         sloughed off more scaly skin, by now half-splintered.
The captured eighteen-pounder fired once more;
         Morales and his howling soldiers entered
         the roofless ruin where resistance centered.
Once in, they squinted, dazzled by the sun
that shared the platform's summit with a gun.

61   Erupting, the twelve-pounder in the apse
         ripped flesh from the Jiménez men and troops
of Matamoros. Dozens there collapsed;
         across their speckled comrades, remnant groups
         now scrambled, chickens scooting from the coops
a shattered truck has scattered on a road.
The Texians had no time to reload

62   the cannon. Stormers rushing up the ramp
         were sliced by Bonham's saber; in his suit
and mask of soot, he seemed prepared to stamp
         a minstrel's jig. He fought, though, like a brute,
         downing attackers, until one could shoot
point-blank and burst his braincase with a ball.
He dropped, an unstrung puppet, by the wall.

63   Defenders fought attackers hand to hand
         inside that stone arena. Cunningham,
a Mississippi bargeman, made his stand
         beside the arsenal; a jagged ram
         punched through him. Charles Smith was the next to slam
the body-latticed ground, beside the form
of William Johnson, percolating, warm.

Esparza, cut off from his family   *64*
     beside a cannon in a darkened room,
fired at white straps, black shakos. Finally
     he slumped. Curled up beside him in the gloom,
     Brigido Guerrero saved himself from doom,
swearing he was a loyal Mexican
held hostage by the rebel garrison.

His comrades from Gonzales all were dead   *65*
     a dozen yards away, but Dickinson
thought only of his wife, his child. With dread
     he saw that Evans had begun to run
     down to the chamber where they kept the gun-
powder, torch in hand. "No! Evans, no!" —
then Dickinson was silenced by a blow.

Now Robert Evans gamboled with the torch,   *66*
     swiping at bayonets, as he drew near
the powder magazine. A bullet scorched
     his temple, then one splashed behind his ear.
     The big, dark, merry Irish volunteer
rolled down the muddy wedge, the smoking brand
extinguished with the exit he had planned.

The graying gunner, Wolf, saw all was lost;   *67*
     he thought no more of Texas, just his boys
inside the sacristy. Pleading, he tossed
     his gun aside, and shouted through the noise,
     "Please, I have children! *Niños!*" But his pleas
did not avert the whirling stocks that struck
him down, the bayonets that dug and stuck.

68 Inside the western room, the women stared
   as Galba Fuqua, a sixteen-year-old boy
 Gonzales sent, reeled through, his features smeared
   with blood. Metal had tunneled to destroy
   his jawbone. What the young man tried to say
 was muffled. Frustrated, he spun to flee
 the chamber, disappeared from history.

69 Just like tornado-catapulted trash —
   bricks, branches — twirling through exploding glass
 into a farmhouse, troops began to crash
   into the chapel room. Amid the mass
   of shadows, Anna Esparza tried to press
 her children closer, while Sue Dickinson
 squeezed Angelina. To that room had run

70 Jake Walker, cousin of the mountain man
   of legend, Joseph Walker, cousin, too,
 of Asa Walker, first among that clan
   to perish at that fort. Asa lay blue
   out in the courtyard, as the soldiers slew
 his cousin in the chapel. Blood corroded
 Jake's mumbling lips, and then his scalp exploded.

71 Like sharks convolving in a scarlet sea,
   the soldiers lurched. The murdered Wolf's young boys
 stood gawking near Susannah. Suddenly,
   a scuffle, and a shrieking, like the noise
   of hell's own hinges creaking. Broken toys
 gazed out through marble. Red began to rim
 the tiny mouths like mustaches of jam.

Gregorio Esparza's orphaned son 72
 Enrique fidgeted in shadow, stared
at butchered playmates. Seeing he was one
  of their own nation, shouting soldiers spared
  the eight-year-old. His mother's wailing flared.
Enrique, gazing at a sergeant's suit,
raised up his narrow arm in a salute.

The women choked on sobs, almost demented. 73
 "Señora Esparza? Mrs. Dickinson?"
— An officer's voice. A swaying lantern glinted
  on shiny corpses. Troops ushered the stunned
  survivors from that darkness. Then a gun
was cracking, and Susannah felt a blow
against her leg. The world blurred in a glow.

One member of the garrison fought on. 74
 Atop the Long Barracks, three stormers lay
beneath the rebel flag that flashed by dawn.
  Lieutenant Torres had ripped down the Greys'
  blue banner, and had just begun to raise
the eagle flag, the green and white and red,
when a sniper's bullet tunneled through his head.

Antonio Fuentes, the thief whom Judge Seguin 75
 had jailed, whom Bowie, drunken, had set free,
occasion for the bitter fight between
  the two commanders, fired impassively
  from the hospital roof, watching targets flee.
Fuentes subsided at a volley's rattle,
the last of all the Texans killed in battle.

BOOK TWELVE

EMBASSIES

THE ARGUMENT

At last Santa Anna comes to enter
the fortress. He rejects surrender.
A grisly labor is begun:
the burning of the garrison.
The victor of the contest shows
his magnanimity to those
he spared. His offer to adopt
an orphan meets with an abrupt
rejection. As survivors ride
to spread the story, back inside
the fort the conqueror looks on
the rival chiefs who died at dawn.

Expanding waves of orange morning raced   *1*
a pair of urgent riders down the road
to San Antonio. The horsemen chased
    their saddled shadows, till the foremost slowed
    and reined the great beast, Saracen, he rode.
As Juan Seguin dismounted, Houston knelt
and pressed his ear against the dewy pelt

of Texas. While the stars had still been bright,   *2*
    the General, flying with Seguin before
their scouting party, had begun this rite;
    till now, like music conveyed by a floor
    from room to room, the thunder of the war
had rattled the Hill Country. Seguin waited
to learn if Central Texas still vibrated.

At length the great gray warrior arose   *3*
    from tranquil ground. His face could not be seen,
and yet from the dejection of his pose
    his comrade knew the truth. Colonel Seguin
    made the cross, blinking in the morning sheen.
Sam Houston began chanting a slow grave
lament the Cherokee sang for the fallen brave.

4   Sometimes, deep in the crater of a drought,
    a rancher as his last recourse will scorch
the prickly pear, so that his cows can mouth
        the juicy pulp; the brutes, ribby and parched,
        will trail their owner as he strolls to torch
another clump. So Santa Anna guided
his aides through fields the battle had ignited.

5   Around them ladders, black against the haze
        as winter trees, were angling. Crooked legs
of slaughtered mules and horses made a maze.
        Entangled with them were the mangled wrecks
        of soldiers. Some had strength enough to flex
and cry for help, some just the strength to cry.
Their master left them there to live or die.

6   A trooper held the reins, as the President
        dismounted near the southern palisade.
Bedazzled by the dawn, he had to squint
        in order to discern the corpses splayed
        across the doubled stakes of the stockade
like seals that throng and glisten on a rock
pulverized by the sea's unceasing shock.

7   As listless as a satiated shark
        that noses round a crater-making boat
where cabined sailors bob, a grisly ark,
        the weary general paced a fortress moat
        planked over now with bodies. Clearing his throat,
he spoke at last: "Order a delegation
from town to bury the soldiers of our nation.

"Burn the rebels. I want to look upon   *8*
    their leaders, though. Have someone point them out."
"Your Excellency!" General Castrillon,
    the courtly Cuban, silvery and stout,
    appeared, striding through bluish rags of cloud.
His grimy soldiers, with jabs to the back,
were herding six men spared in the attack.

The pale Americans — boys, far from home —   *9*
    peered out through sooty faces, as an owl
will blink into a flashlight from the gloam.
    "My order was, No Quarter," came a growl.
    Now it was Castrillon's turn to scowl:
"The rules of war, Your Excellency, state . . ."
Santa Anna snapped, "*My* rules will be obeyed!"

He gestured to the infantry, his hand   *10*
    pristine in white kid leather as a fang.
"You! Execute these rebels!" — his command.
    Then Santa Anna turned. The stockade rang
    with screams and oaths as infantrymen sprang
to action, snuffling hogs turned loose in brakes
and fields to grind up thrashing, baffled snakes.

Ten rivers marble Texas. Of all these,   *11*
    the premier is the river called the Grand,
one of the two titanic arteries
    of our world continent. From antlered land
    that Pecos waters down to ocean sand,
the Rio Grande debouches, all its force
surrendered by degrees along its course.

12   Far north, the prairies quickened by the Red
         and Trinity and Brazos gleam with grass.
     Above the lusher seam of riverbed,
         the budding clouds, like bubbles blown in glass,
         expand at sundown. Deep within their mass,
     like fetal dragons, soundless glows the hue
     of roses pulsate — this is Texas, too.

13   Where noon is twilight, where the silver floss
         festoons the rafters roofing in the slough,
     a river varnishes the logs with moss
         and spangles them with turtles. Gently, through
         a stillness stippled where a heron flew,
     a living log will ease, its passage clean
     but for two eyes like islands in Sabine.

14   Four other rivers drain the spongy chalk
         beneath the domes of cedar and live oak,
     melting their flumes through fossil-riddled rock:
         Nueces, and the Guadalupe, whose choke-
         points force canoers to a frantic stroke;
     the lower Colorado, wild and fickle;
     the San Antonio, a feeble trickle.

15   All ten great rivers, blended with the creek
         named for Saint Peter in San Antonio,
     might have drowned the hills of Bexar for a week
         and still not soaked the blood from the Alamo.
         As it was, the local river's torpid flow
     was dammed by Texan corpses, piled up higher
     than flood-washed cattle swept against bob wire.

Defying orders, some soldiers assigned   *16*
    to grisly duty stuffed the shallow stream.
James Stewart's wreck thus joined some other blind
    unmoving remnants of the Texan team.
      Here Scots-bred David Wilson, who dared dream
of martial fame — or what was left of him —
subsided underneath the rising rim.

Most, though, were fed to three hot cackling hells,   *17*
    the fate of Andrew Jackson Harrison,
the Tennessean; Georgia-born Bill Wells,
    who left behind a daughter and a son;
      young James Buchanan, handy with a gun
or Bowie knife, and Richard Ballentine,
all mingled, where the flames began to shine.

To Texas, Jesse Thompson was no stranger;   *18*
    this settler from Brazoria had fought
the cavalry last autumn as a ranger.
    If he must perish, Thompson always thought,
      a death on horseback was the one he sought.
Impaled by bayonets, his carcass sank
amid a crackle and a smoke that stank.

The body of Sam Evans fed the flame,   *19*
    the young New Yorker — Evans, born the heir
of warriors. His grandfather won fame
    during the Revolutionary War;
      his uncle Jacob Brown topped his career
commanding the Army of the United States.
The embers settled underneath the weights.

20   Within the Alamo, the dismal labor
         of sorting the two sides was undertaken
     by troops who took their profit as a saber,
         a belt, or boots, or trousers, tugged and shaken
         from men who looked as though they might awaken.
     Some soldiers, kneeling, sawed off fingers, ears,
     or genitals as gruesome souvenirs.

21   Among the carts piled high with rebel dead,
         one soldier in a victor's uniform
     was searching every face, with hope and dread
         and no success. James Hannum's corpse, still warm,
         was not the one he sought, nor was the form
     of James Tylee, shot in the lung's red cage,
     survived by wife Matilda, half his age.

22   Together with his son, old Jesse Bowman
         had trapped and hunted down the Ozark trails
     to Texas. Now this nomad, with a yeoman
         named Andrew Nelson, was to feed the bales.
         The two, and William Ward, were stacked like rails,
     beside Bill Sutherland, just seventeen,
     carved up as though by a threshing machine.

23   Impatiently, the questing soldier scanned
         the husks of James L. Ewing, formerly
     invincible in Captain Carey's command,
         and Isaac White. Like an uprooted tree,
         Chris Parker spread, a shoot from chivalry:
     a father blooded at New Orleans, heir
     himself of a father chilled by Forge's air.

268

A friend of Bowie's, Thomas Roberts, lay 24
    among the bayonet-degraded dead,
like William Wills, a farmer, red as clay
    the plough cuts, and Jackson Rusk, Irish-bred,
    a colonist whose waiting land-grant spread
no heirs would ever claim. These dead were not
the dead man whom the somber soldier sought.

Nor was the highest-ranked enlisted man, 25
    the Sergeant Major, Hiram Williamson;
his face was tattered by the swords that ran
    across it, as a kitten's claws will run
    along a scratching post. His one-shot gun,
downing a foe, inspired more to belabor
his nerveless trunk with bayonet and saber.

Spain Summerlin, a Bexar Guard, besieged 26
    the Alamo when Cos was trapped inside;
his stubble showed through skin that death had bleached.
    James Waters Robertson lay slumped beside
    Bill Taylor, whom a bayonet had pried,
like Summerlin, men Tennessee had sent.
The searcher studied them, and on he went.

Bandanna-masked, a soldier spat an oath, 27
    unloading grub-white northerners — Jimmy Brown
and Johnny Wilson, Pennsylvanians both.
    Atop them a new carcass tumbled down,
    John Dillard, from a Tennessean town.
Gregorio Esparza's desperate brother
studied one more Texan, then another.

28   At last, Francisco recognized the face
          upon a corpse akimbo in the court
      before the chapel. Quickening his pace,
          he spanned the lesser yard within the fort.
          Astonished countrymen watched him contort
      his face in effort, or perhaps in grief,
      and hoist the body like a side of beef.

29   He staggered underneath his brother's weight,
          his muscles bunching like a rafter's grain.
      Stooping and slow, he passed the fortress gate,
          and limped beside the wagons of the slain
          mixed up with carts of men crooning their pain.
      His lower lip, with its seditious tremble,
      would sabotage his effort to dissemble.

30   You stand there, as Esparza staggers by,
          beneath his burden, mother of the night,
      invisible to his, to every eye
          but mine. I see you with a second sight;
          I witness you recruiting, in each fight,
      another cohort to replace the brood
      you sank once in a rocky solitude.

31   When Goliad's captives are abruptly told
          to halt, and muskets drop, you see their dread;
      they realize they will not be paroled.
          On that Palm Sunday, ricocheting lead
          drapes leafy boughs atop four hundred dead.
      When bayonets test bodies, you appear
      again, a faint and phosphorescent sphere.

When Houston, spurring on great Saracen,   32
    advances through the San Jacinto grass,
the Texan Fabius, with his few men
    to crush an army with a greater mass,
    unseen you see the vengeful settlers pass,
and hear their cry — "Remember Alamo!
Remember Goliad!" — before the foe.

To Houston, propped beneath the exulting oak,   33
    his foot inclined, the humbled President
of Mexico is brought. You gleam like smoke
    beside Deaf Smith, who cups his ear, intent
    on hearing the transfer of government.
Houston begins, wincing from injury:
"Why, sir, this *is* the nineteenth century!"

Though won, their sovereignty must be defended   34
    by Texans. For the only real frontier
is made of men and guns; that line's extended
    when Rangers cross the river, flinging fear;
    it shrinks, when Mexican forces reappear
in San Antonio, in Forty-Two.
War after war, and, always watching, you.

The Texans, more ambitious than informed,   35
    who attempted to annex New Mexico,
stand in their cell, before the uniformed
    centurions and their chief, their greatest foe,
    Santa Anna, back in power. Slumped and slow,
each Texan draws a bean — the black's the grave,
the white reprieve as Santa Anna's slave.

36   The warlord often has regained the saddle
        since Texas. To the French at Veracruz
in Thirty-Eight he lost a leg in battle,
        interred with pomp by military crews.
        He pauses on his peg leg to abuse
a Texan, yoked up to a cart of dirt;
Sam Walker, though, acknowledges no hurt.

37   A few years later, Captain Walker raids
        with Jack Hays and the other Texas Rangers
when the republic to the north invades
        the Creole state. The Texans are no strangers
        to this opponent; they elude the dangers,
and cannot be distracted by a binge.
They battle, not for empire, but revenge.

38   Resaca de la Palma, Monterrey —
        Llorona, you are there, at each attack.
Hid by a cowl, you see Scott's cannon flay
        collapsing Veracruz. And from each sack,
        from Churubusco and Chapultepec,
you usher your newest adopted sons,
the ruddy *yanquis* and bronze Mexicans.

39   The capitol is ruled by Winfield Scott
        when Santa Anna and his remnant force,
emboldened by defeat, attempt to cut
        the Puebla road. The grim Southwestern wars
        conclude, when Walker's unit of the horse
rides into small Huamantla to surprise
Santa Anna. In the fighting, Walker dies.

His fellow Texas Rangers swear to kill   *40*
 the man whose destiny is locked with theirs —
oh, Lady, will the guns never be still?
 Jack Hays, the greatest of the Rangers, spares
 the fallen warlord, though, when his coach veers
through Texan ranks. In U.S. custody,
the old man rides toward exile and the sea.

His wars are over. Soon his enemies   *41*
 will slaughter one another for the loot,
contesting western lands they fought to seize.
 What legions of the dead you will recruit,
 Llorona, when compatriots dispute
Shiloh, Antietam, the Wilderness,
and Gettysburg, what hordes you will impress!

The lava landscape, though, is cooling fast;   *42*
 when Lee strides out of Appomattox court,
the age of molten borders will be past
 in North America. To the report
 of rifles Maximilian, far from court,
subsides, and with him, France's Mexican
imperium sinks in oblivion.

Confederate, *Cristero*, and Comanch,   *43*
 conquistador, *Villista* — all have followed
Our Lady, now a shy, enticing wench,
 and now a crone. What hordes the floods have swallowed,
 Llorona; yet a soul that grief has hollowed
can be revenged but cannot be replenished.
You linger . . . Ah, your search is not yet finished.

44   Inside the mansion of Ramón Musquiz
         that Santa Anna's staff had commandeered,
      Anna Esparza fought for bread and cheese
            with Indian servants. When Musquiz appeared,
            he warned Esparza's widow that he feared
      she was not safe. He urged her to go back
      to the room holding survivors of the attack.

45   "My children have to eat," Esparza's bride
            insisted, as she nibbled at a crust,
      her grief submerged by hunger. Then, outside,
            the horses nickered and the watchdogs fussed.
            Francisco had arrived. Turned blond by dust,
      he sank down to his knees and gently lay
      the body of Gregorio on the clay.

46   Around that cherished form the widow folded,
            her voice an ululating, wordless wail.
      Rocking her husband's ruin, Anna molded
            her flesh to flesh grown cool as stone and pale.
            The hair his hand once spooled became a veil.
      Francisco, stunned and stoic, as he knelt
      by his brother's corpse and bride, began to melt.

47   This was the scene the President beheld
            as he returned. With somber courtesy,
      Santa Anna doffed his hat. The tears that welled
            from Anna, as Francisco made his plea,
            inspired the man to twitch in sympathy.
      "He was a traitor, but we are merciful.
      Your brother may receive a funeral."

Inside the house, the weary ruler slurped 48
    a steaming cup, then rubbed his eyes in pain,
dictating: "The invaders who usurped
    the garrison at Bexar have all been slain.
    Our losses were but few. Soon this campaign
will be completed. Texas will belong
to Mexico, intact once more and strong . . ."

He looked up as a prisoner was escorted 49
    into the room, a slim young man, a black.
"The slave of Travis," Juan Almonte reported.
    Joe's bandaged arm beside him dangled, slack.
    The slain commander's servant seemed to lack
all knowledge of the battle, when deposed.
A gesture, and the interview was closed.

"His Excellency," Colonel Almonte told 50
    the wary Texan, "wishes to extend
his friendship to you. Here no men are sold;
    in Mexico all slavery is banned.
    His Excellency asks you, as a friend,
if you would like to join us as we crush
the criminals to whom you've lost so much."

Joe glanced from the translator to the man 51
    with tousled hair awaiting his reply.
He chewed his lip, then said, "You understand . . .
    I never want to see nobody die
    no more again. And that's the reason why
I want to head back home. . . . You tell him, please."
Santa Anna's smile dissolved by small degrees.

52 A blanket and two silver coins in hand,
        Joe took his leave. "Perhaps it's just as well,"
    Santa Anna mused. "Perhaps I should have planned
        it thus. For every black who hears him tell
        his story may gain courage to rebel
    on our behalf, should Jackson intervene
    with the army he has set on the Sabine."

53 At last Susannah Dickinson was brought.
        Limping to ease the leg that flak had found,
    she stared in terror at the man who had wrought
        her husband's death while widowing their town,
        Gonzales. In the chair she hunkered down,
    her baby palisaded against harms
    and horrors by a pair of freckled arms.

54 The child was fascinated by the blue
        of Santa Anna's sash. Her eyes were drawn
    away to focus on a ruby hue.
        The irritable parrot pacing on
        its master's chair, a bit of Amazon
    in Texas, spread its fan, a samurai
    reciting verse as he prepares to die.

55 Bemused, the infant dropped her glinting ring.
        It rolled across the floor. A white-gloved hand
    retrieved the pendulum upon the string.
        The stone on what had lately been the band
        Rebecca Cummings placed upon the hand
    of William Travis darkly drank the light,
    educing strangled gurgles of delight.

"A little angel." Santa Anna smiled. 56
   "A little angel, that she is, indeed."
The general gently garlanded the child.
   Almonte, for his chief, began to plead:
   "His Excellency's always guaranteed
the orphans he encounters a new life
on his estates, remote from grief and strife."

"Your little Angelina would be raised 57
   moated by amenity, a daughter to
the President." Susannah listened, dazed.
   "Delights and luxuries unknown to you
   can be your child's, wonders you never knew.
Imagine her upon a patio
where fountains glimmer and great parrots glow . . ."

Susannah tightened. She had seen the grave 58
   that held a woman whom a brave defiled
and made at once a widow and a slave;
   her mind had died before her, when her child,
   at lasso's end, had been hauled through a pile
of bristling cactus pads. This was that ranch,
and General Santa Anna that Comanch.

The widowed adolescent shrank around 59
   the daughter whom her man had bade her raise:
"Don't take my baby!" With a moaning sound,
   Susannah rocked obsessively in place.
   "Tell her," said Santa Anna, "when one weighs —"
Almonte dared to interrupt his chief:
"For God's sake, let us leave her to her grief!"

60   The President responded with a glare.
        The parrot yawped. Its master turned away.
Susannah gulped and rearranged her hair
        and daubed her eyes, her face as red as clay.
        Santa Anna sighed. "You may go on your way
to join the other rebel immigrants . . .
I understand you, too, were happy once."

61   That afternoon, the widow Dickinson,
    atop a mule, her girl child in her clasp,
was guided by a somber Joe past gun
        and bayonet. Silence, but for the rasp
        of banners, and the horses' snort and gasp.
The President, his bicorne lowered, gave
a flourish that evolved into a wave.

62   Susannah started, when the bugles blared.
        Through Mexico's assembled ranks the three
moved slowly eastward. Angelina stared
        at flapping flags. The tiny refugee
        contingent dwindled in immensity.
The troops dispersed, as their commander spurred
his mare to the Alamo without a word.

63   A beekeeper, examining a hive
        whose brood is dying, finds the chamber floor
a scurf of papery mummies. Some, alive,
        twitch feebly underneath the waxen core
        in syrupy corrosion. Others pour
like scales from where they withered in a row.
Thus Santa Anna found the Alamo.

Ruiz, the town's *alcalde,* led the grim   64
    commander past the few remaining crews
still carting off the slaughtered, stopping him
    before a swollen corpse beached on the ooze,
    a land-thrown whale or shark, a killer whose
tremendous grin in death can still prompt fear
in gawking crowds, when hoisted on a pier.

"So this is Veramendi's son-in-law,"   65
    said Santa Anna, eyeing Bowie's rind,
red-striped where bayonets had sought to gnaw.
    "The Mexican by marriage. You will find,
    gentlemen, a vow's too weak to bind
the alien. Don't think a mere embrace
can keep a man from siding with his race."

The somber party crossed the cratered court.   66
    Santa Anna squinted in a barracks room
through leaking smoke, admired the little fort
    of sandbags from which Texan rebels whom
    his troops had killed paid killers back with doom:
"Ingenious." Then the general made his way
north to the wall where one last body lay.

The Alamo's commander sprawled half-stripped,   67
    his jacket gone, his boots and socks a prize,
his bone-white feet projecting. Blood had dripped
    from his exploded brow to ring his eyes,
    congealing in a Mardi Gras disguise.
Barefoot, with mask and stubble, he looked more
the victim of a binge than of a war.

68   Just fifteen years ago, a boy of twelve
        had felt a melting warmth upon his face,
as hunters — kinsmen all — had paused to delve
        into the buck he'd slain. He'd felt them trace
        the sign of the old order of the chase
upon his brow. The hunter who that day
became a man now lay a hunter's prey.

69   The conqueror removed his plumèd crescent,
        a gesture imitated all around
by men who watched their master, grown quiescent,
        study his foe awhile without a sound.
        Then General Santa Anna faintly frowned.
"At last, Guillermo Travis. Why, you are
so young, to have begun so great a war."

70   "This man," he told his aides, "headed the list
        I gave these towns last fall. Had they obeyed,
a firing squad might have averted this
        catastrophe. By God, this young man made
        himself a costly prize. The price we've paid . . ."
The self-described Napoleon of the West
reflected, then said, "Burn him with the rest."

71   Troops lugged the corpse of Travis to a cart,
        like fishmongers tossing a silver plank
atop the staring layers in a mart.
        Beneath the latest weight the wagon sank,
        laden with two armies and every rank.
The wheels protested, then the makeshift hearse
rolled forth, the only obsequy a curse.

"The fort's to be destroyed?" Almonte asked   *72*
   his master. In the stadium of the siege
Santa Anna stood, an actor who has basked
   in warm ovations all alone onstage.
   "We'll leave it to inspire a later age.
As long as Mexicans retell the story
of the Alamo, none shall forget our glory."

Appendix

ON EPIC

GLOSSARY

CHRONOLOGY

ON EPIC

I

CAN A SUCCESSFUL EPIC be written today in the style of Homer? The answer is obviously no.

In Book Eight of *The Odyssey*, Homer provides the earliest portrait of an epic poet (the translation is Robert Fitzgerald's):

> The crier soon came, leading that man of song
> whom the Muses cherished; by her gift he knew
> the good of life, and evil —
> for she who lent him sweetness made him blind.
> Pontónoös fixed a studded chair for him
> hard by a pillar amid the banqueters,
> hanging the taut harp from a peg above him,
> and guided up his hands upon the strings;
> placed a bread basket at his side, and poured
> wine in a cup, that he might drink his fill.
> Now each man's hand went out upon the banquet.
>
> In time, when hunger and thirst were turned away,
> the Muse brought to the minstrel's mind a song
> of heroes whose great fame rang under heaven . . .

If composing epic today meant sitting on a studded chair, strumming a harp, and chanting dactylic hexameters, the experiment might best remain unattempted. If the question is rephrased, however, as to whether it is now possible to write a successful epic, not in the *style* of Homer, but in the *tradition* of Homer, the answer, I will argue, is yes. Each great epic poet in the tradition of Homer has rejected mere mimicry and created what amounts to a new genre, by combining elements of Homeric formula with other literary forms, both sophisticated and popular. Virgil united Homeric epic with Latin legend and Alexandrian style. Dante created something new and unique from the synthesis of Virgil, Ovid, and the medieval allegory. Tasso seriously, and Ariosto facetiously, blended classical epic with chivalric romance. Camões lent the dignity of the Virgilian epic to the Renaissance traveler's tale. Milton fused Greco-Roman epic with Hebrew and Christian Scripture, enriching the compound with elements from a dozen other genres, like Elizabethan blank-verse tragedy. To ignore these tributaries of post-Homeric epic is to make as grave a mistake as someone who, tracing his genealogy, follows only the "illustrious" line of his father or mother, and ignores the contribution to his make-up of the ancestors of the other parent.[1]

The "epic" elements of an epic poem, then, are not the only elements, though they are the elements that define the work as a whole — the catalyst, as it were, for the reaction that produces the alloy. Once epic is understood properly, as an innovative synthesis of older and newer genres rather than as a timeless genre, it is easy to understand why the greatest failures in the history of attempts to write epic have been the poems that were the purest pastiches of past epics, with the least admixture from other genres. Trissino's *Italy Liberated from the Goths* was stillborn, while Tasso's *Jerusalem Liberated* is one of the great masterpieces of the epic tradition. Trissino is far more "correct" than Tasso, in the sense of conforming closely to Greco-Roman models. Trissino uses unrhyming Italian verse, which he thought closer to the classical Greek and Latin hexameters, instead of the rhyming stanzas of medieval and Renaissance narrative poetry. His subject and plotting owe little to what he considered vulgar chivalric romance. The result is as anachronistic as if Trissino had dressed like a Greek of the Dark Ages and strummed on a *kithara* (an affectation not more ridiculous, it should be noted, than that of contemporary professor-poets who adopt the poetic personae of primitive shamans). Trissino, in the manner of a minor epic poet, engages in revival; Tasso, like every other major epic poet, renovates the genre.

If an excess of antique elements in the epic compound produces the brittle alloy of pastiche, too much of the vernacular and contemporary can rob a work of its claim to be an epic at all. In the eighteenth century, Lord Kames remarked that "much useless labor has been bestowed, to distinguish an epic poem by some peculiar mark." Byron, in *Don Juan,* has given us the most concise guide to the conventions that tend to define the epic:

---

1. I am using "epic" as a synonym of "literary" or "secondary" epic, that is, poems by authors aware of Homer's example. Heroic poetry from cultures unaffected by Homeric influence — Hindu, Persian, Norse — should be described by terms other than "primary epic," which ought to be reserved for the two poems attributed to Homer.

My poem's epic, and is meant to be
Divided in twelve books; each book containing,
With love, and war, a heavy gale at sea,
A list of ships, and captains, and kings reigning,
New characters; the episodes are three;
A panoramic view of hell's in training,
After the style of Virgil and of Homer,
So that my name of Epic's no misnomer.

For a work to be an epic, not every feature found in Homer need be imitated. Every epic poem need not have a title ending in "-ad" or "-id," nor need it begin *in medias res,* be divided into twelve (or twenty-four) books, and include battles, speeches, epithets, epic similes, catalogues, councils of supernatural beings, extended flashbacks, and visions of the future. Indeed, as the example of Trissino shows, the surest way to fail in epic poetry is to copy precedent uncritically rather than to select and modify some elements of the tradition while discarding others. It would be difficult, however, to call a poem that contains none of the traditional generic elements an epic.

Ironically, the very prestige of epic has worked against an understanding of the genre, by encouraging both poets and critics to treat it as a form that is exalted and immutable. Beginning with Aristotle and Horace, critics have attempted to prescribe rules for "the epic." Some of these prescriptions are sensible, like Horace's advice that the epic begin *in medias res;* some pedantic, like the dogma of seventeenth-century French critics that the action of epic should take place during a period no greater than a year, as the action of tragedy ought to take place during a period no greater than a day; and some idiosyncratic, like Aristotle's opinion that the ideal epic is about the length of a tragic trilogy, or around 4,000 lines — less than half the length of most major epics (*The Alamo,* at 6,006 lines, is approximately the size Aristotle preferred because a Greek hexameter is longer than an English pentameter line). While critics have pretended to deduce abstract rules from a Platonic idea of epic, poets themselves have often sought to identify their work solely with the epic tradition while downplaying the debt of their poems to other, less prestigious genres. An example would be Tasso's strained efforts to distinguish his chivalric epic from the chivalric romances of Ariosto and Boiardo.

The epic tradition, then, is only one of the elements that goes into the making of an epic poem. This thesis needs to be refined further, by the observation that the epic tradition itself will be perceived differently, by different poets.

There are several reasons for this. The most obvious is that not all great epic poets have had access to all of the works of predecessors in the genre (a fact that modern critics, accustomed to the availability of the classics both in the original and in translation, forget at their peril). Dante never read a line of Homer, who to him was merely a venerated name. Chaucer misread a line in Horace as describing an ancient epic poet who was the equal of Homer named Lollius; in fact Lollius was the addressee of Horace's epistle. (One must admire the slyness with which Chaucer claimed that a work by the vanished Lollius was the source for his tale in *Troilus and Criseyde,* rather than his contemporary Boccaccio's *Filostrato*).

Whether a poet is part of the epic tradition also depends to a large degree on the fate of his language. Milton had the good fortune to write a great English epic just before Britain and then the United States became the dominant powers in the world. Were Brazil to become the dominant world power, who is to say that Camões would not be more familiar than Milton? Translation can help, but this, too, has its vagaries. The decline of Tasso's reputation in the English-speaking world, and the ascent of Dante's, is in part the result of an absence of any modern translation of *Jerusalem Liberated* as fine as the many contemporary englishings of *The Divine Comedy.*

The vagaries of literary survival and transmission are not the only reason that each epic poet has his own sense of the tradition. From the group of prior writers of epic, each major epic poet selects some to be models and neglects others. A poet's understanding of the epic poets who are great and, even more important, useful for his purposes, may not fit the critical consensus of succeeding generations, or even of his own. In the *Inferno* (4.86), Dante names himself as "sixth" in "that high company" that includes Virgil, Homer, Horace, Ovid, and Lucan. In *Troilus and Criseyde* (which is surely an epic), Chaucer describes himself as following in the footsteps of Homer, Virgil, Ovid, Lucan, and Statius.[2] Milton described the "diffuse epic" as "that epic form whereof the two poems of Homer, and those other two of Virgil and Tasso, are a . . . model."

Modern critics do not think that Ovid was writing in the same genre as Homer and Virgil. Today Tasso, one of the greatest poets of the Renaissance, is neglected, Lucan held in low esteem, and Camões and Statius utterly forgotten. Before we chuckle at the poor taste of our predecessors, however, we should recall that the contemporary conception of the epic pantheon widespread in the English-speaking world, as a trinity containing Homer, Dante, and Milton, dates back only

---

2. The Penguin Classics translation of Chaucer's bow to his epic predecessors — "Virgile, Ovide, Omer, Lucan, and Stace" — drops Lucan altogether — "Homer, Virgil, Ovid, Statius." In addition to being a shocking violation of the ethics of translation, this is proof of the depths to which the reputation of this Latin epic poet has sunk.

to the late Romantic era. Since Romanticism was largely a movement of cultural revolt centered in Protestant Germany and Britain and directed against French classicism and its Italian Renaissance sources, the Romantics naturally downgraded the status of Virgil (whom the French had tended to prefer to the "primitive" Homer) and of Tasso (the poet of Counter-Reformation Catholicism). Dante was exempted from the ban on the classical, the Catholic, and the Mediterranean only because his complex allegory appealed to the Romantics for all the wrong reasons, seeming to them fanciful and "sublime." Modernism finalized the canonization of Dante and the displacement of Virgil and the other Roman epic poets.

It is not my intent to propose an authoritative canon of epic poets to replace the orthodox Homer-Dante-Milton trinity inherited from the Romantics. The genuine epic tradition is defined anew by every major epic poet; there are as many canons as there are epic poets drawing on the works of predecessors whom they admire. If Tasso is part of our epic tradition, then Lucan becomes part of it too because Tasso draws upon Lucan, incorporating him by reference, as it were.

T o mention reference is to raise another subject of profound importance in understanding epic: allusion. Epic alludes to the past in several ways. There are, of course, textual allusions, which may be either allusions of detail (like the lifting of an epic simile from one poet by another) or design (the modeling of incidents or plots on examples in previous epics, like Virgil's combination of an "Odyssey" in the first half of the *Aeneid* with an "Iliad" in the second half).

Quite apart from these textual allusions, every epic, or at least every epic since Homer's, sets up an implicit comparison between the poet and previous epic poets, and between the poet's society and prestigious states and cultures of the past. Whatever their social and political values, most epic poets share the goal of proving that their societies are the equivalents or superiors of the most admired societies of antiquity (republican or imperial Rome, or Homeric Greece) and that their languages — Dante's *illustre volgare* — are equal to Latin and Greek as vehicles for great literature. In Dante, as perhaps in Tasso, the idea of the *translatio studii* is linked with the dream of the *translatio imperii,* the actual reunification of the nations of the West in a new Roman Empire under Emperor or Pope. In early modern Europe and the modern global state system, the "Augustan" impulse typically has been channeled not into a quest for universal political and cultural empire, but into the more modest enterprise of turning one's nation-state into one of many coexisting "New Romes." Milton expressed this vernacular cultural nationalism when he expressed his ambition that "what the greatest and choicest wits of Athens, Rome, or modern Italy, and those Hebrews of old, did for their country, I . . . might do for mine." In a postimperial, partly westernized world of sovereign nation-states, each nation may have its language and history ennobled by its own epic poets, who unite elements of a shared Greco-Roman tradition with indigenous, perhaps non-Western, literary traditions.

This assumes, of course, that both nations and national literatures will continue to exist, even in a world with a high degree of international commerce and intellectual exchange. The barriers of language alone will ensure that, even in the most united and homogeneous world, national literatures will be less like currents in an ocean than like lakes connected here and there by canals and locks. The works of a few authors, like Shakespeare, will become detached from their national cultures and become part of the common civilizational heritage of a variety of nations, if only in translation; many equally great authors like Goethe will remain little known, except by specialists, outside of the languages in which they wrote. Even within a family of nations sharing a common language — the English-speaking world, the Spanish-speaking family of nations — differences between national literatures will always exist because of different political, religious, and social histories, and even different landscapes. An English-speaking Texan, or Australian, or Western Canadian is unlikely to experience the same pleasure that an inhabitant of England feels on hearing Shakespeare's lines in *A Midsummer Night's Dream:* "I know a bank, whereon the wild thyme blows, / Where oxlips and the nodding violet grows / Quite over-canopied with luscious woodbine, / With sweet musk-roses, and with eglantine." North American and Latin American poets, however conservative they may be in their employment of English or Spanish poetic techniques, must find cognates in their own continent for the nightingale, the acanthus, the lion. Ultimately the Rockies and the Andes, the Mississippi and the Rio Grande and the Amazon, must become as patinaed with associations as Mount Olympus and Mount Fuji, the Jordan and the Rhine and the Ganges.

Literary intellectuals schooled by Romanticism and Modernism tend to be appalled by the idea that a national literature is something consciously constructed, from a mix of local and imported materials, on the model of prestigious foreign literatures, rather than something that arises spontaneously from individual genius or the national folk-soul. Indeed, what might be called the Augustan conception, in which a more or less codified system of literary genres, along with a code of laws and perhaps a model constitution, is "received" by a peripheral country from a metropolitan country or region, and then adapted to local conditions by means of appropriate excisions, additions, and modifications, has lost out in recent generations to the romantic version of literary nationalism. The two might be contrasted as national classicism and national romanticism. National classicism is the compromise between the cosmopolitan ideal of one global culture and national romanticism, that is, extreme xenophobic cultural nationalism or nativism. The national-classical ideal is a single civilization with many national cultures, related but distinct, like dialects of a language. National classicists want to adapt Mediterranean wine to new lands and climates; national romantics want no wine at all but pure springwater bubbling up from the untouched soil. National romanticism denounces classical form as Latin or French or European or cosmopolitan or Old World as opposed to Teutonic or American or New World. In the United States, national romanticism, identified with Walt Whitman, has tended to have a liberal and populist flavor. This is ironic because national romanticism is much more reactionary and parochial in its conception of literature than national classicism, which, though not necessarily cosmopolitan, is by definition pan-Western. The complement of national Romanticism in culture is usually fascism or some other form of xenophobic populism in politics.

Cultural Augustanism, then, is far from being an instrument of parochial or reactionary politics. Indeed, classicism in culture is a familiar accompaniment to reformist and revolutionary politics, both good and bad. The renovation of ancient models can lend dignity to (or disguise) the revolutionary's work of reforming or rejecting more recent or more local traditions. Similar classical traditions may be invoked to justify and ennoble quite different projects of reform. Bourbon absolutists and French republicans alike used the artistic languages of antiquity to lend solidity to their innovations. Revolutionary classicism has been employed both by republican radicals like Milton and Shelley and by innovating monarchists (in seventeenth-century France) and triumphalist defenders of the papacy (like Tasso during the Counter-Reformation). Dante the imperialist and Milton the Protestant republican were not merely artistic, but theological and political radicals, albeit of very different kinds.

Though it is sometimes said that epic is an "aristocratic" art form, its greatest appeal from the Renaissance until now has been to the foes of the feudal aristocracy — monarchists and republicans. The supporters of aristocratic values have found little appeal in epic, preferring the chivalric romance, and the country-house poem. The rejection of epic by the early Modernists in English like Eliot and Yeats, and their downgrading of the Miltonic and Romantic heritage, was linked to their reactionary political views and their anti-democratic conception of literature as an esoteric art for coteries of aristocrats or mandarins.

II

The implications of my argument for the subject of contemporary epic are obvious. If the question is whether it is possible to write a successful contemporary Homeric or Virgilian or Tassonian or Miltonic epic, the answer is clearly no. Such a poem would be a mere pastiche, an archaeological reconstruction, lacking the context of a living tradition. As we have seen, however, none of the great epics in the Western tradition have been pastiches of this kind. If the question is whether it is possible to blend conventions from epic predecessors with elements of living genres of fiction, drama, and cinema, and techniques of contemporary poetry, in the same way that Virgil and Dante and Tasso and Camõens and Milton renovated epic by hybridization, the answer is clearly yes. Such creative renovation of the form is as possible in the twentieth century as it was in the sixteenth, or the first century B.C.; and it will be possible in the thirtieth or fortieth century, if there are writers and audiences who still value works that allude to the tradition of Homer and his successors. If a modern epic fails, the failure must be blamed on the author, and not "an age too late."

Against this argument it will be objected that not only epic verse, but any narrative poetry, is somehow obsolete. By the end of the twentieth century, Dana Gioia has observed, "The panoply of available genres would seem reduced to a few hardy perennials which poets [have] worked over and over again with dreary regularity — the short lyric, the ode, the familiar verse epistle, perhaps the epigram, and one new-fangled form called the 'sequence' which often seemed to be either just a group of short lyrics stuck together or an ode in the process of falling apart." Today "poem" and "lyric" tend to be treated as synonyms.

For two and a half millenia, Western critics considered either epic or tragedy the chief literary genre. The peculiar idea that the lyric poem is the highest — perhaps the *only* — form of poetry appeared for the first time in the nineteenth century. According to John Stuart Mill, "Poetry is feeling, confessing itself to itself in moments of solitude." From this definition followed the conclusion that lyric poetry is "More pre-eminently and peculiarly poetry than any other." An epic poem "in so far as it is epic . . . is not poetry at all," according to Mill, but merely a means for linking together a number of brief lyric passages that express the emotions of the poet, who is conceived of as a sort of human divining rod, given to fits of significant quivering. This was also the conclusion of Edgar Allan Poe: "I hold that a long poem does not exist." The reason is that "elevating excitement," the *raison d'être* of poetry, "cannot be sustained throughout a composition of any great length. After the lapse of half an hour, at the very utmost, it flags, fails, a revulsion ensues, and then the poem is, in effect, and in fact, no longer such." Samuel Johnson had written, "In every work, one part must be for the sake of others; a palace must have passages; a poem must have transitions." Ignoring this commonsensical observation, Poe held that an epic could be genuinely poetic "only when, losing sight of that vital requisite in all works of art, unity, we view it merely as a series of minor poems." Poe's attempt to redefine poetry along the lines of music results in contradiction, of course, inasmuch as a symphony produced on his principles would be nothing but a series of crescendos. (Poe was nothing if not consistent. Having concluded that epics were impossible, he proceeded to dismiss the novel as a genre and to declare that the short story is the highest form of prose fiction.)

Already in the nineteenth century the identification of poetry with lyric led Walter Savage Landor to inform a friend that "the greater part of Homer is trash." Nevertheless, the rising prestige of the lyric did not prevent Romantic poets from writing long narratives, odes, elegies, and dramas in verse. Keats, that master of the lyric, observed that the greatest "test of Invention" is "a long poem. . . . Did our great poets ever write *short* pieces?" Only with the triumph of Modernism did the lyric come close to driving the grander genres of poetry out of existence. Now that formerly insurgent Modernism has become the intolerant establishment, a prejudice against not only epic, but any kind of coherent narrative verse is the orthodoxy in the academy, publishing, and the prestige press. In recent years in the United States, however, there has been an impressive reaction against an exhausted Modernism, taking the form of a renascence of storytelling in verse in the work of Vikram Seth, Frederick Turner, Dana Gioia, Robert McDowell, Mark Jarman, David Mason, Frederick Feirstein, and many others. With the exception of Turner, who has written two remarkable science-fiction epics, most of the Americans in the New Narrative movement have avoided epic in favor of brief narratives in colloquial language in the tradition of Frost, Robinson, Jeffers, Wordsworth, and Crabbe. Even so, their work has made it easier, not only to appreciate the great epics of the past on their own terms, but to create new poems in the genre.

Temporary though it has been, the abdication of narrative by many major poets has appeared to give credence to the argument that the novel and cinema have usurped the domain of epic and other narrative verse. The argument is not new. As early as 1755, Fielding wrote, "I must confess I should have honoured and loved Homer more had he written a true history of his own times in humble prose, than those noble poems that have so justly collected the praise of all ages." Homer should have written novels! Matthew Arnold made a similar criticism of Virgil in his inaugural lecture as Professor of Poetry at Oxford. "*Is he adequate?* Does he represent the epoch in which he lived, the mighty Roman world of his time, as the great poets of the great epoch of Greek life represented them, in all its fullness, in all its significance?" Arnold was confused. Homer did not write about Greek civilization in his time, but about what was already a remote and idealized past. At any rate, the same criticism might be made of Shakespeare, none of whose tragedies or histories are set in Elizabethan England. Perhaps Shakespeare should have written novels about coming of age in Stratford.[3]

---

3. When Arnold tried to write an epic, it was not set in Victorian Britain or the British Empire, but in medieval Central Asia: *Sohrab and Rustum.*

The epic-to-novel argument is based on a misreading of literary history common in the English-speaking world, which holds that the novel was invented in the seventeenth or eighteenth centuries, by Fielding or Richardson or Defoe. Sometimes this is accompanied by the idea of the "death of the novel" and its replacement by silent movies, or television, or virtual reality, or the electronic medium of the moment. The fact is that "the novel," even more than "the epic," is a rubric for a variety of forms, many of which date to antiquity. There has never been a time, since the spread of literacy in antiquity, when epics were as common as prose romances or novels, for the simple reason that good epic verse is much more difficult to write than even highly artful prose.

Stories in verse have always coexisted with stories in prose, with verse usually being reserved for subjects of greater civic or religious importance. In any society in which verse exists as a technique for heightening and emphasizing language, writers will have the option of treating stories of particular significance to the community in verse. Epic poetry can no more be replaced by novels, or for that matter by lyric poetry, than civic centers and houses of worship and great libraries and museums can be replaced by houses and apartments and shopping malls. Indeed, there is no reason that the writer of a major epic should not be able to write a first-rate lyric, a good novel, and a fine play or screenplay, in the same way that an accomplished architect is able to design a capitol building, a single-family home, and a doghouse. Ancient tradition ascribes to Homer not only the *Iliad* and the *Odyssey* but a comic poem, the *Margites*. Virgil's fame would have been secure on the basis of his *Eclogues* and *Georgics*, even if he had never written the *Aeneid*. Shakespeare wrote tragedies, comedies, sonnets, and narrative poems. Literature is not divided vertically by occupational categories into novelists, poets, and playwrights, but horizontally between major writers and minor writers.

Major writers write in major genres — and sheer scale and complexity are part of the definition of a major genre. "Aristotle said that in order to be magnificent a literary work must have magnitude; after all, in one sense *great* and *large* are synonyms," observes the critic Gary Taylor in *Cultural Selection* (1996). "It is more difficult to create large works than small ones; larger works create more obstacles and therefore give a maker greater challenges — and more opportunities to dazzle us by seeming to overcome those obstacles effortlessly. Moreover, a large work is capable of far more complexity than a small one." In short, there are aesthetic as well as social reasons why immense epics like Homer's and Virgil's have been preserved in their entirety with loving care for more than two millenia, while most of the lyric poetry of antiquity survives only as isolated lines or phrases.

III

Epic, then, is available to writers today, as in any time, as a genre to be reinvented, not merely resurrected. A case can nonetheless be made that, although epic might be written successfully today, it should not be written, for moral or political reasons extrinsic to literature. Epic, it has been said, is un-Christian, militaristic, imperialistic, or (more narrowly) un-American.

Today's secular Western intelligentsia is unlikely to be concerned with the Christian objection to epic, but its historical importance makes it worth considering. Arguing in *A Preface to Paradise Lost* (1942) that the *Aeneid* really "symbolized the destiny of Man," C. S. Lewis concludes, "The real question is whether any epic development beyond Virgil is possible. But one thing is certain. If we are to have another epic it must go on from Virgil. Any return to the merely heroic, any lay, however good, that tells merely of brave men fighting to save their lives or to get home or to avenge their kinsmen, will now be an anachronism. You cannot be young twice. The explicitly religious subject for any future epic has been dictated by Virgil; it is the only further development left." What is really anachronistic, it can be argued, is not epic poetry, but rather Lewis's neomedieval Christian conception of epic. Lewis updates the long-discredited conception of Virgil as a predecessor of Christianity: "It is not thanks to the Fourth Eclogue alone that he has become almost a great Christian poet." In reality, Virgil was not a proto-Christian poet, and his epic is not an allegory. For Virgil, if not for St. Augustine and C. S. Lewis, Rome is not a symbol of the city of man; it is a real city, a real nation.

Christians are within their rights to view history as a comedy, in which the triumph of justice at the end of time has been assured from the beginning. For those with such a worldview, what Lewis calls "the merely heroic" is trivial. If, however, one does not share such a reassuring faith, then the merely heroic cannot be so easily dismissed. The sack of a city or the founding of a state is of profound importance, if it is your city, or your state. Even if it is not, the fact that we can be moved by the suffering and triumph of nations not our own means that the "merely heroic" is of universal interest. What is more, not only the fate of individual nations, but of civilization itself may depend on prowess in arms. It was the "merely heroic" efforts of the democracies and their allies that prevented the world in the twentieth century from being dominated by a militarized German or Soviet Europe. Hitler was defeated, and Stalin deterred, by armies, not by prayers.

Christians of all persuasions, finding themselves in government, have almost always found it necessary to employ, and justify, the military and diplomatic means that Christian pacifists condemn. At any rate, Christians who believe in a God capable of angrily drowning almost all of humanity in a flood and planning from eternity for his son by a human woman to be tortured to death are not very convincing when they decry the immorality of Zeus. After rejecting the Arthurian stories of courteous knights as too frivolous and immoral as a subject for an epic, Milton wrote a tragedy about Samson, a barbarian who slaughters more opponents than Achilles and finally commits suicide in order to annihilate innocent women and children along with Philistine men — all according to the will of Yahweh. In *Paradise Lost* (though not in *Paradise Regained*), Milton contradicts his stated preference for "the better fortitude / Of Patience and Heroic Martyrdom" rather than "Wars, hitherto the only Argument / Heroic deem'd," when he devotes the sixth book to a pseudo-Homeric War in Heaven, complete with chariots, in loyalty to epic precedent.[4]

Related to this disparagement of "the merely heroic" is the suggestion that the modern epic must be internalized. One sometimes reads that, with Milton, or Wordsworth, or Whitman, the intellectual or spiritual development of the poet — Blake's "mental fight" — replaced the struggles of warriors as the proper subject of narrative poetry of epic scope. The sequence of Achilles, Rinaldo, and Wordsworth (or Whitman) brings to mind Carlyle's unintentionally funny list of "heroes," which begins with the Norse god Odin and ends with Samuel "Dictionary" Johnson.

It simply is not true that moral courage is more important than physical courage, or in any way a substitute for it. Almost all of the examples of great moral courage that come to mind involve the danger of physical harm, like the nonviolent disobedience of Gandhi and King (both of whom fell to the bullets of assassins). Political dissent is courageous if its possible consequences include exile, imprisonment, torture, or execution — but not if they are limited to the denial of tenure, patronage, or friendship. One could write an epic about civil rights demonstrators, or prisoners of war, or labor organizers facing company goons, or "enemies of the people" in concentration camps. An epic poet can even write about himself, if he has experienced great adventures (like Camões) or participated in wars (like Ercilla). But an epic by a sedate and bookish poet about his own life or thoughts is impossible, except as a parody.[5]

---

4. The argument of some modern scholars that Milton actually intended the War in Heaven to be ludicrous is unconvincing; the incident is treated seriously in Milton's biblical sources, and the Son's victory would be meaningless if the rebel angels did not pose a serious threat.

5. The subject of Wordsworth's projected "epic," *The Recluse,* was to have been "the sensations and opinions of a poet living in retirement" that would "consist chiefly of meditations in the Author's own person." *The Prelude,* all that remains of this scheme, was to have borne the same relation to *The Recluse* "as the ante-chapel has to the body of a gothic cathedral."

Today the liberal objection to military epic is likely to be more influential than the older Christian objections to the form. Juan Luis Vives, a humanist scholar of the sixteenth century, claimed, "The name of Achilles enflamed Alexander, Alexander Caesar, Caesar many others: Caesar killed in various wars 192,000 men, not counting the civil wars." Defoe denounced "the Tyrannies, the horrid Desolations, the inhuman and unnatural Lusts, the Murthers, and other Crimes they committed." Richardson complained about the *Iliad:* "I am afraid this poem, noble as it truly is, has done infinite mischief for a series of ages; since to it, and its copy the Eneid [*sic*], is owing, in a great measure, the savage spirit that has actuated, from the earliest ages to this time, the fighting fellows, that, worse than lions or tigers, have ravaged the earth, and made it a field of blood."

This viewpoint was particularly influential in the early United States. The young John Quincy Adams was shocked when he read the *Iliad,* describing the Greek gods as "despicable beings" who thought nothing of "avenging a trifling injury, by the slaughter of thousands." Thomas Paine rejected the *Iliad* as "a book of false glory, tending to inspire immoral and mischievous notions of honor." In 1789, Benjamin Rush called for the elimination of classical studies from the American university curriculum, which "by enabling us to read agreeable histories of ancient crimes often lead us to imitate or tolerate them." Rush combined the offices of Savonarola and Cato when he wrote: "Were every Greek and Latin book (the New Testament excepted) consumed in a bonfire, the world would be wiser and better for it. 'Delenda, delenda est lingua Romana' should be the voice of reason and liberty and humanity in every part of the world." (Rush seems not to have been troubled by the paradox of denouncing antiquity in a classical language.)

The influence of epic on the great conquerors of antiquity was real enough; Alexander, for example, if Plutarch is to be believed, kept a copy of the *Iliad* under his pillow together with a dagger while campaigning. Napoleon adopted the counterfeit Scottish epic *Ossian* as his own.[6] Might Homer have spared the world many wars had he composed an influential epic about fishing? Curiously, the military monarchs of Sumer, Akkadia, Babylon, Assyria, Egypt, Persia, India, China, Japan, Mexico, and Peru devoted themselves to war and conquest, even though they knew nothing of Homer. Subsequent history has refuted the hope of eighteenth-century optimists that a republic like the United States would have no need for the art of war or the celebration of military prowess. In addition to suffering a postindependence invasion by Britain in the War of 1812 and a devastating civil war, the United States, to date, has fought numerous wars of imperial

---

6. "Alexander had chosen Homer for his poet . . . Augustus had chosen Virgil . . . As for me, I had nothing but *Ossian:* the others were taken." Napoleon is quoted in David Quint, *Epic and Empire* (1993).

conquest or regional domination, two world wars, and one cold war, that is, a world war fought indirectly by attrition and proxy. So long as states with liberal and republican constitutions have interests and ambitions that bring them into intense conflict with other states, liberal republics no less than monarchies and dictatorships will have to be prepared to fight wars and to celebrate valor and patriotic sacrifice. George Washington, the soldier who presided over the establishment of the first great liberal democracy of the modern era, owned a statue of Aeneas carrying his father Anchises out of the ruins of burning Troy.

The celebration of martial virtue in the service of legitimate ends by liberals and republicans must be accompanied by an unflinching acknowledgment of the costs of war. Here the best model among the epic poets is Homer, who can describe the emotions of men and women in wartime and clinically analyze the wounds that bring agony and death with a terrifying clarity. Homer is no less a national poet than Virgil; he was probably employed by a king who claimed descent from one of his heroes. Even so, the impartiality of Homer in the *Iliad* is as genuine as it is famous. An epic may, like the *Aeneid* and *Jerusalem Liberated,* be a tale of manifest destiny; but the example of Homer shows that it need not be. A tragic epic in the manner of the *Iliad* will commemorate a war important to the poet's people without romanticizing combat and without identifying the success or defeat of the rival sides with the design of Providence. Epic should neither idealize nor vilify war, but treat it as what it is — a perennial part of the existence of human communities, in which what is best and worst in human nature is shown in sharp relief.

IV

The objection that epic is un-American, then, is easy to refute if by "American" one means liberal or democratic. I have already dealt with the kind of literary nativism that claims that epic along with other Old World forms must somehow die out on this continent, as some eighteenth-century French philosophes claimed European people, animals, and plants would inevitably wither away in the insalubrious Western Hemisphere. The question of whether an American epic can be written has already been settled by Joel Barlow and Stephen Vincent Benét.

Joel Barlow's *The Vision of Columbus* (1787; recast in 1807 as *The Columbiad*) was the first best-seller in the United States. Even in Barlow's day, the poem was more often bought than read; Thomas Jefferson (who wanted Barlow to write a pro-Republican history of the United States) praised the book's ornate binding, but confessed he could not find the time to read the poem. George Washington sent a copy of *The Vision of Columbus* as a gift to an acquaintance with the accompanying note: "Genl Washington takes the liberty of offering his respectful compliments to Mrs. Penn — and the Vision of Columbus. — It is one of several copies for which he subscribed some years ago and received since he came to this city. — To the merit, or demerit of the performance, the General can say nothing — not having had time to read it."

The Columbiad is boring because of Barlow's decision to write a visionary encyclopedic epic, rather than a historical epic. A radical Jeffersonian and well-wisher of the French Revolution, Barlow spoke for many critics of ancient epic during the Enlightenment when he complained that "Vergil wrote and felt like a subject, not a citizen" and argued that Homer's "existence has really proved one of the signal misfortunes of mankind" because of Homer's tendency "to inflame the minds of young readers with an enthusiastic ardor for military fame." Barlow's pacifist political philosophy denied him the usual subject of epic, warfare, and left him with no option but to write an encyclopedic, visionary poem, which like most such extended visions is a stilted pageant. Shelley and Hugo were great poets, but no one reads *Queen Mab* or *La Légende des siècles*. A verbal mural portraying the progress of humanity is doomed to be dull. Visions tend to be more exciting in life than in poetry. Most readers, unfortunately but understandably, skip two thirds of Dante and a good half of Milton. Barlow's Columbus speaks for many readers of encyclopedic epic when he begs the pedagogic Angel: "Unfold no more; but grant a kind release, / Give me, 'tis all I ask, to rest in peace."

Stephen Vincent Benét worried that his American historical poem would be "the most colossal flop since Barlow's *Columbiad*." His anxiety was unfounded. *John Brown's Body* (1928) sold hundreds of thousands of copies, was read by Raymond Massey on the radio, and won the Pulitzer and Guggenheim prizes. Three generations after its publication, Benét's highly readable and intelligent poem remains in print. Despite its weaknesses, *John Brown's Body* is likely to be read outside of the academy long after the extended poems of the Modernists — Eliot's *The Waste Land*, Pound's *Cantos*, Williams's *Paterson* — have been forgotten.

For all its virtues, *John Brown's Body* lacks the coherence of classical epic. Benét hesitated to call *John Brown's Body* an epic, calling it a "cyclorama" or a "long poem." *John Brown's Body* is a "closet movie" in the sense that Thomas Hardy's *The Dynasts* is a closet drama. Like Hardy chronicling the Napoleonic Wars in *The Dynasts*, Benét ignores the commonsensical rules of thumb (not dogmas!) of classical epic — a dominant character; a short time span; concentration on a few episodes; a single, unifying verse form — and opts for a looser and more cinematic treatment, which fails to make a lasting impression in the memory precisely because the parts obscure the design, if any, of the whole.

Once a qualified exception is made for Benét, the rest of the history of American epic can be summed up in the observation that heretofore the best American poets have not written epic, and the American poets who have written epic have not been the best. Longfellow and a few other nineteenth-century Americans had the skill to write an American epic. Later, E. A. Robinson and Robert Frost possessed the means; so did the leading Southern Fugitives, like Robert Penn Warren, Allen Tate, and David Donaldson. All of these poets wrote substantial narratives in both traditional and unusual verse forms. Why were they not drawn to epic?

The answer has to do with both literary fashion and the regional and class prejudices of American literary elites. With respect to the first, it is enough to note that, with the exception of the Federalist period, the history of the United States to date has been more or less coterminous with the history of Romanticism and Modernism. During the nineteenth and twentieth centuries, the legendary and historical epic had fallen into disfavor among the advanced writers and critics of the entire Western world. The Romantic encyclopedic epic, as the comprehensive vision of human history, had not; and it is surely significant that Longfellow, alert to the trends in transatlantic civilization, not only translated Dante but attempted a kind of encyclopedic epic of his own, a counterpart to Hugo's, in his three-part cycle of plays about Christianity. While the vision, that familiar element of epic tradition, expanded until it shattered the frame of narrative in the Romantic epic, the subjects of legendary and historical epic continued to be treated by major poets, but seldom in classical epic form. (That tended to be done, badly, by minor poets.) Most of the significant narrative poets of the nineteenth century, reacting against neoclassicism, looked away from classical antiquity and the Renaissance to models found in the Middle Ages, the Dark Ages, and non-Western traditions. Tennyson called his great Arthurian poems "idylls," not epic. Swinburne and Morris retold medieval legends and Viking sagas in styles that owed little to the Greco-Roman legacy. Goethe, Browning, and Hardy chose closet drama, rather than epic, as their preferred vehicle for legendary or historical narratives. Though Longfellow's *Evangeline* is in the English equivalent of Homeric hexameters, it is a melodramatic romance, like Goethe's "bourgeois epic" *Hermann und Dorothea,* not an epic (although the scene of the burning of Grand Pré shows what Longfellow might have done, had temperament and worldview not led him to shrink from the depiction of combat that is at the heart of classical epic). For his most sustained work of legendary narrative, *Hiawatha,* Longfellow chose the style of primitive Finnish folk poetry. The irony that the great age of narrative poetry, the nineteenth century, was the Dark Ages of classically inspired epic seems even greater when one reflects that the most successful sustained narrative in the manner of Tasso and Ariosto was Byron's mock epic, *Don Juan.*

On Epic

The legendary and historical epic, in neoclassical and Miltonic forms, appealed not to the advanced writers in the nineteenth-century United States, but to less sophisticated Americans whose tastes were a generation or two behind those of intellectuals like Longfellow. As John McWilliams points out, "Between Timothy Dwight's The Conquest of Canaan (1785) and Alfred Mitchell's The Coloniad (1858) at least nineteen epic poems were completed and published by American authors." A boomlet in heroic poetry also attended the Columbian quatercentennial: "John Campbell's Republica (1891), Henry Iliowizi's Quest of Columbus (1892), Samuel Jefferson's Columbus: An Epic Poem (1892), John Howell's Columbus (1893), and Franklyn Quinby's The Columbiad (1893)."[7] It is easy to sneer at the various "Columbiads" and "Booniads" and "Mexiads." William Faulkner's grandfather, in the fashion of the conquistador-poets of Spain and Portugal, wrote an inadvertently comic Homeric pastiche about his own Mississippi regiment's adventures in the Mexican War in which Jefferson Davis appeared as "Jeff the Bold." Even more preposterous was the *Fredoniad* of Dr. Richard "Pop" Emmons, at 33,000 lines — twice that of a Homeric epic — possibly the longest epic poem ever written, and possibly the worst. In this *reductio ad absurdum* of messianic Jacksonian ideology, the goddess Fredonia — a sort of animated Miss Liberty — repeatedly intervenes on behalf of the valiant Americans in a series of battles with British and Indians, who are helped out by Satan and his minions. (One imagines the epic staged outdoors in the manner of Tchaikovsky's *1812 Overture*, complete with cannon and fireworks.) These poems failed because their authors were crude and imitative poets who simply poured American content into the molds of *Paradise Lost* or Pope's and Dryden's translations without that reinvention of the genre which every major epic poet has accomplished.

Though the minor epic poets of nineteenth-century America were not up to the task they had imposed on themselves, there was nothing wrong with their choices of subjects for legendary or historical American epics. They were correct in thinking that these should be stories of broad interest that were already familiar to their compatriots. As Emerson observed, "The poet needs a ground in popular tradition on which he may work, and which, again, may restrain his art within the due temperance. It holds him to the people, supplies a foundation for his edifice; and, in furnishing so much work done to his hand, leaves him at leisure, and in full strength for the audacities of his imagination." Just as Tasso and Spenser, in their different ways, gave classical form and dignity to the subjects of chivalric romance, which humanist intellectuals in their era regarded with contempt, so the contem-

---

7. No historical figure appears to have inspired more epic verse than Columbus. Tasso devotes two stanzas of *Jerusalem Liberated* to his encomium of Columbus.

porary American epic poet should work his transformative magic on the apparently worthless materials of popular fiction and cinema.

The most appropriate subjects for an American legendary epic, it can be argued, are familiar tales from the Bible, chivalric romance (in its modern form as post-Tolkien fantasy fiction), and science fiction. All three are flourishing genres of popular fiction (including Christian fiction, though it is neglected by secular critics). All three can provide contemporary epic poets with subjects equal to the Matter of Troy or the Matter of Romance, subjects already somewhat familiar to readers. The American legendary epic, it should be noted, is a legendary epic written by an American; its subject need not have any particular connection with America. Nor, for that matter, need the American historical epic, which might take its subject from any part of the globe, at any time, from the Ice Age to the present. The epic of American history — a division, as it were, of the American historical epic — *does* require an American subject.

Most of the successful epics in a tradition now three millenia old have been historical, even if the historical characters and events they described were as shrouded with legend as those of Homer and Virgil (Achilles and Aeneas, it is important to remember, were thought to have been historic individuals). We may think of Lucan as a historical poet and Homer and Virgil as mythological poets, but the ancients did not make this dichotomy. Tasso, defending his choice of a historical subject, the Second Crusade, in his *Discourses on the Art of Poetry,* made an argument on behalf of historical epic in general: "Considering [stories] false, people do not so easily consent to being moved now to wrath, now to terror, now to pity — or to being, by turns, delighted, saddened, held in suspense or in rapture. In sum, they do not follow the sequence of events with the same expectation and delight as they would if they deemed that sequence true, either wholly or in part." A historical foundation is not a drawback because an epic's "novelty does not principally consist in the subject's being invented and unheard of before but in the novelty of the plot's crisis and its resolution." What is more, the successful historical epic (unlike the legendary or mythological) is usually based on national history and saga. The *Iliad* and the *Odyssey* are not just poems in Greek by a Greek, but poems about Greek history. The *Aeneid* is the epic of the founding of the Roman nation; the *Lusiads,* of the founding of the Portuguese maritime empire. An American can write a historical epic on a non-American subject; but it will lack the communal significance of an epic by an American about the history of the American nation.

Tasso is equally persuasive in writing of the historical periods in which the poet can find the best subjects: "histories of times neither very modern nor very ancient do not entail the annoyance of outmoded customs nor deprive us of freedom for invention." For Tasso in the 1560s, "the times of Charlemagne and Arthur and those which either preceded or succeeded them by a little" were best; for modern Americans, it can be argued, the comparable period that is "neither very modern nor very ancient" is that of the "heroic age" of North American history, between the voyage of Columbus and the consolidation of the modern states of the U.S., Canada, and Mexico just after the American Civil War (by "heroic," I am referring only to violent and chaotic — and thus dramatic — social conditions). The four great sources of subjects for epics of American history, it can be suggested, are the homeland wars, that is, the wars with the French, Indians, British, and Mexicans for the present-day American homeland; the civil wars (the American Revolution having been more of a genuine "civil war" than the War Between the States); the bloody history of American slavery, which provides battles in the form of insurrections and adventure in the form of slave escapes; and the exploration and settlement of the territory of the United States. That these subjects, until now, have not attracted American poets of the first rank says less about their suitability for heroic poetry than about the regional and political biases of the American literati.

The United States has had not one, but two great literary intelligentsias — the New Englanders of the nineteenth century, and the Southerners of the twentieth. For reasons having less to do with art than with politics, the poets of New England and the South have been unsympathetic to obvious subjects of American historical epic like the wars with the French and the Mexicans. Postbellum Southerners, for obvious reasons, were not going to write poems about the defeat of the enemies of the Union. Similarly, New England Brahmins, dwelling in a territory long since taken by force from French and Indian opponents, indulged themselves by condemning the war with Mexico and romanticizing Indian nations that were safely debellated.[8] The exceptions prove the rule. Longfellow in *Evangeline* issued a sort of retroactive apology for the defeat of the French, and issued another to the Indians in *Hiawatha*. Perhaps it is no accident that the two greatest failures of Longfellow the New Englander and of Robert Penn Warren the Southerner are their poems taking the side of Indians so idealized as to be insipid — Hiawatha and Chief Joseph. The author of a heroic poem may sympathize with the defeated rivals of his nation; he cannot, however, *prefer* them to his own people, without

---

8. During the Mexican War, Nathaniel Hawthorne sneered: "*Is* old Joel Barlow still alive? Unconscionable man! Why, he must have nearly fulfilled his century! And *does* he meditate an epic on the war between Mexico and Texas, with machinery contrived on the principle of the steam-engine, as being the nearest to celestial agency that our epoch can boast?" His friend and fellow New Englander Melville, though, noted the potential of frontier folklore, remarking that Hercules was "an antique Crockett."

falling into a fallacy as reprehensible as chauvinism. Homeric impartiality is not to be confused with jingoism in reverse. As Abraham Lincoln once observed, a woman could objectively determine who was winning in a fight between her husband and a bear without alternately shouting, "Go, husband!" and "Go, bear!"

To the parochial regionalism of the historic American literati, the pride of class and caste must be added as a reason for the absence of major American epic on national themes. Snobbery, more than any other single factor, prevented the composition of epics on modern themes in early modern Europe; Voltaire observed that the word "colonel" could not be used in an epic without making the elite of his day laugh. Hegel and Toqueville both predicted that citizens of the United States, freed from such extraliterary inhibitions, would produce magnificent epics of the common man (a category including colonels without hereditary titles). They failed to perceive that the democratization of American politics would not necessarily be accompanied by an alteration of the oligarchic constitution of the American intelligentsia, whose ranks — editors and publishers more than writers — have always been disproportionately made up of downwardly mobile children of the rich, for whom literature is less a calling than a caste credential. From the Connecticut Wits, who railed against artisans and Irishmen, to the *soi-disant* left of the post–World War II era, whose members have been so pathetically eager to prove that they are "highbrow" and not "middlebrow," members of every generation of the American literary elite have posed as a saving remnant in a mobocracy on the verge of destroying civilization. (In every generation, civilization, somehow, has survived.)[9]

An American historical epic, whether based on war, slave escapes, or frontier exploration, requires sympathetic, though not sentimental, portrayals of the very sorts of people whom the American literati have tended to despise. In "Monadnoc," Emerson writes that among mountaineers, "I thought to find the patriots / In whom the stock of freedom roots." Instead, ascending the mountain he discovered "a churl, / With heart of cat and eyes of bug, / Dull victim of his pipe and mug." The Brahmin concludes by wishing genocide for the rural proletariat of Massachusetts: "But if the brave old mould is broke, / And end in churls the mountain folk, / In tavern cheer and tavern joke, / Sink, O mountain, in the

---

9. The very distinction between "highbrow" and "lowbrow" — popularized in the early twentieth century by Van Wyck Brooks — has more to do with American class anxieties than with universal aesthetic criteria. As Brooks noted to his astonishment in 1915: "I have proposed these terms (highbrow and lowbrow) to a Russian, an Englishman, and a German, asking each in turn whether in his country there was anything to correspond with the conceptions implied in them. In each case they have been returned to me as quite American, authentically our very own."

swamp! / Hide in thy skies, O sovereign lamp! / Perish like leaves, the highland breed! / No sire survive, no son succeed!"[10] Emerson could no more write an epic featuring Daniel Boone or David Crockett than T. S. Eliot could write one whose heroes were Jewish immigrants or Irish longshoremen.

In the twentieth century, the alienation of American poets from the lower orders has been even more extreme. American poets and critics in the twentieth century have tended to be either downwardly mobile Anglo-American gentry, or upwardly mobile European-American scholarship students. The former dominated American poetry until the fifties (perhaps even later, depending on how one assesses the influence of the Merrill Lynch heir James Merrill in the poetry world). The leading figures of high Modernism, T. S. Eliot and Ezra Pound, both hated the United States so much they not only became expatriates, but renounced their citizenship, like Henry James. Eliot's *The Waste Land* contains references to many nations and regions of the world — and, by design, not one allusion to his native country. The Southern Agrarians/Fugitives, responsible for the New Criticism, regretted being governed from Washington instead of Richmond. Expatriates and neo-Confederates alike agreed that the United States was very far from the model of an ideal Anglo-Saxon, Christian, and rural society, free if possible of both Jews and blacks (Allen Tate regretted the absence of a deferent white peasantry in the South). They were naturally sympathetic to antidemocratic and anti-American reaction abroad. Eliot was influenced deeply by Charles Maurras; Pound became a voluntary propagandist for Mussolini and Hitler. Robert Lowell, a déclassé Brahmin, refused to serve in World War II, on the grounds that it was an unjust war. His moving in with Allen Tate, at one point, symbolized a union of two declining regional elites against the rest of American society.

The second half of the twentieth century saw the displacement of the Anglo-American literati by first- and second-generation European-American literary intellectuals, usually on the political left. One would have expected that this infusion of new blood would have resulted in a rejection of the esoteric mandarin literature cultivated by anti-Semites, fascists, and neo-Confederates, in favor of a vigorous and popular art wedding American vernacular traditions with European folk and art traditions. Indeed, something like this happened, on Broadway and in Hollywood, both largely the creation of immigrant Jews. In American poetry, however, the new intelligentsia all too often took over and extended the coterie culture of the expatriates and Southerners. Appreciation of abstruse poetry, visual

---

10. As Thomas Disch suggests in *The Castle of Indolence* (1995), one would give a great deal "to have a proper, gossipy account of Emerson's contretemps with the churls of Monadnoc."

art, and music served to distinguish ambitious scholarship students from their relatives in the tenement district, Little Italy, or the rural hinterland, and, moreover, was awarded by the Anglo-Americans — many of them reactionary Southerners teaching in northern universities — in whose power tenure rested. This explains the curious fact that the postwar educational enfranchisement of the American masses, following the triumph of American arms, and the partial triumph of American ideals, in World War II, failed to produce an efflorescence of confidently national and democratic art, of the sort foreshadowed in some of the work of the New Deal era. Instead, the G.I. Bill and the Fulbright program and the Rhodes scholarship turned hordes of Jewish, Italian, Irish, and German Americans into imitation Englishmen, often with British accents as acquired as those of Eliot and James. Rugged veterans of World War II returned to Europe as Fulbright Fellows and wrote precious poems about Italian villas and English summer houses. The Beats who rebelled against this kind of tweedy formalism belonged to the same academic coterie, which has now perpetuated itself for several generations on the campuses of universities with "creative writing" programs.

In *The Genteel Tradition at Bay,* George Santayana remarked on the contrast between the robustness of American vernacular culture and society and the preciosity of the Atlantic seaboard literati. Almost a century later, the situation has hardly changed. To American academic intellectuals whose status depends on their skill in interpreting the esoteric, ironic lyrics of mid-twentieth-century fashion, as to the displaced blue bloods from whom they inherited Modernist poetics, the very idea of an epic in rhyming stanzas about an American historical event like the battle of the Alamo is a challenge not merely aesthetic but social.

V

Samuel Johnson observed that "The subject of an epic poem is naturally an event of great consequence" such as "the destruction of a city, the conduct of a colony, or the foundation of an empire." All three topics are included in the subject of *The Alamo.* That subject is the Texas Revolution, the critical event in the complex and gradual takeover of northern Mexico by Anglo-Americans which culminated with the Mexican War and fixed the territories of the two major nation-states of North America. This is not a story of merely regional interest. The history of Texas is of crucial importance to the history of the United States; the history of the United States, to that of modern global civilization.

Inasmuch as the Texas Revolution is one of the formative episodes in the history of the American nation-state, it will possess a continuing relevance to all Americans, no matter their race or ancestry, who take an interest in the past of their nation. Popular fascination with American history from Jamestown to the twentieth century did not diminish when the descendants of recent European immigrants came to outnumber old-stock Anglo-Americans in the white population. It is not unreasonable to expect that the projected nonwhite or mixed-race majority of North America a century or two from now will consider all of American history, and not just that pertaining to predecessors of their race, ethnic group, or religion, to be "their" history.[11]

The story of the Alamo has inspired not only dozens of historical accounts, novels, movies, and plays (including a feeble play in pseudo-Shakespearean blank verse by the antebellum Southern novelist William Gilmore Simms), but impressive quantities of unimpressive verse. The earliest poem on the subject that I have been able to discover appeared in the New Orleans *Commercial Bulletin* shortly after the battle: "Vengeance on Santa Anna and his minions / Vile scum, up boiled from the infernal regions . . . / The offscouring baseness of hell's blackest legions, / Too filthy far with crawling worms to dwell / And far too horrid and too base for hell." As recently as 1979, in a small-press poem entitled *The Alamo* by one Viola Riley Berry, one can find similar sentiments in similar verse: "Then, like a demon near the gates of Heaven, / Who sees their bliss but cannot mar its joy, / Who hear their song borne on the breath of eve'n [*sic*] / Peans [*sic*] of triumph which nothing can alloy, / . . . [Santa Anna] determines to quench it by the power of his might . . ."

This kind of jingoism has not gone uncontested. An event as central in American history and consciousness as the battle of the Alamo has naturally inspired battling interpretations. It is sometimes said (usually by those who do not know Texas very well) that the story of the Alamo is "nothing but" a racist myth, serving the white-supremacist interpretation of America's westward expansion as the providential progress of a superior people. Though this interpretation was set forth sometimes in the nineteenth century, Texans themselves have seldom linked the Texan war with the saga of Anglo-American pioneers elsewhere in the west. Instead, in Texas the war with Mexico has usually been treated as a repetition of the American Revolution, with Santa Anna taking the place of King George — ironically, it must be said, for Santa Anna fits the model of a tyrant much more

---

11. A few years ago, after the airing of a TV drama that incorporated the battle of the Alamo, I happened to hear three office workers in Manhattan — one black American, one Puerto Rican American, and one Italian American — discussing the battle in terms of "us" Americans. "*We* had Long Rifles, and *they* only had muskets," the black American explained, identifying imaginatively with nineteenth-century white Southerners who were part of *his* nation — even though they would have denied that he was part of theirs.

closely than the much-maligned British monarch. In other words, for most An-
glo- and Euro-American Texans, the Texas Revolution was not "about" the west-
ward expansion of the American people, but rather it was "about" liberal democ-
racy versus dictatorship. Nor did this traditional historical myth conflate Mexicans
and American Indians as comparable barbarians who stood in the way of white
progress (as revisionists sometimes allege). Rather, Mexicans, or at least the Mexi-
can Creole elite, were considered a people incapable of sustaining republican
institutions — an incapacity which they shared, in the eyes of generations of
Anglo-Americans, with French and Russians and Spaniards. Their incapacity for
democracy was attributed as much to the debilitating effects of Catholicism or
Orthodoxy and monarchy as to bad genes. This was self-serving and chauvinist
Anglo-American mythology, to be sure, but it is mythology of a quite different
kind from that which informed the relations of white Americans and Indian
nations, to say nothing of the myths governing the relations of white and black
Americans.

In rejecting the traditional Texan myth of the Texas Revolution as a replay of
the American Revolution, revisionists have recently promoted an equally mislead-
ing account of the Texan War of Independence as a version of the conquest of
Third World nations by European colonialists. It will not do, however, to replace
one cartoon version of history with another — and not just because General Santa
Anna resembled Gandhi far less than he resembled King George. For one thing, a
majority — about three out of four — of the settlers in Texas at the time of the
revolt were Anglo-American or European immigrants. For another, the Mexican
province of Yucatán seceded around the same time as Texas, and existed, like
Texas, as an independent republic for about a decade before being reannexed by
Mexico. Earlier the Central American states — Guatemala, Honduras, and Sal-
vador — had seceded from Mexico. If Texas (and California) were "stolen" from
Mexico, then the Central American republics must be considered Mexican *irre-
denta* as well. The fact is that the borders of empires and republics in North
America were in constant flux between the arrival of Columbus and the consolida-
tion of the present boundaries of the United States, Canada, and Mexico in the
middle of the nineteenth century, and it does violence to language and logic to
speak of the cession, sale, or conquest of thinly populated territories like those of
Texas, California, and Alaska using the same terms that describe the imposition of
rule by foreign minorities on indigenous majorities. North American Indian na-
tions, to be sure, have cause for complaint — but it was probably inevitable that
they would come under the rule of one or another European or white-settler
government in the nineteenth century. From the Indian viewpoint, of course, the
Mexicans are conquerors as much as the Americans and the British and French
in Canada.

The circumstances of the Texas Revolution, then, prevent it from being described accurately as "imperialism," in the modern sense of the term, as the conquest and domination of a majority nationality by a nationality that is at least a local minority. The closest parallel to the struggle for the present-day southwestern United States during the Texas Revolution and the Mexican War can be found in the much more lethal South American War of the Triple Alliance (1864–70) that left Paraguay shorn of much of its territory. I do not mean to deny that the United States has engaged in classical imperialism, nor to suggest that such imperialism can be justified or celebrated. The brutal American conquest and occupation of the Philippines, and the overthrow of the Hawaiian monarchy by American planters, *do* fit the conventional definition of imperialism, and unlike the Texas Revolution and the Mexican War should be remembered with regret by contemporary Americans.[12]

The truth about the Texas Revolution, then, is not simple. Neither is it single. Among the Texan leaders there were American nationalists who sought to turn Texas into a new state, or states, annexed to the U.S.; Southern imperialists who wanted to expand the zone of slavery in North America; a few who genuinely wanted to found an independent republic; and, at least among the *Tejanos,* in the beginning, some who wanted Texas to remain in Mexico under a restored liberal and federalist constitution. The motives of ordinary Texans were just as diverse. There were long-settled farmers who fought to protect their families and properties from the invading army, and opportunistic soldiers of fortune from the U.S. and Europe out for land and glory. There were *Tejanos* who supported rebellion, and Anglo settlers who favored rapprochement with the Mexican government. In *The Alamo,* I have attempted to do justice to all of these various, and often conflicting, factions.

In addition, I have tried to do justice to the role of the *Tejanos* in the revolution. In the old days, Anglo-Texan historians tended to ignore figures like the Vice-President of the Texas Republic, Lorenzo de Zavala, and the Seguin family. In

---

12. My great-grandfather Richard Augustus Hearon, one of the first deans of Southern Methodist University in Dallas, Texas, wrote "A Plea for the Filipinos": "O my brother! Why this carnage? / Why the blood you daily pour / From the life-cup of your manhood / On this distant alien shore? / Do you seek to conquer peoples / Fiercely struggling to be free, / Battling, as your fathers battled / Foeman from across the sea?" In the same year that my great-grandfather wrote his poem, 1899, a much more accomplished poet, Rudyard Kipling, praised American imperialism in "The White Man's Burden," subtitled "The United States and the Philippine Islands": "Take up the White Man's burden — / Send forth the best ye breed — / Go bind your sons to exile / To serve your captives' need; / To wait in heavy harness / On fluttered folk and wild — / Your new-caught, sullen peoples, / Half devil and half child."

recent years, the reputation of these *Tejano* leaders has not been helped by the reassessment of Texan history by the politically correct left, which has tended to view them as upper-class "collaborators" with "the enemy," that is, the Anglo-Texans. For radical Mexican Americans, the leading *Tejanos,* being mostly rich white landowners, were not "authentic" Mexicans, that is, mestizo or Indian "Chicanos." Taken to an extreme, this approach would render any account of the Texas Revolution suspect, unless it were from the perspective of impoverished and powerless *Tejanos* who would be exploited whether Santa Anna or Houston won.

Ironically, the degradation of the Mexican Creole elite by the revisionist left is strikingly similar to the vilification of the same class by traditional Anglo-American Protestant historians. For centuries, Anglo-Americans, British, and Dutch have spread the "black legend" of Spain, which holds that the Spanish empire, embodying the worst aspects of Catholicism and despotic monarchy, committed one of the greatest atrocities in history in its conquest of the Aztecs. Long before today's multicultural left began idealizing American Indians, Anglo-American Protestants were bemoaning the fate of the enlightened philosopher-prince Montezuma at the hands of that despicable Catholic, Hernan Cortés, and his band of ruffians. In reality, of course, Cortés was able to conquer Mexico only because he mobilized a revolution by the Indian nations whom the Aztec military caste oppressed. It is doubtful that anyone lacking an unjustifiable animus against the Spanish, or Catholics in general, would be distressed by the obliteration of a Neolithic empire resting on war and human sacrifice by Renaissance Spaniards, vicious though the latter could be. So deeply rooted, though, is the *leyenda negra* in the Anglo-American Protestant imagination, that William Prescott's magnificent epic history, *The Conquest of Mexico,* was attacked by many of Prescott's fellow Americans when it was published, for being too kind to the Spanish and too unsympathetic to the Aztecs.[13]

In the twentieth century, the romanticization of the Indian and the derogation of the Spanish heritage by *indigenista* Mexican intellectuals has added a new version of the black legend to the old Northern European Protestant version.[14] To

---

13. In Viola Riley Berry's *The Alamo,* the Anglo-Texans are actually compared to the Aztecs, as similar victims of Spanish American Creole oppression: "These monuments of ancient worth, / In ruin still august and grand, / Bear testimony of the truth / Of Montezuma's glorious reign, / And Austin felt that bond sublime . . . So looked he back in sympathy / To him who died without a sign, / Upon a bed of burning coals, / A victim of Spain's cruelty."

14. The greatest Mexican thinker of the twentieth century, José Vasconcelos, never made the mistake of identifying vice or virtue with one or another of the strains that have gone into the making of a mestizo nationality, *la raza cosmica.*

compound the irony, Santa Anna, since the Mexican Revolution, has been treated as a villain in Mexico as well as Texas, though for different reasons; he is blamed for retarding Mexican progress in the era following Mexican independence. One need not be a defender of the Mexican Creole aristocracy from which Santa Anna sprang — that equivalent of the Southern planters or the German Junkers — to doubt that all of the problems of Mexico can be blamed plausibly on one class, much less on one individual. In *The Alamo*, I have presented what I believe is the fairest and most objective portrait of this charismatic *caudillo* to be found in historical fiction. One can only wonder whether the General would have appreciated the irony that the least unsympathetic portrayal of him in literature would be in an epic about the Alamo by a sixth-generation Texan.

L ike the major epics of the past, *The Alamo* is the product of an act of synthesis. In the poem, elements from classical and Renaissance epic are blended with the realism of the historical novel, the pace of cinema, and the vividness of imagery characteristic of the best Romantic and Modernist lyric poetry. The stanza, evocative of medieval and Renaissance Provençal and Italian verse, is the rhyme royal stanza used by Chaucer and Shakespeare for narratives. In its design, the poem follows the model of Virgil's *Aeneid*, which combines an "Odyssey" in its first half with an "Iliad" in its second half. The first third of *The Alamo* follows the linked but episodic adventures of its hero, William Barret Travis; the remaining two-thirds are devoted to the siege and battle of the Alamo. This division in the action corresponds to the distinction between what Spenser, in his letter to Raleigh about *The Faerie Queene*, described as the moral virtues (those of an individual hero) and the politic virtues (those of a commander and leader of a community). The supernatural "machinery" is limited to the allegorical figure of La Llorona, the Weeper, a character from the contemporary folklore of Mexican Americans and Mexicans along *la frontera*. The use of such a figure as a Muse was suggested by the employment of the Furies in *Troilus and Criseyde* by Chaucer (who got the idea from the invocations to Tisiphone and her sister Furies in the *Thebaid* of Statius).

In *The Alamo*, I have attempted to avoid repeating the mistakes that made Barlow's American epic a failure and compromised the success of Benét's. The digressive and visionary parts of the poem are strictly subordinated to the story — a tale of real people in the midst of a real war. The poem is unified in form, and no attempt is made to portray the Texas Revolution in its entirety. *The Alamo* begins *in medias res* at the point at which the hero's fortunes are at their lowest ebb. For Travis, this occurs when his second attempt to launch a revolution is repudiated by a transient majority of his fellow Texan colonists and he is forced to go into hiding not only from the Mexican authorities, but from his neighbors. The poem ends with the death of Travis and his troops. Voltaire, noting that "the *Iliad* ends with the death of Hector, the *Aeneid* with that of Turnus," complained that "the tribe of commentators have upon that enacted a law that a house ought never to be finished, because Homer and Virgil did not complete their own; but if Homer had taken Troy, and Virgil married Lavinia to Aeneas, the critics would have laid down a rule just the contrary." The ending of *The Alamo* is justified not by precedent, but by the fact that the subject of the poem is not the war as a whole, but merely the part played in the Texas Revolution by William Barret Travis and the soldiers he commanded.

I have followed history closely, although in the interest of drama or clarity I have occasionally employed the accepted devices of historical fiction, such as the omission of insignificant detail and the invention of minor scenes. In choosing between varying accounts of what happened at the Alamo, I have used plausibility, not dramatic value, as the criterion. For example, I have not included the well-known scene of Travis drawing the line in the sand for his troops to cross because it almost certainly never happened. The tale was told in 1873 by William P. Zuber, a veteran of the Texas Revolution who was also one of the prodigious liars of Texas history. In 1877 Zuber admitted that he had invented Travis's supposed speech, and also "threw in" one paragraph that made a better story — no doubt the one describing the line in the sand. Susannah Dickinson, prompted by reporters years after Zuber's tale became famous, later claimed to remember the incident — but she put it on the first day of the siege (she had never mentioned the supposed incident before Zuber wrote about it).

Quite apart from its tainted source, the tale of the line in the sand can be rejected because of its absurdity. Are we to believe that Travis took all of the pickets from the walls of the Alamo, to give them a chance to cross the line? If not, how were the pickets given the choice of staying or trying to escape? But there is a more serious objection. If Travis drew the line in the sand on March 4, the night before the battle, then the choice he offered his men was no choice at all. The couriers had barely been able to get in and out of the Alamo through enemy lines; by March 4, few if any of the Texan rebels would have been able to escape, even at night. The appropriate response by the members of the Alamo garrison to the offer Travis is supposed to have made would have been bitter laughter. Aristotle thought that, in poetry, a probable impossibility was preferable to an improbable possibility. The story of Travis's line in the dust is an improbable impossibility.

Zuber claimed to have been told the story by the French immigrant Louis Rose, who was supposed to have recuperated at his parents' farm after escaping from the Alamo. There really was a Louis Rose, a fifty-year-old veteran of Napoleon's campaign in Russia who fought in the Battle of Bexar in the winter of 1835 when the Texan forces captured San Antonio. He lived until 1850 in Texas and Louisiana, telling anyone who asked why he had not stayed at the Alamo, "By God, I wasn't ready to die." Because he could not have taken an offer to escape by Travis that Travis never made, his departure from San Antonio must have occurred before the arrival of Santa Anna's army, during the siege, or during the battle. It is inconceivable that Travis would not have raised an alarm about a French deserter heading eastward in his letters to his fellow Texans. It is possible that Rose fought in the battle and survived somehow. It seems most likely, though, that he left before or during the investment of San Antonio and was never in the Alamo at all. In the poem, Rose flees as the Mexican army arrives.

How David Crockett died at the Alamo has been another subject of sometimes bitter debate. In Hollywood versions of the Alamo story, Crockett always goes down swinging, in his trademark coonskin cap. From the beginning, though, there have been accounts that Crockett was personally executed by Santa Anna, who is known to have ordered the execution of half a dozen or so Texan prisoners. (Some accounts in the months and years following claimed Crockett was still alive in the mines of Mexico and would return — evidencing their nature as folklore, like tales of the disappearance and future return of other national heroes like King Arthur and Barbarossa.) The accounts of Crockett's execution, appearing in pro-Texan U.S. newspapers, are suspect, given their evident purpose of inflaming hostility toward a Santa Anna who personally ordered the cold-blooded murder of an American celebrity. What is more, a confrontation between Santa Anna and Davy Crockett looks suspiciously like a cliché from the sort of historical fiction that arranges to have the famous figures of an era or a war meet — "President Wilson, allow me to introduce Pablo Picasso."[15] The fact that William Zuber is a source of one of these tales of Crockett's execution should make us even more suspicious (Zuber also has Bowie surviving the battle and giving a lecture on democracy to a Mexican officer, who cuts out Bowie's tongue and burns him alive on the funeral pyre of the other Texans).

In recent years, historians have claimed that tales of Crockett's execution have been vindicated by the alleged diary of the campaign in Texas of Colonel José Enrique de la Peña, who fought at the Alamo and in 1839 wrote (but never published) a pseudonymous document denouncing Santa Anna for executing prisoners. "Among those had been a man who pertained to the natural sciences, whose love of it conducted him to Texas, and who locked himself up in the Alamo

---

15. One charming Alamo legend has Santa Anna himself sneaking into San Antonio in disguise before the invasion and infiltrating the Texan fandango.

not believing it safe by his quality of foreigner, when general Santa Anna surprised Bejar." This does not sound very much like Crockett, unless hunting bears is thought to have constituted scientific research. Nor does it fit the attested behavior of Crockett, a veteran of the Indian wars. "The Hon. David Crockett was seen at all points animating the men to do their duty," Travis wrote in his dispatch from the Alamo on March 24, 1836. Finally, if De la Peña meant Crockett, why did he not mention him by name? Although Mexican officers might not have been familiar with Crockett before the battle, by 1839 De la Peña would be well aware of the American celebrity who died at the Alamo.

In the recently published "diary" ascribed to De la Peña, the cryptic account in his 1839 manuscript is elaborated upon:

> Some seven men had survived the general carnage and, under the protection of General Castrillon, they were brought before Santa Anna. Among them was one of great stature, well proportioned, with regular features, in whose face there was the imprint of adversity, but in whom one also noticed a degree of resignation and nobility that did him honor. He was the naturalist David Crockett, well known in North America for his unusual adventures, who had undertaken to explore the country and who, finding himself in Bejar at the very moment of surprise, had taken refuge in the Alamo, fearing that his status as a foreigner might not be respected. Santa Anna answered Castrillon's intervention in Crockett's behalf with a gesture of indignation and, addressing himself to the sappers, the troops closest to him, ordered his execution.

One of the leading authorities on the battle of the Alamo, Bill Groneman, has made a persuasive argument that the De la Peña diary, like many manuscripts connected with the Texas Revolution, is a modern hoax, possibly perpetrated by the late John A. Laflin, a master forger whom some believe to have fabricated a famous letter from the Alamo defender Isaac Millsaps to his blind wife.[16] If the diary is authentic, it is possible that De la Peña padded his own recollections with accounts gleaned from American newspapers of the alleged surrender of Crockett and also the heroic death of Travis, which the diarist implausibly claims to have witnessed.

If either of these possibilities is the case, then the most reliable account of Crockett's death is that of Susannah Dickinson, who told one J. M. Morphis: "I recognized Col. Crockett lying dead and mutilated between the church and the two story barrack building." This is believable; Dickinson and the other women

---

16. Bill Groneman, *Defense of a Legend: Crockett and the De la Pena Diary* (Plano, Texas: Republic of Texas Press, 1994). See also Gregory Curtis, "Forgery, Texas Style," *Texas Monthly* (March 1989).

and children would have been led out of the chapel by Mexican officers through the area that Crockett and the other Tennesseans were assigned to defend, between the palisade, the chapel, and the two-story building that housed the hospital and the Long Barracks. Revisionists to the contrary, then, the best evidence supports the conclusion that David Crockett did not surrender but died fighting at his assigned post in the Alamo. Perhaps it does not matter much, in the final analysis; the likelihood that Crockett, like most of the other defenders, was bayoneted makes the distinction between death in battle and death upon surrender somewhat less clear than a stark contrast between heroism and cowardice. The four hundred Texan soldiers who were massacred in cold blood at Goliad on Santa Anna's orders after they surrendered on assurances of good treatment were no less courageous for the manner of their deaths.

While I have followed history closely, *The Alamo* is not intended to achieve the comprehensiveness of the encyclopedic epic. Those who wish to learn about "Optics and Astronomy, Botany, Metallurgy, Fossilism, Chemistry, Geology, Anatomy, Medicine" — Coleridge's idea of what a proper epic ought to include — as well as those who want God's ways to be justified to men, will have too look elsewhere.[17] It is a flaw of the epics of Milton and of Spenser that they require readers far more erudite than even the sophisticated audiences of Virgil and Lucan, to say nothing of Homer's audience. Virgil presumes an acquaintance with two sets of myth and history — the Greek and the Latin-Roman — and with Mediterranean geography. Spenser and Milton retain these preconditions, while adding onerous new requirements — a detailed knowledge of the Hebraic-Christian tradition, of chivalric lore in Spenser, and, in Milton, all sorts of recondite (and, by now, mostly obsolete) scientific and geographic learning. To their contemporaries, Spenser and Milton were much more difficult to understand than Virgil was to his readers and listeners.

In *The Alamo*, I have attempted to write an epic that is as accessible to Americans with a general education as the *Aeneid* was to educated Romans. Much of what seems exotic to us in Virgil would not have seemed so to his fellow Romans. To non-American readers, or future generations of Americans, a reference to Tennessee whiskey may seem as exotic as an allusion to Falernian wine. In this connection, there is more to be learned from Spenser's naturalizing of the eclogue

---

17. For example, to Victor Hugo's *The Legend of the Ages,* which includes, among other characters, Eve, Mohammed, and Napoleon. In his encyclopedic epic, Hugo sought, according to his preface, "To express humanity in a sort of cyclical work; to depict [humanity] successively and simultaneously in all its aspects — history, fable, philosophy, religion, science, all of which reduce to a single and immense movement of enlightenment."

in the rural Britain of his day than from the archaeologically correct pastiches of Pope and other neoclassicists.

In the early years of the American republic, an educated audience would have had little problem recognizing allusions to Scipio Africanus or Cato or Cincinnatus; by the mid-nineteenth century, the situation had changed, and it seems unlikely that the lesser figures of Greco-Roman lore and history will ever again be familiar to educated American readers. Most biblical lore is now as remote to Americans as Babylonian mythology was to Romans of Virgil's day (the exception being the minority of contemporary American Protestant evangelicals who are intimately familiar with the Bible). To allude to any figures less familiar than Caesar or Samson is to write for the professoriat, not the public. Where I have done so, the context usually provides sufficient explanation.

In place of now-recondite classical and biblical lore, I have employed familiar North American and global history, and drawn much of my imagery from the fauna, flora, and landscape of North America, particularly though not exclusively of Texas and the southwest. I have also drawn images from rural life, and the aspects of daily life that are least likely to be transformed as technology improves. The arcane knowledge prized by theorists of the encyclopedic epic could only mar a historical epic. The neoclassical prejudice against "terms of art" drawn from science and technology was justified. The suggestion that a contemporary poet should prove his contemporaneity by referring to contemporary appliances and contemporary theories of natural science, if followed, would render even a poem of the first rank dated and quaint in a very short time.

I have occasionally waived the rule against adverting to the unfamiliar when it comes to Mexican geography and history. It is a scandal that, for so many Americans, Mexico is simply a terra incognita, from which armies, bandits, and illegal immigrants have occasionally and unaccountably emerged, and not a great and long-suffering nation with whose destiny the fate of our own people will forever be entwined. A comprehensive glossary of personal and place names, including both the exotic and the familiar, follows this essay.

The Alamo is a public and commemorative poem about an event that is central to the consciousness and identity not only of Texans, but of all Americans who share in the national culture. In the spirit of the architect of a war memorial, I have worked into the narrative at least one mention of every Alamo defender whom current scholarship identifies, as well as, in some cases, biographical information and anecdotes about the soldiers that historians have discovered.[18] I have also done the same for a number of Mexican soldiers, all of whom, except for the

---

18. Bill Groneman's study, *Alamo Defenders* (Austin, Texas: Eakin Press, 1990), has been an indispensable resource. No roster of those present at the Alamo can be definitive.

officers, are invented — a necessity because of the lack of documentation on the Mexican side. The number of individuals thus mentioned is lower than the sum of those named by Homer in the *Iliad,* according to C. B. Armstrong in *Greece and Rome* 16:30–31 (1969). "The named casualties of officers total 238, and unnamed 26. Other ranks are not recorded." It seems appropriate, in an epic about volunteers fighting to found a republic, to commemorate the enlisted men as well as the officers whose decisions drove events. After all, *The Alamo* is the epic of the extraordinary ordinary man whose creation in America Hegel and Tocqueville predicted.

GLOSSARY

This glossary includes all of the proper names of people, places, animals, and items that appear in *The Alamo*. Spanish words that have not been anglicized are also given. The titles of characters are those they possessed at the time of the Battle of the Alamo.

Only the first appearance of the name or word is given, by book, stanza, and line number within the stanza. For example, 6.77.7 refers to the seventh line of the seventy-seventh stanza in Book Six.

The names of Mexican characters should be given their Mexican-Spanish pronunciation. Place names in Texas that have been anglicized, however, are given their anglicized pronunciation. Thus the final "e" is dropped in pronouncing the names of the Rio Grande and Guadalupe Rivers, and Anahuac is AN-a-wak, not ah-NAH-wahk.

Hiatus — the following of a vowel by a vowel — is to be avoided by elision, where indicated by the meter. For example, in most places "the Alamo" should be read as a "cretic foot" of one unstressed syllable enclosed by two stressed syllables: "Thyalamo."

The name of Santa Anna in most cases should be pronounced as three syllables, with the stress on the second: Sahn-TAHN-a. In a few instances, it should be pronounced with four syllables: SAHN-ta AHN-a. The position of the name in the line provides the appropriate metrical cues.

Similarly, depending on its placement in the line, New Orleans may be pronounced as a dissyllabic word — NAH-luns — or a trisyllabic word — New AH-luns. It is never pronounced New Or-lee-uns.

The states in which cities in the United States are located are identified. The same practice is not followed in the case of cities in Mexico, because the boundaries of Mexican states are not necessarily the same now as they were in the 1830s.

AARON (5.28.1) Brother and spokesman for Moses in the Bible.

ABAMILLO, JUAN (11.18.6) Alamo defender.

ACAPULCO (6.56.7)   City in Mexico.

ACCADIA (7.41.1)   French ("Cajun") Louisiana.

ACHAEAN (6.17.7)   Term for a Greek in the epics of Homer.

ADAM (3.26.1)   First human being, according to the Bible.

ADELITA (7.54.1)   Soldier's lover in a traditional Mexican ballad.

aguador (7.4.1)   (Sp.) Water vendor.

ALABAMA (2.6.1)   State in the Southern United States.

ALAMO, THE (1.11.5)   Fortress in San Antonio, Texas. Originally a Spanish Franciscan mission, called San Antonio de Valera, the Alamo was converted into a fort by the Spanish imperial government in 1793. A company of Indian-fighting Spanish cavalry, the Second Flying Company of San Carlos de Parras, gave the fort the name of their hometown in Mexico, Alamo (Cottonwood).

alcalde (1.8.6)   (Sp.) Mayor.

ALEXANDER (5.64.7)   Alexander the Great (355–323 B.C.) Macedonian monarch who conquered much of the ancient Mediterranean and Middle East.

ALLEN, ROBERT (11.18.7)   Alamo defender.

ALMONTE, COLONEL JUAN (1.10.4)   Aide to Santa Anna.

ALSBURY, HORACE (8.21.3)   Texan settler, absent from San Antonio when his wife, Juana, was trapped in the Alamo with the Texan garrison.

ALSBURY, JUANA (7.18.3)   Alamo survivor and wife of Horace Alsbury.

AMADOR, GENERAL JUAN (10.17.1)   Mexican officer.

AMAT, GENERAL (9.33.4)   Mexican officer.

AMAZON (12.54.5)   River in South America.

ANAHUAC (1.43.6)   Town on the Texas coast (anglicized pronunciation: AN-a-wak).

ANAYA, AMBROSIO (9.46.1)   Mexican soldier.

ANDRADE, JUAN JOSÉ (6.14.4)   Mexican officer.

ANDROSS, MILES (11.4.4)   Alamo defender.

ANGELINA DICKINSON (7.11.3)   Alamo survivor; daughter of Almeron and Susannah Dickinson.

ANTICHRIST (5.53.5)   False messiah to appear during the Last Days, according to Christian prophecy.

ANTIETAM (12.41.6)   Battle of the U.S. Civil War.

APPOMATTOX (12.42.2)   Town in Virginia; site of courthouse where General Robert E. Lee surrendered to General Ulysses S. Grant in 1865, ending the U.S. Civil War.

AROCHA, ANTONIO CRUZ (5.45.1)   Texan cavalryman who rode with Seguin as a courier from the Alamo after the siege had begun.

ARREDONDO, GENERAL JOAQUIN DE (1.11.6)   Spanish General who crushed the attempt of Texas to secede from then-Spanish Mexico in 1813. In his ranks was a nineteen-year-old Lieutenant named Santa Anna.

AUNT BEA (8.64.5)   Relative of Joe.

AUSTIN, JOHN (2.35.5)   Texan settler; veteran of the filibustering expeditions of James Long.

AUSTIN, STEPHEN (1.27.7)   The most important of the impresarios who brought Anglo-American and European settlers to Texas, and one of the most influential leaders of the Texas Revolution.

AUTRY, MICAJAH (10.57.1)   Alamo defender.

AZTECS (6.59.6)   Native American nation that governed much of present-day Mexico until overthrown by Spanish invaders.

BADILLO, SERGEANT JUAN (10.10.6)   Alamo defender.

BAILEY, PETER JAMES III (10.58.4)   Alamo defender.

BAKER, CAPTAIN WILLIAM CHARLES M. (8.43.7)   Alamo defender.

BAKER, ISAAC G. "IKE" (11.48.5)   Alamo defender.

BALLENTINE, JOHN J. (10.70.1)   Alamo defender.

BALLENTINE, RICHARD W. (12.17.6)   Alamo defender.

BAUGH, CAPTAIN JOHN J. (8.42.4)   Alamo defender; adjutant to Travis.

BAYLISS, JOSEPH (11.2.7) Alamo defender.

BEAST (5.53.7) Satanic being in the Christian Bible's Book of Revelation.

BEXAR (1.11.4) City of San Antonio, Texas (full name, San Antonio de Bexar), or the surrounding county of Bexar.

BEXAR GUARDS (8.43.6) Unit of the Texan Alamo garrison.

BLAIR, JOHN (11.4.3) Alamo defender.

BLAIR, CAPTAIN SAMUEL (11.15.1) Alamo defender.

BLAZE (4.4.2) Wild mustang.

BLAZEBY, CAPTAIN WILLIAM "BILL" (8.43.3) Alamo defender.

BONAPARTE, NAPOLEON (5.21.5) French military dictator who conquered much of Europe in the late eighteenth and early nineteenth centuries. The model for Santa Anna, who called himself the "Napoleon of the West."

BONHAM, COLONEL JAMES BUTLER (2.3.2) Alamo defender.

BOONE, DANIEL (4.37.7) Celebrated eighteenth-century American frontiersman.

BOOTES (8.67.3) A constellation.

BOURNE, DANIEL "DAN" (10.37.4) Alamo defender.

BOWIE, COLONEL JAMES "JIM" (4.40.1) Also Don Santiago (Sp. for James), 5.6.1. (1795–1836) Alamo defender; cocommander of the Alamo garrison; influential Texan leader. A self-made planter from a poor family in Lousiana who entered the slave trade as a partner of the pirate Jean Laffite, Bowie became famous as a duelist, using the Bowie knife that his brother Rezin invented. In the early 1830s he moved to San Antonio and married Ursula Veramendi, the daughter of the Vice Governor of Coauhila-Texas. Most of the Veramendi family, including Ursula, died in the cholera epidemic of 1833.

BOWIE, URSULA (7.19.6) Wife of James Bowie; d. 1833.

BOWIE KNIFE (3.30.5) Unique knife that Rezin Bowie invented and that Jim Bowie made famous.

BOWMAN, JESSE B. (12.22.1) Alamo defender.

BRADBURN, COLONEL JOHN DAVIS (1.59.5) American-born commander of the Mexican garrison at Anahuac in 1832.

BRAZORIA (2.35.4)   Town on the Brazos River in East Central Texas.

Brazoria (2.46.4)   Ship used by the Texan rebels in the Battle of Velasco in 1832.

BRAZOS (3.33.2)   Brazos de Dios. River in Texas.

BRINDLE (4.3.5)   Wild mustang.

BRISCOE, ANDREW (.58.4)   Texan settler.

BROTHER LOU (6.53.6)   Character in one of David Crockett's tales.

BROWN, GEORGE (10.44.2)   Alamo defender.

BROWN, JACOB (12.19.5)   U.S. general; uncle of Alamo defender Samuel B. Evans.

BROWN, JAMES "JIMMY" (12.27.2)   Alamo defender.

BROWN, ROBERT (7.42.3)   Member of the Alamo garrison; sent out as a courier, he survived the fall of the Alamo.

BUCHANAN, JAMES (12.17.5)   Alamo defender.

BUCKNER, STRAP (2.45.1)   Texan settler killed in the Battle of Velasco.

BURLESON, GENERAL EDWARD "ED" (4.16.6)   Texan officer.

BURNS, SAMUEL E. (10.37.6)   Alamo defender.

BURR, AARON (3.38.4)   Vice President of the United States, 1801 to 1805. Accused of treason against the United States for plotting a filibustering expedition into Mexico, but acquitted. An ally in Burr's scheme who betrayed him, General James Wilkinson of the U.S. Army, was a relative of Jane Long, a central figure in the subsequent Anglo-American attempts to seize Texas from Mexico.

BUSTAMANTE, GENERAL ANASTASIO (1.31.7)   Mexican military dictator, 1830–1832. Overthrown by Santa Anna.

CAESAR, GAIUS JULIUS (1.25.3)   The popular Roman military leader who established a personal dictatorship. His assassination in 44 B.C. by a group of senators led to a civil war, in which his nephew Octavian triumphed. Octavian, renamed Augustus Caesar, preserved republican forms but effectively turned Rome into a despotic monarchy. The title Caesar was adopted by subsequent Roman Emperors, as well as post-Roman monarchs (Kaiser, Tsar).

CAIN, JOHN "JOHNNY" (10.70.3)   Alamo defender.

CAMPBELL, ROBERT (10.65.2)   Alamo defender.

CANALES, HIPOLITO (9.13.1)   Mexican soldier.

CAREY, CAPTAIN WILLIAM R. (7.14.3)   Alamo defender; chief of the Texan artillery company nicknamed "The Invincibles."

CAROLINA (2.3.4)   South Carolina; state in the Southern United States.

CASTRILLON, GENERAL MANUEL, 5.38.4   Mexican officer.

CATORCE, 9.47.3   Town in Mexico.

caudillo, 1.10.1   (Sp.) Strong man; political boss; military dictator.

CENTAURUS, 8.66.2   Constellation.

CHAPULTEPEC (12.38.5)   Fortress overlooking Mexico City; site of a battle during the war between the United States and Mexico (1846–1848).

CHARLESTON (2.3.3)   City in South Carolina, United States

CHAVEZ, MARIANO (9.43.4)   Mexican soldier.

CHEROKEE (1.33.4)   Native American nation resident in what became the Southern United States. Sam Houston was an adopted member of the Cherokee nation.

CHURUBUSCO (12.38.5)   Town in Mexico. Site of a battle during the Mexican War.

CICERO, MARCUS TULLIUS (1.25.6)   Roman republican statesman, orator, and man of letters, assassinated on the order of the triumvir Mark Antony in 43 B.C.

CIRCE (2.40.6)   In Greek mythology, an enchantress who turned men into animals.

CLAIBORNE (4.53.2)   Town in Alabama where Travis lived before he moved to Texas in 1831, leaving behind his wife, Rosanna, his son, Charles Edward, and an unborn daughter.

CLARK, CHARLES HENRY (10.4.1)   Alamo defender.

CLARK, M. B. (10.39.1)   Alamo defender.

CLOUD, DANIEL W. (7.6.2)   Alamo defender.

COAHUILA (1.11.2)   State in Northeastern Mexico. Until the Texas Revolution, Texas was officially a province of Coahuila.

COCHRAN, ROBERT E. (11.10.6) Alamo defender.

COLT, SAMUEL (6.41.1) American inventor of the revolver.

COMANCHE (4.58.3) Comanch; member of a Native American nation that frequently warred with the settlers in Texas and Northern Mexico and other Native American nations in the eighteenth and nineteenth centuries.

CONSTITUTION OF 1824 (4.21.6) After Mexico won its independence from Spain in 1821, a Mexican General, Agustín de Iturbide, installed himself as Emperor in 1822, only to be deposed in 1823 and executed in 1824. The constitution of 1824 established a liberal republican government for Mexico — at least on paper. In the 1830s, rebels against centralizing, authoritarian governments in Mexico, including some Texan revolutionaries, at times claimed that their goal was the restoration of the liberal 1824 constitution.

CONSULTATION (4.24.2) Interim government of revolutionary Texas.

CORINTH (5.22.6) Ancient Greek city.

corrido (4.49.6) Mexican ballad.

CORSICA (5.22.1) Island off the Italian coast; birthplace of Napoleon Bonaparte.

CORTÉS (6.60.7) Spanish conqueror of Mexico.

COS, GENERAL MARTIN PERFECTO DE (1.11.1) Mexican officer.

COTTLE, GEORGE WASHINGTON (8.7.5) Alamo defender.

COURTMAN, HENRY (11.11.2) Alamo defender.

CRAWFORD, LEMUEL (11.4.3) Alamo defender.

CRETE (6.60.2) Island in the Aegean. According to Greek mythology, King Minos of Crete demanded a tribute of youths from Athens who were sacrificed to the Minotaur, a monster that was half human and half bull.

"CRIPPLE CREEK" (6.70.7) American folk tune.

Cristero (12.43.1) Catholic rebels against the anticlerical government of Mexico in the 1920s.

CROCKETT, COLONEL DAVID (4.37.7) (1786–1836) Alamo defender; American frontiersman and folk hero; member of the U.S. House of Representatives. Like Will Rogers in the twentieth century, the "Congressman from the

Canebrake" became a celebrity by personifying the plain-speaking, wise-cracking, crude but decent American democrat. A Whig from Tennessee, Crockett was defeated in a congressional election by President Andrew Jackson's Democrats. In 1835, after telling the voters who had turned him out of office "Y'all can go to hell; I'm going to Texas," Crockett set out for Texas hoping for a new start.

CROSSMAN, ROBERT (11.3.2)   An Alamo defender.

CUBA (3.5.5)   Island in the Caribbean.

CUMMINGS, DAVID P. (11.49.7)   Alamo defender.

CUMMINGS, REBECCA (2.5.1)   Texan settler; lover of William Barret Travis.

CUNNINGHAM, ROBERT (11.63.3)   Alamo defender.

DARST, JACOB "JAKE" (8.8.2)   Alamo defender.

DARST, MARGARET (8.8.2)   Texan settler, wife of Jacob Darst.

DAVIS, JOHN (11.49.1)   Alamo defender.

DAY, FREEMAN H. K. (10.50.3)   Alamo defender.

DAY, JERRY C. (11.48.7)   Alamo defender.

DAYMON, SQUIRE (10.70.4)   Alamo defender.

DEARDUFF, WILLIAM (11.45.7)   Alamo defender.

DEFIANCE, FORT (3.50.6)   Fortress on Galveston Island where Jane Long, her daughter, and her slave Kian spent the winter of 1819 to 1820 during the filibustering campaign against Mexico led by her husband, James Long.

Deguello (1.5.3)   Mexican bugle call, signaling No Quarter.

DELLET, JUDGE JAMES (4.54.3)   Mentor of the young Travis in Claiborne, Alabama.

DENNISON, STEPHEN "STEVE" (11.29.3)   Alamo defender.

DESPALLIER, BLAZ (7.41.2)   Texan soldier; brother of Charles Despallier.

DESPALLIER, CHARLES (7.41.2)   Alamo defender; brother of Blaz Despallier.

DEWALL, LEWIS (10.39.2)   Alamo defender.

DEWITT, EVALINE (8.12.3)   Texan settler.

DIABLO (7.37.5) Bowie's horse, borrowed by Juan Seguin during his trip through enemy lines after the siege of the Alamo began.

DICKINSON, LIEUTENANT ALMERON (7.11.1) Alamo defender.

DICKINSON, ANGELINA ELIZABETH (7.11.3) Alamo survivor; infant daughter of Almeron and Susannah Dickinson

DICKINSON, SUSANNAH ARABELLA (8.19.5) Alamo survivor; wife of Almeron Dickinson; mother of Angelina.

DILLARD, JOHN HENRY (12.27.5) Alamo defender.

DIMKINS, JAMES R. (11.29.7) Alamo defender.

DIONYSIUS (5.23.6) Tyrant of ancient Syracuse; overthrown by Timoleon of Corinth.

DOÑA PETRA (7.37.6) Petra Gonzales. James Bowie's maid.

DORSETT (11.35.4) Texan settler.

DRACO (8.70.3) Constellation.

DUQUE, COLONEL FRANCISCO (9.22.1) Mexican officer.

DUVALT, ANDREW (11.3.6) Alamo defender.

EAGLE ISLAND (2.49.6) Plantation of Texan settler Jared Groce.

EIRE (10.37.7) Ireland.

escopetas (5.45.6) Muskets used by Mexican army.

ESPALIER, CARLOS (10.50.5) Alamo defender.

ESPARZA, ANNA SALAZAR (8.19.3) Alamo survivor; wife of Gregorio Esparza and mother of Enrique Esparza.

ESPARZA, ENRIQUE (8.62.6) Alamo survivor, aged eight. One of four children of Gregorio and Anna Esparza who survived the Battle of the Alamo by hiding in the mission chapel. The others were Francisco (three), Manuel (five), and Maria de Jesús Castro Esparza (ten).

ESPARZA, FRANCISCO (7.15.2) Mexican soldier; brother of Gregorio Esparza.

ESPARZA, JOSÉ "GREGORIO" (7.15.3–4) Alamo defender

EVANS, ROBERT (8.44.7) Alamo defender.

E V A N S, S A M U E L B. "S A M" (12.19.1)   Alamo defender.

E W I N G, J A M E S L. (9.19.6)   Alamo defender.

F A B I U S (12.32.3)   Quintus Fabius Maximus Verrucosus. Roman republican leader whose strategy of wearing out Hannibal's invading Carthaginian army while avoiding direct confrontations earned him the title Cunctator (Delayer). George Washington in the American Revolution, and Sam Houston in the Texas Revolution, both employed "Fabian" strategies.

F A N N I N, C O L O N E L J A M E S (8.30.7)   Commander of the Texan garrison at Goliad.

F A U N T L E R O Y, W I L L I A M K E E N E R (10.58.3)   Alamo defender.

F I N K, M I K E (4.37.7)   Fabled American frontiersman of the early nineteenth century.

F I S H B A U G H, W I L L I A M (10.44.6)   Alamo defender.

F L A N D E R S, J O H N (11.51.1)   Alamo defender.

F L I C K (4.4.3)   Wild mustang.

F L I C K E R (4.4.3)   Wild mustang.

F L O Y D, D O L P H I N W A R D "D O L P H" (11.42.6)   Alamo defender.

F L O Y D, E S T E R B E R R Y H O U S E (11.54.7)   Texan settler; wife of Dolphin Floyd.

F O R G E (12.23.7)   Valley Forge; winter camp for George Washington's army during the American Revolution.

F O R S Y T H, C A P T A I N J O H N H U B B A R D (5.52.3)   Alamo defender.

F U E N T E S, A N T O N I O (5.7.3)   Alamo defender.

F U Q U A, G A L B A (11.68.2)   Alamo defender.

G A L L O, J U A N A (7.50.6)   (Sp.) "Juana Rooster." A Mexican *soldadera*.

G A L V E S T O N (3.39.4)   Island along the Texas coast.

G A O N A, G E N E R A L A N T O N I O (6.14.4)   Mexican officer.

G A L L A R D O, T O M A S (9.24.1)   Mexican soldier.

G A R N E T T, W I L L I A M (5.51.2)   Alamo defender.

GARRAND, JAMES W. (10.3.3)   Alamo defender.

GARRETT, JAMES GIRARD "JIMMY" (11.37.3)   Alamo defender.

GARVIN, JOHN E. (11.10.4)   Alamo defender.

GASTON, JOHN E. (10.65.2)   Alamo defender.

GASTON, SIDNEY (8.10.4)   Texan settler; wife first of Thomas Miller and then of Johnny Kellogg; sister of John E. Gaston.

GEORGE, JAMES (11.45.2)   Alamo defender.

GERTRUDIS (7.13.5)   Sister-in-law of James Bowie.

GETTYSBURG (12.41.7)   Battle of U.S. Civil War.

GNASHER (4.4.1)   Wild mustang.

GOLIAD (8.33.3)   Town in Texas; site of fortress and Texan garrison commanded by Colonel James Fannin during the siege of the Alamo. Two weeks after the fall of the Alamo, on March 20, 1836, Fannin surrendered, on condition that his men be treated as prisoners of war. Instead, on Palm Sunday, March 27, 1836, Fannin and almost all of his four hundred unarmed men were shot and stabbed to death on the orders of Santa Anna. The United States and several European powers denounced the massacre.

GONZALES (7.34.3)   Town in Texas.

GOODRICH, JOHN C. (10.12.6)   Alamo defender.

GRANICUS (5.64.7)   River in Asia Minor where Alexander the Great and his Macedonian army defeated the Persians under Darius in 334 B.C.

GRIMES, ALBERT CALVIN (10.13.5)   Alamo defender.

GROCE, JARED (2.48.7)   Texan settler.

GUADALAJARA (6.20.5)   City in Mexico.

GUADALUPE (12.14.4)   River in Texas.

GUANAJUATO (6.16.1)   City in Mexico.

GUERRERO, BRIGIDO (5.10.1)   Member of the Alamo garrison.

GUTIÉRREZ, BERNARDO (10.66.6)   Leader of the Texan revolt against Spain in 1813.

GWYNNE, JAMES C. (10.37.5)   Alamo defender.

H A I T I (3.5.5)   Island in the Caribbean.

H A N N U M, J A M E S (12.21.4)   Alamo defender.

H A R R I S, J O H N (10.5.1)   Alamo defender.

H A R R I S B U R G (1.64.6)   Town in Texas.

H A R R I S O N, A N D R E W J A C K S O N (12.17.2)   Alamo defender.

H A R R I S O N, C A P T A I N W I L L I A M B. "B I L L" (6.36.5)   Alamo defender.

H A W K I N S, J O S E P H M. (10.39.1)   Alamo defender.

H A Y S, J O H N C O F F E E "J A C K" (12.37.2)   Celebrated Texas Ranger who served in the period between the Texas Revolution and the Civil War.

H A Y S, J O H N M. (10.51.3)   Alamo defender.

H E C T O R (7.56.7)   Rooster.

H E I S K E L L, C H A R L E S M. (10.71.1)   Alamo defender.

H E R C U L E S (2.45.1)   Mythical strong man of ancient Greece.

H E R N D O N, P A T R I C K H E N R Y (10.50.3)   Alamo defender.

H E R O D O T U S (3.20.7)   Ancient Greek historian.

H E R R E R A, C A R L O S (9.45.1)   Mexican soldier.

H E R R E R A, J U A N (9.45.1)   Mexican soldier.

H E R S E E, W I L L I A M D A N I E L (11.8.4)   Alamo defender.

H E S S I A N S (3.4.5)   Mercenaries from the German state of Hesse, employed by the British government to fight the American colonists during the American Revolution.

H I D A L G O (2.28.7)   Father Miguel Hidalgo y Costilla. Mexican priest who helped to lead an abortive revolution against Spain in 1810. September 16, 1810, the day of the beginning of his uprising, is celebrated as Mexican Independence Day. In 1811, Hidalgo was defeated by Spanish forces and shot.

H I L L C O U N T R Y (12.2.6)   Region of West Central Texas to the north of San Antonio.

H O L L A N D, T A P L E Y (10.43.3)   Alamo defender.

HOLLOWAY, SAMUEL (10.3.7)   Alamo defender.

HORSESHOE BEND (1.36.3)   Site on the Tallapoosa River in Tennessee where U.S. forces under General Andrew Jackson fought the Creek Indian faction known as the Red Sticks in 1814. While storming the Red Stick barricade, young Third Lieutenant Sam Houston suffered a severe wound from an arrow that never completely healed.

HOUSTON, SAM (1.34.1)   (1793–1863) Commander in chief of the Texan army. A runaway who grew up among the Cherokees of Tennessee, Sam Houston returned to them when his marriage collapsed and he was hounded from office as Governor of Tennessee in 1829. For several years he lived among the Cherokees, possibly plotting to detach Texas or other parts of Northern Mexico with Cherokee help. In 1832, Houston traveled to Texas and quickly became a leader of the "War Dogs," the settlers who favored secession from Mexico. When war broke out, Houston became commander in chief. After the fall of the Alamo and the subsequent massacre of the Texan garrison at Goliad by Santa Anna's forces, Houston retreated eastward. On April 21, 1836, Houston led his outnumbered men to attack the Mexican army at San Jacinto, near present-day Houston; caught by surprise, the Mexicans were devastated, and Santa Anna, taken prisoner, was forced to acknowledge the independence of Texas. Houston became the first President of the Republic of Texas and, after Texas was admitted to the United States in 1845, a U.S. Senator from Texas. A Unionist like his mentor Andrew Jackson, Houston, serving as Governor in 1861, tried to prevent the secession of Texas from the United States, but was unlawfully deposed by pro-Confederate Texans. Refusing President Abraham Lincoln's offer to reinstate him as Governor with the help of federal forces, Houston died in 1863 without seeing the Union restored. "His figure is athletic; everything about him indicates physical and moral energy," wrote Alexis de Tocqueville after meeting Houston in 1831. "This man has an extraordinary history."

HOWELL, WILLIAM D. (11.5.7)   Alamo defender.

HUAMANTLA (12.39.6)   Village in Mexico where one of the last battles in the Mexican War took place in October 1847. During the fighting with what remained of Santa Anna's army, Texas Ranger Captain Samuel Walker was killed.

INDEPENDENCE DAY (10.72.2)   Fourth of July, the anniversary of the signing of the U.S. Declaration of Independence.

INVINCIBLES (7.27.2)   Nickname of Captain William Carey's ordnance company, part of the Texan garrison at the Alamo.

ITURBIDE, AGUSTÍN DE (6.61.3) Mexican general who had himself crowned Emperor of Mexico in 1822, only to be deposed in 1823 and executed in 1824 after a failed attempt at a coup d'état.

JACK, PATRICK (2.23.1) Texan settler.

JACKSON, GENERAL ANDREW (1.36.4) President of the United States, 1829–1837.

JACKSON, LOUISE COTTLE (8.7.2) Texan settler; wife of Thomas Jackson.

JACKSON, THOMAS (8.7.3) Alamo defender.

JACKSON, WILLIAM DANIEL (11.10.1) Alamo defender.

JAMESON, GREEN B. (5.19.2) Alamo defender.

JENNINGS, GORDON C. (11.11.1) Alamo defender.

JESÚS, MARÍA DE (9.32.4) Mexican *soldadera*.

JOAN (8.64.6) Relative of Joe.

JOE (1.72.1) Slave of William Barret Travis.

JOHN (7.14.3) Slave of William Carey.

JOHNSON, COLONEL FRANCIS "FRANK" (4.37.2) Texan settler.

JOHNSON, LEWIS (11.14.7) Alamo defender.

JOHNSON, WILLIAM (11.63.7) Alamo defender.

JONAH (3.50.1) Hebrew prophet kept alive in the wilderness, according to the Bible.

JONES, LIEUTENANT JOHN (10.2.4) Alamo defender.

JONES, CAPTAIN RANDALL (4.8.6) Officer in the Texas cavalry.

KARAKANKAWAYS (33.44.7) Karankawa Indians; inhabitants of sections of coastal Texas, in the early nineteenth century.

KELLOGG, JOHN BENJAMIN "JOHNNY" (8.11.1) Alamo defender. Husband of Sidney Gaston.

KENNY, JAMES (10.71.2) Alamo defender.

Glossary

KENT, ANDREW (8.8.5)   Alamo defender.

KENT, ELIZABETH ZUMWALT (8.8.4)   Texan settler; wife of Andrew Kent.

KERR, JOSEPH "JOE" (10.35.1)   Alamo defender.

KERR, NATHANIEL (10.35.1)   Member of the Alamo garrison; died before the siege.

KIAN (3.39.2)   Slave of Jane Long.

KIMBELL, LIEUTENANT GEORGE C. (8.24.5)   Alamo defender.

KIMBELL, PRUDENCE NASH (8.6.1)   Texan settler; wife of George Kimbell.

KING, WILLIAM PHILIP "BILLY" (11.40.6)   Alamo defender.

KING, JOHN G. (11.57.4)   Texan settler; father of Billy King.

KRAKEN (6.67.7)   Submarine monster mistaken for an island, in Northern European legend.

"LA CUCARACHA" (7.55.6)   Traditional Mexican ballad.

La Maison Rouge (3.54.2)   Home of pirate Jean Laffite on Galveston Island in the early nineteenth century.

LA VILLITA (6.63.2)   Shantytown near the Alamo.

LAFFITE, JEAN (3.54.2)   Celebrated French pirate who operated in the Caribbean and Gulf of Mexico in the first few decades of the nineteenth century.

LAKE TRAVIS (7.6.7)   Lake on the Lower Colorado River named for William Barret Travis.

LEE, GENERAL ROBERT E. (12.42.2)   Commander in chief of the army of the Confederate States of America during most of the U.S. Civil War.

LEWIS, MARY (11.12.6)   U.S. citizen; mother of William Lewis.

LEWIS, WILLIAM IRVINE (11.12.2)   Alamo defender.

LIGHTFOOT, WILLIAM J. "BILL" (10.34.2)   Alamo defender.

LINDLEY, JONATHAN L. "JON" (10.36.7)   Alamo defender.

LINN, WILLIAM "BILL" (10.8.1)   Alamo defender.

LIPAN (4.61.6)   Division of the Apache nation.

LLORONA, LA (5.1.6)   (Sp.) "The Weeper," a figure from Mexican and Mexican-American folklore, the ghost of a woman who drowned her children and who now haunts the world luring others to their doom.

LONG, DOCTOR JAMES (2.36.6)   Filibuster from the United States who led two ill-fated attempts to seize Texas from Spain in 1819 and 1820, only to be executed in Mexico City; husband of Jane Long.

LONG, JANE (2.39.3)   Texan settler; widow of James Long.

LOSOYA, TORIBIO (8.23.2)   Alamo defender.

LOWER COLORADO (12.14.6)   River in Texas.

MADISON, JAMES (10.66.4)   Fourth president of the United States; uncle of James Rose.

MAIN, GEORGE WASHINGTON (11.9.2)   Alamo defender.

MALONE, WILLIAM T. "BILL" (5.10.2)   Alamo defender.

MARDI GRAS (12.67.5)   Annual festival in New Orleans following Lent.

MARIUS, GAIUS (2.16.1)   Dictatorial Roman consul who massacred his political rivals on being restored to power by an army of proletarians in 87 B.C.

MARSHALL, WILLIAM "WILL" (11.34.1)   Alamo defender.

MARTIN, ALBERT (7.29.6)   Alamo defender.

MATAMOROS (6.10.5)   Town in Mexico.

MAXIMILIAN (12.42.5)   Emperor of Mexico installed by Louis Napoleon of France and overthrown by Mexican nationalists in 1867.

McAFFERTY, EDWARD "ED" (10.34.6)   Alamo defender.

McCOY, JESSE (11.34.5)   Alamo defender.

McDOWELL, WILLIAM "WILL" (10.59.5)   Alamo defender.

McGEE, JAMES (11.4.1)   Alamo defender.

McGREGOR, JOHN (8.25.7)   Alamo defender.

McKINNEY, ROBERT (10.50.2)   Alamo defender.

MEDINA (5.43.5)   River south of San Antonio; site of massacre of Texas revolutionaries by Spanish forces under Arredondo in 1813.

MIER Y TERAN, GENERAL (2.14.7)   Mexican general charged with supervision of Texas during the turmoil of 1832.

MELTON, ELIEL (8.43.1)   Alamo defender.

MENÉNDEZ, JULIO (9.25.1–2)   Mexican soldier.

MEXICAS (6.59.5)   Native Americans who inhabited Mexico before the Spanish Conquest and gave the country its name.

MIFFLIN COUNTY (10.59.7)   County in Pennsylvania.

MILAM, BEN (2.37.2)   Texan settler; veteran of James Long's filibustering expeditions.

MILKY WAY (8.70.2)   Galaxy in which the Sun and the solar system are located.

MILLER, J. B. (1.26.1)   Texan settler.

MILLER, THOMAS R. (8.10.6)   Alamo defender. Ex-husband of Sidney Gaston.

MILLS, WILLIAM "WILL" (10.34.7)   Alamo defender.

MILLSAPS, ISAAC (8.14.3)   Alamo defender.

MILLSAPS, MARY (8.14.5)   Texan settler; wife of Isaac Millsaps.

MISSISSIPPI (1.38.3)   River in the United States; state in Southern United States.

MITCHASSON, EDWARD F. "Ed" (11.4.6)   Alamo defender.

MITCHELL, EDWIN T. "Ed" (1.11.1)   Alamo defender.

MITCHELL, NAPOLEON B. (11.23.2)   Alamo defender.

MONROE, JAMES (10.67.7)   Fifth President of the United States, 1817 to 1825.

MONTCALM (6.46.6)   Marquis de Montcalm. Commander of French forces against the British and Anglo-American forces in the Battle of the Plains of Abraham (1759) during the French and Indian War (1754 to 1763).

MONTERA (2.31.1) Mexican soldier in the garrison at Anahuac in 1832.

MONTERREY (12.38.1) City in Mexico.

MOORE, ROBERT B. (9.38.1) Alamo defender.

MOORE, WILLIS (9.38.4) Alamo defender. Cousin of Robert B. Moore.

MORA, CAPTAIN (9.28.4) Mexican officer.

MORALES, COLONEL 8.59.1 Mexican officer.

MORELOS (2.28.7) Father José María Morelos, a mestizo priest who assumed leadership of the abortive Mexican revolution of 1810 to 1815, after the execution of Father Hidalgo. He was defeated, and executed in 1815.

MOUNTED VOLUNTEERS OF TENNESSEE (6.39.1–2) Unit of the Texan garrison at the Alamo.

MUSQUIZ, RAMON (12.44.1) Citizen of San Antonio.

MUSSELMAN, ROBERT (10.6.7) Alamo defender.

NACOGDOCHES (2.14.4) City in East Texas.

NANCY (8.7.4) Nancy Cottle. Texan settler; wife of George Cottle.

NAOMI (8.12.5) Texan settler; daughter of Evaline Dewitt.

NAPOLEON OF THE WEST (5.21.7) Nickname of Santa Anna.

NAVA, ANDRES (11.19.6) Alamo defender.

NEGGAN, GEORGE (11.42.3) Alamo defender.

NEILL, COLONEL JAMES C. (5.12.1) Commander of Texan regulars at the Alamo garrison, who turned over command to William Barret Travis when departing on family business shortly before the siege and battle of the Alamo.

NELSON, ANDREW M. (12.22.4) Alamo defender.

NELSON, EDWARD (10.50.2) Alamo defender.

NELSON, GEORGE (11.7.6) Alamo defender.

NEW MEXICO (12.35.2) State in Northern Mexico, annexed by the United States after the U.S.-Mexican War.

NORTHCROSS, JAMES (11.14.5) Alamo defender.

NOWLAN, JAMES (11.7.5) Alamo defender.

NUECES (12.14.4) River in Texas.

NULLIFIERS (3.4.3) Radical opponents of the federal government during the crisis of 1832, during which South Carolina came close to seceding from the United States.

Ohio (1.52.2) Ship used by Travis in his attack on the Mexican garrison at Anahuac, Texas, in 1835.

OLD EIGHTEEN (11.39.6) Nickname of the Texan settlers at Gonzales who repelled a Mexican force attempting to retake the town's garrison in the autumn of 1835.

OLD GLORY (5.57.7) Flag of the United States of America.

OLD HICKORY (3.14.6) Nickname of Andrew Jackson, who was President of the United States at the time of the Texas Revolution.

OLD WORLD (5.20.7) Term used for the entire land mass of the earth with the exception of North and South America; the Eastern Hemisphere.

PADILLO, IGNACIO (9.28.2) Mexican soldier.

PAGAN, GEORGE (10.51.3) Alamo defender.

PALM SUNDAY (12.31.4) The Sunday before Easter, celebrated by Christians who commemorate the entry of Jesus into Jerusalem before his crucifixion.

PALO DURO (4.5.5) Canyon in the Texas Panhandle.

PAREDES, ANTONIO (9.44.1) Mexican soldier.

PARKER, CHRISTOPHER ADAMS "Chris" (12.23.5) Alamo defender.

PARKS, WILLIAM (10.65.7) Alamo defender.

PAULLUS (5.66.5) Roman republican consul who defeated the Macedonians in Greece in 167 B.C. and returned in triumph to Rome.

PEARL (6.51.7) Character in one of David Crockett's tales.

PECOS (12.11.5) River in Texas.

PEÑA, JUAN BAUTISTA (9.12.2) Mexican soldier.

PENTECOST (11.30.6) Christian holiday on the seventh Sunday after Easter that commemorates the descent of the Holy Spirit on the Apostles, as related in the New Testament.

PERRY, RICHARDSON (10.70.2)   Alamo defender.

PHARAOH (2.17.4)   Title of despotic monarch of ancient Egypt.

PHILIPPI (1.25.5)   Site of the defeat and suicide of Marcus Junius Brutus, one of the republican Senators who assassinated Caesar, by Antony and Octavian in 42 B.C.

PICO, GONZAGO (9.44.4)   Mexican soldier.

PIEDRAS, COLONEL (2.14.3)   Commander of the Mexican garrison at Nacogdoches, Texas, during the conflict of 1832.

PLAINS OF ABRAHAM (6.46.6–7)   Battlefield near Quebec, Canada, in which the British and Anglo-American forces under General James Wolfe defeated the French, led by the Marquis de Montcalm.

PLUTARCH (3.20.7)   Lucius Mestrius Plutarchus. Author of *Lives,* a celebrated comparison of eminent Greeks and Romans.

POINSETT, JOEL (2.37.7)   U.S. ambassador to Mexico in the 1830s.

POLLARD, AMOS "DOC" (8.42.5)   Alamo defender.

presidarios (2.24.7)   Troops assigned to a Mexican *presidio* or fortress. *Presidarios* were often convicts.

PUEBLA (12.39.4)   City in Mexico.

pulque (7.46.1)   Mexican drink made from the maguey plant.

QUERÉTARO (6.15.4)   City in Mexico.

QUETZALCOATL (6.59.1)   God of enlightenment in ancient Mexican mythology; portrayed as a feathered serpent. In some accounts, Quetzalcoatl was a sage who departed across the Atlantic but promised to return. Montezuma, the last Aztec emperor, thought for a time that Cortés might be the god Quetzalcoatl.

RAMÍREZ Y SESMA, GENERAL JOAQUÍN (6.9.2)   Mexican officer.

RAPIDES PARISH (5.29.2)   Parish in Louisiana, a state in the Southern United States.

RED RIVER (12.12.1)   River in Texas.

RESACA DE LA PALMA (12.38.1)   Battle of the U.S.-Mexican War.

REYNOLDS, JOHN PURDY (10.59.1)   Alamo defender.

REZIN (4.44.2)   Rezin Bowie. Brother of James Bowie; inventor of the Bowie knife.

RHODES (9.5.5)   Island in the eastern Mediterranean, home of an advanced mercantile society during much of Antiquity. In the Hellenistic period, after surviving a siege by Demetrius, a member of the Antigonid dynasty, the Rhodians melted down some of the metal from weapons and armor abandoned on the battlefield and used it in constructing a statue of Apollo that stood by the harbor — the Collosus of Rhodes, one of the seven wonders of the ancient world.

RIO GRANDE (5.58.4)   River in Texas.

ROBERTS, THOMAS H. "Tom" (12.24.1)   Alamo defender.

ROBERTSON, JAMES WATERS (12.26.4)   Alamo defender.

ROBINSON (11.3.7)   Alamo defender.

ROBINSON, ED (2.58.6)   Texan settler killed in the Battle of Velasco in 1832.

ROSE, JAMES M. (10.68.1)   Alamo defender.

ROSE, LOUIS (7.27.6)   Member of the Texas Alamo garrison who survived by leaving before or during the siege.

RUSK, JACKSON J. (12.24.4)   Alamo defender.

RUTHERFORD, JOSEPH (10.27.1)   Alamo defender.

RYAN, ISAAC (10.71.2)   Alamo defender.

SABINE (1.72.6)   River that marks the boundary between Texas and Louisiana; before the Texas Revolution, the Sabine also marked the border between the United States and Mexico.

SAINT ANTHONY (5.14.5)   Patron saint of San Antonio, Texas.

SAMSON (2.21.7)   Hebrew strong man.

SAN ANTONIO (1.11.7)   Town in Bexar County, Texas; site of the Alamo fortress.

SAN ANTONIO RIVER (12.14.7)   River in Texas.

SAN FELIPE DE AUSTIN (1.22.3)   Town in Texas established by Anglo-American colonists.

SAN FERNANDO (6.62.3)   Original cathedral in San Antonio, Texas.

SAN FRANCISCO (5.66.3)   Port city and bay in California.

SAN JACINTO (12.32.2)   Site near modern Houston, Texas, where Sam Houston's Texan forces routed the Mexican army, captured Santa Anna, and won the independence of the Republic of Texas on April 21, 1836.

SAN PEDRO (6.34.2)   River in San Antonio.

SANTA ANNA, GENERAL (1.8.1)   Antonio Lopez de Santa Anna-Perez de Lebron (1794–1876). Mexican President and commander in chief of the Mexican Army; victor of the Battle of the Alamo. A charismatic and resourceful opportunist from a Mexican Creole background, Santa Anna became dictator of Mexico several times, and acted as a king-maker at other times, between his equally frequent periods of exile abroad. An able general, he prevented the reconquest of Mexico by Spain in 1829 and stopped a French invasion of Veracruz in 1838, losing his leg in battle. He was less fortunate in his wars with the Anglo-Americans, losing the war against the Texan settlers in 1836 and leading the Mexican Army to defeat in the Mexican War of 1846 to 1848. The dominant figure of Mexican politics during the first half of the nineteenth century, Santa Anna died impoverished and forgotten in Mexico City. In his homeland, the "Napoleon of the West" remains a reviled figure.

SANTA FE (5.65.7)   Capital of New Mexico.

SARACEN (4.31.3)   Horse that General Sam Houston rode in the Battle of San Jacinto. During the battle, Houston was shot and severely wounded.

SCAMANDER (5.64.6)   River on the plain before Troy, in Homer's *Iliad*.

SCOTT, WINFIELD (12.39.1)   Commander in chief of the U.S. Army during the invasion and occupation of Mexico in the U.S.-Mexican War.

SCURLOCK, MIAL (10.37.1)   Alamo defender.

SEGUIN, DON ERASMO (6.4.3)   Rancher, judge, and leading citizen of San Antonio; father of Juan Seguin.

SEGUIN, CAPTAIN JUAN (6.6.6)   Officer of the Texas Cavalry, and member of the Alamo garrison. Sent out as a courier by Travis, Seguin was spared the fate of his comrades at the Alamo; after the war, he would bury their ashes in a public ceremony in San Antonio. Seguin led a contingent of *Tejanos* at the Battle of San Jacinto. He became Mayor of San Antonio, but the hostility of Anglo-American newcomers, exacerbated by his ambiguous behavior during an invasion of Texas by the Mexican Army under General Adrian Woll in 1842, forced him and his family to flee Texas and seek the protection of the Mexican government.

Seguin spent the rest of his life a bitter man, trusted neither in Texas nor in Mexico.

SEMINOLES (10.7.4) Native American nation in Florida, augmented by significant numbers of runaway slaves from the American South. The U.S. military savagely repressed the Seminoles in the 1820s.

SERRANO (1.6.4) Mexican officer.

SEWELL, MARCUS L. (11.8.1) Alamo defender.

SHIED, MANSON (10.64.1) Alamo defender.

SHILOH (12.41.6) Battle in the U.S. Civil War.

SIMMONS, CLEVELAND KINLOCH "CLEVE" (11.37.4) Alamo defender.

SMITH, CHARLES S. (11.63.5) Alamo defender.

SMITH, ERASTUS "DEAF" (4.46.1) Texan settler; scout for the Texan army.

SMITH, JOHN (7.7.3) Alamo courier.

SMITH, JOSHUA G. (10.10.2) Alamo defender.

SMITH, WILLIAM H. (11.14.4) Alamo defender.

soldaderas (5.36.1) Mexican female camp followers.

STARR, RICHARD "DICK" (10.8.3) Alamo defender.

STEWART, JAMES E. (8.73.2) Alamo defender.

STOCKTON, RICHARD L. (10.64.3) Alamo defender.

SUE (6.51.7) Character in one of David Crockett's tales.

SULTAN (4.6.1) Wild mustang.

SUMMERLIN, A. SPAIN (12.26.1) Alamo defender.

SUMMERS, WILLIAM E. (10.44.6) Alamo defender.

SUTHERLAND, DOCTOR JOHN (7.7.2) Alamo courier.

SUTHERLAND, WILLIAM DE PRIEST "Bill" (12.22.6) Alamo defender.

SYRACUSE (5.23.1) Sicilian city; ancient city-state. According to Plutarch,

Syracuse was liberated from the tyrannical rule of Dionysius in 343 B.C. by Timoleon of Corinth, leading a joint force of native Syracusans and Corinthian immigrants.

TAMPICO (6.21.5)   Mexican coastal city where Santa Anna foiled a Spanish invasion attempt in 1829.

TAURUS (8.70.4)   Constellation.

TAYLOR, EDWARD (11.35.5)   Alamo defender.

TAYLOR, GEORGE (11.36.1)   Alamo defender.

TAYLOR, JAMES "JIM" (11.36.1)   Alamo defender.

TAYLOR, WILLIAM "Bill" (12.26.5)   Alamo defender.

Tejano (1.12.4)   Native Texan of Mexican/Spanish descent.

TENNESSEE LONG RIFLE (6.56.3)   Distinctive firearm of Anglo-American frontiersman in the first half of the nineteenth century.

TENORIO, CAPTAIN ANTONIO (1.59.1)   Commander of the Mexican garrison at Anahuac, Texas, at the time of Travis's raid in 1835.

TEXAS RANGERS (12.34.4)   Border guard of the Texas Republic; later the state police of the state of Texas.

THOMAS, B. ARCHER M. (9.19.2)   Alamo defender.

THOMAS, HENRY (11.30.1)   Alamo defender.

THOMPSON, JESSE G. (12.18.1)   Alamo defender.

THOMSON, JOHN W. (10.65.1)   Alamo defender.

THURSTON, JOHN M. (11.19.3)   Alamo defender.

TIMOLEON (5.22.6)   Subject of one of Plutarch's *Lives*. An eminent citizen of ancient Corinth, who assassinated his brother for attempting to become tyrant of Corinth. Later Timoleon led a fleet of Corinthians to Sicily, where with local help he overthrew Dionysius, tyrant of Syracuse, and established a republican constitution. He died in Syracuse around 337 B.C.

TOLSA, GENERAL (6.14.4)   Mexican officer.

TOLTECS (6.59.5)   Early dynasty in pre-Columbian Mexico and Central America.

TORRES, LIEUTENANT (11.74.4)   Mexican soldier.

TRAMMEL, BURKE (10.26.3)   Alamo defender.

TRAVIS, CHARLES EDWARD (3.23.7)   Son of William Barret Travis.

TRAVIS, LIEUTENANT COLONEL WILLIAM BARRET (1.15.5) (1809–36). Alamo defender; commander of the Texan garrison at the Alamo. Born in South Carolina, Travis grew up in Alabama, then a U.S. territory. Something of a prodigy as an adolescent, he became a lawyer, a teacher, and a journalist, and married Rosanna E. Cato, with whom he had two children. In 1831, Travis abandoned his wife and children and arrived in Texas, under mysterious circumstances; according to family tradition, he killed a man he suspected of having an affair with his wife, in a duel or ambush. Eventually Travis divorced his wife and obtained custody of his son, Charles Edward. In 1832, Travis and a friend named Patrick Jack were among the leaders of a rebellion by the inhabitants of the coastal settlement of Anahuac against the local Mexican commander, an Anglo-American named John (or Juan) Davis Bradburn. In 1835, Travis returned to Anahuac to seize the fortress, in an attempt to spark a Texas-wide revolution against the Mexican government, then a dictatorship under General Santa Anna. Though the settlers repudiated Travis's action at first, the War Party eventually prevailed and the Texas Revolution began. During the war of the winter of 1835 to 1836, Travis served as a cavalry officer. After the initial expulsion of Mexican forces from Texas, in early February 1836, Travis inherited the command of the Alamo garrison when his superior officer, Colonel James C. Neill, left San Antonio because of sickness in his family. At the time of his death during the Battle of the Alamo, Travis was twenty-seven.

TRINITY (12.2.2)   River in Texas.

TRUDGE (4.3.6)   Wild mustang.

TUMLINSON, GEORGE W. (11.53.4)   Alamo defender.

TURTLE BAYOU (2.32.2)   Site near Anahuac where the rebellious Texan settlers in 1832 drew up the Turtle Bayou Resolutions stating their grievances.

TWINS (8.70.2)   Gemini, a constellation.

TYLEE, JAMES (12.21.6)   Alamo defender.

TYLEE, MATILDA (12.21.7)   Texan settler; wife of James Tylee.

UGARTECHEA, COLONEL DOMINGO DE "DOM" (2.14.2)   Commander of the Mexican fortress at Velasco, Texas, in 1832.

URREA, GENERAL JOSÉ (8.37.2)   Mexican officer.

vaqueros (4.5.2)   (Sp.) Cowboys.

VARELA (9.43.6)   Mexican soldier.

VELASCO (2.14.3)   Texas coastal town; site of battle between Mexican government soldiers and Texan settlers in 1832.

VERACRUZ (12.36.2)   Mexican port city.

VERAMENDI, DON JUAN (4.74.2)   Eminent citizen of San Antonio and Saltillo; Vice Governor of Coahuila-Texas; father-in-law of James Bowie. Along with a number of relatives, including his daughter, Bowie's wife, Ursula, Veramendi died of cholera in 1833.

VIESCA (1.23.6)   Governor of Coahuila-Texas; deposed by Santa Anna in 1835.

Villista (12.43.2)   Follower of rebel general Pancho Villa during the Mexican Revolution of 1911 to 1921.

WALKER, ASA (11.70.3)   Alamo defender. Cousin of Jake Walker.

WALKER, JACOB "Jake" (11.70.1)   Alamo defender. Brother of Joseph Walker.

WALKER, JOSEPH (11.70.2)   Famous American mountain man of the early nineteenth century.

WALKER, SAMUEL "Sam" (12.36.7)   Celebrated Texas Ranger; taken prisoner after the failed attempt of the Texas Republic to conquer New Mexico in 1842, and later released; killed in one of the final battles of the Mexican War.

WAR DOGS (1.34.3)   Faction of Texan settlers including Houston and Travis who favored separating Texas from Mexico, by war if necessary.

WARD, WILLIAM B. (12.22.5)   Alamo defender.

WARNELL, HENRY. (8.73.1)   Alamo defender.

WASHINGTON, D.C. (5.66.4)   Capital of the United States of America.

WASHINGTON, GEORGE (6.66.1)   Commander in chief of the U.S. military during the American Revolution; President of the Constitutional Convention in Philadelphia in 1787; first President of the United States of America.

WASHINGTON-ON-BRAZOS (8.1.7)   Town in Texas; site of Convention that issued the Texas Declaration of Independence on March 2, 1836.

WATER STREET (8.6.4) Street in Gonzales, Texas.

WATERS, THOMAS "TOM" (10.27.1) Alamo defender.

WEBSTER, DANIEL (10.72.4) Massachusetts Senator; U.S. Secretary of State; distinguished American orator and nationalist leader.

WEEPER (1.17.4) Another name for La Llorona.

WELLS, WILLIAM "BILL" (12.17.3) Alamo defender.

WHARTON, WILL (2.49.7) Texan settler; member of the War Party.

WHITE, ISAAC (12.23.4) Alamo defender.

WHITE, CAPTAIN ROBERT (8.43.6) Alamo defender.

WILDERNESS (12.41.6) Battle of the U.S. Civil War.

WILKINSON, GENERAL JAMES (3.38.5) U.S. General, involved in numerous intrigues throughout his career. During the Revolutionary War, he participated in the Conway Cabal, a plot to oust George Washington as commander in chief; later, as a U.S. military commander in the Southwest, he first conspired with Vice President Aaron Burr to launch a filibustering expedition in Texas and other parts of Mexico, then betrayed Burr to President Jefferson, who sought unsuccessfully to have Burr hanged as a traitor. His nephews were involved in the unsuccessful Texas Revolution of 1811 to 1813, and his niece Jane was the wife of James Long, leader of two later and equally unsuccessful attempts to conquer Texas with teams of Anglo-Americans and native *Tejanos*. Wilkinson died in 1825 in Mexico. In recent generations, U.S. historians discovered that for most of his time as a U.S. military officer he had been a secret agent for the government of Spain, Number Thirteen.

WILLIAMSON, SERGEANT MAJOR HIRAM JAMES (8.42.7) Alamo defender.

WILLS, WILLIAM (12.24.3) Alamo defender.

WILSON, DAVID L. (12.16.5) Alamo defender.

WILSON, JOHN "JOHNNY" (12.27.3) Alamo defender.

WOLF, ANTHONY (12.67.1) Alamo defender. Father of two young boys killed in the Battle of the Alamo.

WOLFE, GENERAL JAMES (5.66.4) Commander of the British and Anglo-American forces that routed the French under General Montcalm at the

Plains of Abraham on September 13, 1759, winning French Canada and the Ohio River Valley for the British empire.

WRIGHT, CLAIBORNE (11.48.6)   Alamo defender.

WRIGHT, LEMUEL (1.30.2)   Texan settler.

XIMENES, DAMACIO (10.11.6)   Alamo defender.

yanqui (1.13.2)   (Sp.) Yankee. Citizen of the United States; Anglophone American originally from the U.S. or Canada.

ZACATECAS (1.5.7)   City in Mexico.

ZANCO, CHARLES (10.14.1)   Alamo defender.

zapador (10.8.2)   (Sp.) Sapper in the Mexican Army.

ZAVALA, DON LORENZO DE (1.9.1)   Eminent Mexican liberal politician, diplomat and intellectual; opponent of Santa Anna's dictatorship; first Vice President of the Republic of Texas.

CHRONOLOGY

1811–1813   With covert backing from the United States, residents of Texas rebel against Spanish rule. The rebels are suppressed in the Battle of Medina near San Antonio by Spanish troops commanded by General Joaquin de Arredondo. Serving in Arredondo's force is the nineteen-year-old Lieutenant Antonio Lopez de Santa Anna.

1819   A New Orleans doctor, James Long, leads a band of American adventurers and *Tejanos* in a failed attempt to capture Texas from Spain.

1820   Long leads a second attempt to seize Texas. He is imprisoned in Mexico City along with John Austin and Ben Milam. Long is executed. His widow, Jane, remains in Texas as a settler.

1821   Mexico wins its independence from Spain.

1821   The American colonial impresario Stephen F. Austin begins to settle colonists peacefully in Texas with land grants obtained from the Mexican government.

1824   The Mexican government consolidates Texas and Coahuila into a new state, Coahuila-Texas.

1829   Santa Anna, now a General, saves Mexico from Spain's attempt at reconquest at the Battle of Tampico.

1829–1837   In this period of turmoil, Mexico has seventeen Presidents.

1830

    FEBRUARY.   James Bowie emigrates from Louisiana to Texas.

    APRIL 6.   The Law of April 6, 1830, is passed in an attempt to halt American immigration. The Mexican government strengthens its Texas garrisons with convict-soldiers (*presidarios*). The law is not effectively enforced.

1831   William Barret Travis moves from Alabama to Texas.

APRIL 25. In San Antonio, James Bowie weds Ursula Veramendi, daughter of the vice governor of Coahuila-Texas.

1832

APRIL–JULY. In Anahuac, Texas, tensions between the settlers and the local Mexican garrison, commanded by an immigrant from the U.S. named John Davis Bradburn, erupt into a confrontation. Bradburn arrests Travis and another dissident, Patrick Jack, and stakes them to the ground, threatening to shoot them if the settlers attack. The settlers issue the Turtle Bayou Resolutions, setting forth their grievances. Texan volunteers bringing arms by ship to the rebel camp at Turtle Bayou engage in a battle with the Mexican garrison at Velasco, leaving several dead and wounded. Piedras, the commander of the garrison at Nacogdoches, intervenes on the side of the colonists. Travis and Jack are freed, and Bradburn, after resigning, flees Texas to escape the vengeance of the settlers.

DECEMBER. Sam Houston immigrates to Texas.

1833   Santa Anna overthrows Bustamante and becomes President of Mexico.

1835

MAY 10. The Rape of Zacatecas: Santa Anna defeats liberals who have rebelled against his autocratic rule. His troops go on a spree of rape, looting, and destruction, killing 2500 Zacatecan women and male civilians.

JUNE 21. Secret letters to the Mexican garrison commander at Anahuac intercepted by Texan settlers in San Felipe de Austin.

JUNE 27. William Barret Travis leads two dozen settlers to seize the Mexican garrison at Anahuac, Texas.

JULY 4. Travis and his men arrive in Harrisburg, Texas, with the captured Mexican garrison.

JULY 17. Peace Party leaders at San Felipe condemn Travis's raid in a resolution. Other communities issue similar condemnations.

AUGUST 1. General Cos sends a letter to Texas, demanding "the apprehension of the ungrateful and bad citizen, Juliano Barret Travis, who headed the revolutionary party. . . ."

The arrest of Lorenzo de Zavala and other "agitators" is also ordered. Fearing that Santa Anna is planning an invasion of Texas, the Texan settlers close ranks behind the rebels. The colonies agree to send representatives to a Consultation at Washington-on-Brazos on October 15.

SEPTEMBER 17.   General Cos arrives in Texas with his army.

SEPTEMBER 1–2.   Settlers in Gonzales, Texas, repel Mexican soldiers attempting to seize the town's cannon. The Texas Revolution begins.

OCTOBER 3.   In Mexico City, Santa Anna dissolves all state governments and institutes a personal dictatorship.

SEPTEMBER 19.   Stephen F. Austin, long identified with moderation, declares, "War is our only recourse."

OCTOBER 11.   Austin is elected commander in chief of the Texan army. He leads the army toward San Antonio to confront the force under Cos.

NOVEMBER 3.   The Consultation appoints Sam Houston commander of the regular army to be organized.

NOVEMBER 14.   The Consultation chooses to support a restoration of the Mexican constitution of 1824 rather than to declare independence. The body is adjourned until March 1, 1836.

NOVEMBER 24.   Austin resigns from his command to become an emissary to the United States. Edward Burleson is elected to replace him, with Francis Johnson as second in command.

DECEMBER 5–10.   Led by Ben Milam, a veteran of the Long expeditions, the Texans capture San Antonio and the Alamo. Milam dies during the fighting. Cos and his troops are allowed to leave Texas.

1836

FEBRUARY 2.   Travis arrives in San Antonio, as second in command to Colonel James Neill. At some point in the next few days, Neill, leaving because of a family illness, turns over the command to Travis. Bowie insists that he is in command of the volunteers in Bexar. Bowie releases all the prisoners in San Antonio's jail. Travis consents to an election, which Bowie wins.

FEBRUARY 8.   David Crockett and the Tennessee Mounted Volunteers under the command of Captain William Harris arrive in San Antonio.

FEBRUARY 12.   Santa Anna and his army reach the Rio Grande. Around this time, Travis and Bowie agree on a joint command.

FEBRUARY 21.   Santa Anna arrives at the Medina River near San Antonio. Heavy rain impedes his progress.

CHRONOLOGY

FEBRUARY 22. While members of the Texan garrison celebrate Washington's Birthday, scouts from Santa Anna's army reach the outskirts of San Antonio.

FEBRUARY 23 The siege of the Alamo begins.

FEBRUARY 24. Bowie, gravely ill, turns over the command to Travis. Travis sends his famous appeal for help, vowing, "I shall never surrender or retreat."

FEBRUARY 25. In a letter to Houston, Travis praises Charles Despallier and Robert Brown for setting fire to houses of La Villita that the enemy had used for cover. Travis writes that during a skirmish Crockett was "seen at all points, animating the men to do their duty."

MARCH 1. Thirty volunteers from Gonzales slip through enemy lines to join the Alamo garrison.

MARCH 2. Texan delegates meeting at Washington-on-Brazos declare the independence of Texas.

MARCH 6. Shortly before dawn, Santa Anna's troops storm the Alamo. All of the defenders are killed, except for one, Brigido Guerrero, who claims he was a hostage. Santa Anna permits Susannah Dickinson; her infant, Angelina; and Travis's slave, Joe, to join the Texan forces in the east. They reach the camp of Houston on March 11.

MARCH 19. Colonel James Fannin, riding to relieve San Antonio, is captured by Mexican forces. Promised parole to New Orleans for his men, Fannin surrenders his garrison at Goliad.

MARCH 27. On this Palm Sunday, at Santa Anna's orders, healthy Texan prisoners, told they are being paroled, are marched from the Goliad fortress and shot. Sick prisoners in the fortress hospital are then butchered. Around four hundred Texans in all are executed.

MARCH–APRIL. The Runaway Scrape. Texan settlers flee east, abandoning their towns to Santa Anna's armies, which put the settlements to the torch. Houston pursues an unpopular but ultimately effective strategy of luring Santa Anna into East Texas.

APRIL 21, 1836. At San Jacinto, Houston surprises the army of Santa Anna. The Texans, shouting "Remember the Alamo!" and "Remember Goliad!" kill as many as six hundred of the enemy. Santa Anna, captured and brought before the wounded Houston, agrees to order his remaining forces in Texas to leave. Houston allows Santa Anna to travel to Washington, D.C., where he meets President Andrew Jackson. In Mexico, Santa Anna is denounced for losing Texas.

1845

MARCH 1. A joint resolution of Congress invites the Republic of Texas to join the United States.

DECEMBER 29. Texas is formally admitted to the United States.

APRIL 25. Mexican troops attack U.S. troops on the Texan side of the Rio Grande.

MAY 13. The United States declares war on Mexico.

1846

AUGUST 16. Santa Anna, allowed by the U.S. Navy to return from exile in Cuba after promising to work for peace, arrives in Mexico. Reneging on his promise, he seizes power and assumes command of the Mexican military effort.

1847

SEPTEMBER 16. Having failed to expel the U.S., Santa Anna resigns the presidency of Mexico. The U.S. army of occupation allows him safe conduct out of the country into renewed exile.

1848   The treaty of Guadalupe Hidalgo is ratified by the Mexican Senate, ending the U.S.-Mexican War. Mexico surrenders its claim to Texas and cedes California and the American Southwest, in return for $15 million and the forgiveness of all debts owed by Mexico to the United States.

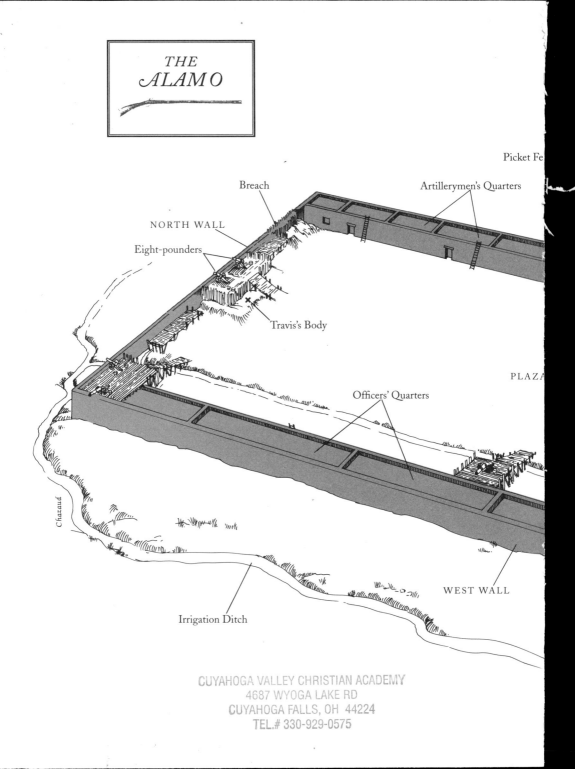

THE
ALAMO

Picket Fe

Breach

Artillerymen's Quarters

NORTH WALL

Eight-pounders

Travis's Body

PLAZ

Officers' Quarters

Chazaud

WEST WALL

Irrigation Ditch